December's A  May

A Collection of **50** (or thereabout)
Inspiring Personal and Formal Essays

Dr. Grace Allman Burke

Epigraph

How tedious and tasteless the hours

When Jesus no longer I see

Sweet prospects, sweet birds and sweet flowers,

Have all lost their sweetness to me.

The midsummer sun shines but dim,

The fields strive in vain to look gay;

But when I am happy in Him

December's as pleasant as May.[1]

---

[1] Lyrics by John Newton. 1725 – 1807. (Public Domain)

To Yvette + Felix Griffin

In Memory Of
Sarah Javonne Davis

Many Blings!
Dr. Gene Burke
11/11/2023

ISBN: 9798550642023

Library of Congress Control No.: 2020920941

Published by: GRACE BURKE BOOKS, Prosper, Texas

Scripture quotations are from the Authorized King James Version, World Bible Publishers, Inc. Copyright 1998

Selected scripture quotations are taken from the following:

New King James Version. Copyright © 1982 by Thomas Nelson, Inc. Used by permission. All rights reserved.

NEW AMERICAN STANDARD BIBLE. Copyright 1960-1995 by the Lockman Foundation. Used by permission.

New Living Translation. Copyright 1996 – 2015 by Tyndale House Foundation. Used by permission of Tyndale House Publishers, Inc. All rights reserved.

NEW INTERNATIONAL VERSION. Copyright ©1973-1984 by International Bible Society. Used by permission. All rights reserved worldwide.

THE MESSAGE, copyright ©1993,2002,2018 by Eugene H. Peterson. Used by Permission of NavPress. All rights reserved. Represented by Tyndale House Publishers.

Disclaimer: The essays in this collection are all true. Most were experienced by the author, with a few "as told to" the author. I have tried to recreate events, locales, and conversations from my memories of them. In some instances, to maintain anonymity, I have changed the names of individuals, places of residence, and occupations.

Cover Design by Willis Davis; Author Photo by Casandera Brown

Publisher Website: www.graceburkebooks.com; email: gburke333@gmail.com

Table of Contents

Acknowledgements

I would like to acknowledge and express appreciation, To God, first and foremost, my Creator, Savior, Lord and Comforter, who inspired me to write, craft, and create.

To my helpmate, Neville, of many years, whom God sent to support, love, and affirm me throughout this process. You are my rock. To special young people:

- my children, Cranston, Jhanna, and Jie
- my nephew, Richard
- my grandchildren, Grace, Alexandria, Sarah (in heaven), Nehemiah, and Nadiah
- my great grandchildren, Charlotte, and Kayden
- my godchildren, Amanda (in heaven), Matthew, Jacob, Benjamin, Nicole, Mario, Jermaine, Ashley, Steve, Deja, Osasere, Sarah, and Kevin
- my church grandchildren, Marcus, and Angie, whom I delivered into this world, and those whom I blessed and anointed the moment they arrived, Raymon, Kayla, Joanna, Kennedy, Noah, Arthur, Aaron, Nylan, and Augustine

To my siblings, Luther and Marilyn; DiAne Gates and the members of my Edit Group; Michelle Brown; and the many friends who encouraged and supported me, To all, I say "thank you," you are the members of my Village, who sustained me and brought lots of joy as I reflected back while writing this book.

Endorsements

"December's As Pleasant As May" is a charming and inspiring collection of essays by my friend, author, and edit partner Grace Burke. A perfect read for the coming winter shivers, snuggled by a crackling fire, sipping hot chocolate.

Dr. Burke grew up in a delightful household and after reading the stories about her father, I'm eager to meet him when we all get home!

In these days of tension and trials, this book offers the reader glimpses of a time when life was real and so was God. A time when families enjoyed each other —aunts, uncles, cousins, grandparents — everyone! A time and heritage God intended for all of His children — rooted and grounded in love for one another and for Him.

Dr. Burke's conversational writing style, laced with humor, a twinkle in her eye, and an abundance of joy, will warm your heart, bring a smile, and perhaps a tear.

Because of Dr. Burke's attention to character details, I'm sure we'll recognize and meet these dear people for all eternity.

Super book —Definitely a five-star read. Thank you, Grace!

DiAne N. Gates, Author, Illustrator, GriefShare Facilitator

Dr. Grace Allman Burke writes with an easy style from an approach that is faith-based. I could hardly put down her previous book ***Broken Pieces...Mending the Fragments Through Adoption.***

In her new book, ***December's As Pleasant As May,*** she keeps the reader riveted and totally engaged as she recounts true stories from her life. It's a must-read that provides messages of hope and encouragement throughout its pages.

Linda P. Jones, Pastor, Transformational Leader, Author and Speaker

December's As Pleasant As May" is a unique collection of inspirational essays drawn from the various stages of the author's life. From a strong faith-based perspective, Dr. Grace Allman Burke writes with authenticity and candor while illustrating these experiences. I strongly recommend this book to anyone seeking inspiration and affirmation. It is definitely a good read.

James M. Hutchins, Senior Pastor New Life Community Church

Without hesitation, it gives me great delight to endorse Dr. Grace Burke's book ***December's As Pleasant As May***. I have known Dr. Burke for over thirty years as an outstanding nurse and trainer of midwives. I vividly recall Dr. Burke, along with her husband, Neville Burke, traveling to Zambia, Africa, with my wife, Rev. Dr. Gloria Broomes and me, during one of our missionary visits there. While in that country, she visited and helped the local midwives in their professional practice.

Dr. Burke's prior five books have been insightful and compelling. I am confident each reader will be impacted in a positive way by this outstanding book.

**Rev. Dr. Winston Herman Broomes, Retired Pastor,
Missionary, and Church Planter**

Readers know when a narrative casts a spell the minute they open the book. Grace Allman Burke is that type of writer and is a delightful story- teller. Her new book, ***December's as Pleasant as May***, takes us on a riveting walk down memory lane that engages the reader from start to ending.

Delna Bryan, Faculty, Young Men's Leadership Academy

Part I
Personal Essays

Section A. Springtime

Harlem Tales

I grew up in the 1940s and 1950s in New York City's Harlem, an area forty-blocks square, going North to South and crossing East to West. I lived in a stately Brownstone house on East 124th Street which my parents purchased when I was four years old. I attended Public School 68 and Ebenezer Church, both on the West Side. My dad had emigrated many years earlier from Barbados in the West Indies and my mom from Panama. They were God-fearing people and raised my siblings and me to love God and cherish a good education. Though they never stifled our curiosities, they were rather strict in their upbringing.

In the first seven Essays, I want to share with you snippets of my life during my early years in Harlem— a place I still call home. The people, the time, the places are indelible in my memory and sometimes I long to experience those simpler days again.

> *"My people will live in peaceful dwelling places, in secure homes in undisturbed places of rest."*
>
> Isaiah 32: 18 (NIV)

Fond Memories of Harlem
(A Personal Reflection)

Our House

When our family moved to 124th Street, our house was officially classified as a "Rooming House," and, thus, was purchased, with tenants, who continued to occupy rooms in the two top floors of the four-story building. We kids had plenty of room to run, jump and play in the lower two levels, outside in the front, and in the backyard. We had ample space also to entertain our large extended family in the parlor on the second floor whenever they visited. My mom, the quintessential cook and baker, took pride in her kitchen, from which delightful aromas emitted daily. I often wondered how she did it after her tiring days at work as a Registered Nurse at Harlem Hospital.

What made our house so interesting were the tenants who lived upstairs. Their many foibles are etched in my memory.

Three single Caucasian men—all immigrants from Sweden—each occupied a room. Wallin and Sandberg, for the most part, were okay. They went out to work daily, paid their rent on time, and lived quietly upstairs. Olsson, on the contrary, was full of resentment against us. Belligerent and insulting, he made it clear he did not like that we Black people had become his landlords.

George and Millie Colton, a childless middle-aged couple, occupied a kitchenette room on the second floor. Daddy, who did not smoke, asked George to temper his cigarette smoking since the fumes wafted downstairs to our quarters.

Mr. Henry, a bachelor, had a girlfriend named Eva. Despite Daddy's strict rules for the house, Henry often snuck Eva into his room for overnight or weekend trysts.

Over the years, tenants came and went but one family, in particular, struck a notable chord—the Millers. Charles Miller, at first, rented a room as a single man. After a while, he advised us he was returning home to Mississippi to live, permanently.

To our surprise, a few years later, Charles reappeared with a family in tow. "This here is my wife, Lillie Mae, and my two little boys." Gesturing, "This one here is Henry Lee, he's four. Joe Nathan, here, is two."

He pleaded with Daddy to rent him a large room for his family. "As soon as we find an apartment, we'll move. Right now we have no place to go."

Lillie Mae stood quietly. Ma and Daddy had compassion on them and rented them a large, vacant room with a small kitchen. They looked undernourished and had obviously poor dental care. It was clear the parents had little schooling and were backward in their behavior, though not rude or disrespectful. What we didn't realize at the time, Lillie Mae was expecting a third child.

One summer afternoon, Ma caught a whiff of smoke in the house. Glancing upstairs, indeed, thick black fumes were billowing downward. Ma rushed us outside while Daddy called the Fire Department. Soon the Colton's window opened and George threw a thick blackened, smoldering mattress down to the sidewalk.

"I'm sorry," he explained. "I guess I fell asleep smoking. I did not mean any harm. I promise I won't do it again."

Meanwhile, next day, Sandberg, with urgency, rang the bell at the gate outside our quarters. "I haven't seen Olsson for a few days. I hope he's all right."

Daddy went upstairs to investigate and smelled a strong odor coming from Olsson's room. Although, as landlord, he had a key to the room, he summoned the Police instead of going in himself.

"We have a dead body in here," the officer said, bluntly, holding a handkerchief over his nose.

This sent a chill over all the tenants. I wanted to go upstairs to see Olsson, but Ma wouldn't let me. The medical examiner said he died of natural causes as there were no signs of foul play. I felt traumatized by that experience for a long time.

A few months after Olsson's passing, Lillie Mae gave birth to her third son, naming him William.

"You can't have five people living in one room," Daddy warned Charles. "Please try harder to find an apartment."

By then, the Millers were well settled in, even calling my parents "Mom" and "Dad!" I was delighted since I loved babies and young children. From time to time, I went upstairs and brought all the Miller kids down to our quarters. I bathed and fed them, changed their clothing, read to them, and loved them. I really believed they were a part of our family.

Late one night, after we'd already gone to bed, we were awakened by a shrill woman's voice calling loudly outside. "Lillie Mae! Lillie Mae! is this the house where you live?"

Ma glanced outside and saw a taxicab which had brought an elderly woman to our door. "I'm Ms. Maralee Turner from Sledge, Mississippi," she informed in a thick Southern drawl. "I'm Lillie Mae's grandmother. Did she have the baby yet?"

Ma nodded in the affirmative, urged her to pay the taxi driver so he could leave, then brought her into the house. Upstairs she went to join the Millers, becoming the sixth person to live in that room! She stayed a long time and did not return to Mississippi until Lillie Mae, one year later, delivered her first baby girl. The child was named Maralee, after her great-grandmother. When big Maralee left, at last, the family moved out.

"I told you overnight ladies are not allowed in single men's rooms in my house," I heard Daddy scold Henry one Sunday morning. "I ought to put you out." Daddy had observed Eva departing an hour earlier.

"I'm sorry, Sir. Please don't let me go. I promise to do better." As before, soft-hearted Daddy let him stay.

There are many more incidents I could recall where our tenants are concerned. I'll stop here for now, though, as I share with you tales about our neighborhood.

Our Neighborhood

My parents were very protective of my two siblings and me while growing up. Although, at the time, the streets were relatively safe, we weren't allowed to wander or roam much farther than in and around our immediate neighborhood. They wanted us to be vigilant and have a plan or purpose in mind when going anywhere away from home.

The neighbors on our block were nice, peaceful, people. Hard-working homeowners, mostly of West Indian origin, they shared the same values as my parents. I never knew why we didn't go into their homes, nor they into ours, but we still considered each other friends. Our families attended our respective weddings, funerals, and special occasions. We kids laughed, talked, and played games outside of our houses. Our mothers all shopped "under the bridge" at the market on 116th Street and Park Avenue for fresh fruit, vegetables, and fish.

Across the street was Mt. Morris Park (later renamed Marcus Garvey Park, after the internationally known Jamaican political activist). Several varieties of elegant maple trees lined its periphery. There were play areas for kids of all ages, and small mountains in the center to climb for fun and picnicking at the top. We were allowed to play freely in the park and also to run through it to the other side to my grandparents' house on Mt. Morris Park West. I have fond memories of delicious cakes and rolls baked by Grandma and dripping ices, shaved by Grandpa when my cousins spent summers with us in Harlem.

My parents' concerns were not unfounded, I came to understand. Truth be told, there were many negative influences from which they were trying to shield us. For example, Fifth Avenue around the corner was considered unsafe. Several apartment buildings, bar and grills, and small shops there allowed shady-looking characters to hang out in front of them. One day, while my brother was playing outside our house, a young man grabbed his piggy bank and took off running toward Fifth Avenue.

"Run, Daddy!" we yelled as my father followed in hot pursuit.

When the guy ran into one of those notorious apartment buildings, Daddy stopped short, reckoning it would have been unsafe for him to enter just to get a few pennies back.

Two establishments, including the small grocery store and our hairdressing salon, were the only places we could go to alone on Madison Avenue around the eastern corner from our house.

Mrs. Jefferson, Ms. Adams, Ms. Turner, the salon proprietor, and Deloris, part-time African dancer, were the beauticians in the salon. Each of them had a lot to say. Women from throughout the neighborhood went there to get their hair done. Community characters of all descriptions hung out there, passing the time away. It was also a hub for sale, at reduced prices, of "hot" or stolen goods. I enjoyed going to the salon while growing up and I learned a whole lot. My dad and my brother went to the barbershop on Lenox Avenue to get haircuts. Only the Lord knows what went on over there.

Further down the block was the ominous Turkish Baths which the police were always raiding. I never knew what went on as people descended a long winding staircase to the baths. I knew though we might not live to tell the story if we tried to find out!

Our Community

Each morning as I walked to school, I passed many interesting characters and fascinating sights. As I travelled West on 124th Street and crossed Fifth Avenue– the dividing line in New York between East and West--were Harlem Travel Agency, Handmaids of Mary Catholic Convent, the Harlem Branch of New York Public Library, Sans Souci (meaning *Without Care* in French)—a mysterious-looking six-story apartment building, and Rice High School, a Catholic school for boys. Every day I bumped into a cadre of blond-haired, uniformed, unsmiling, "eyes straight-ahead," briefcase-holding White boys, who'd descended into Harlem via the commuter train from affluent Westchester County, to attend this school.

Turning North on Lenox Avenue, I crossed bustling 125th Street, an indoor and outdoor shopping mall. I looked West and glimpsed in the distance, the marquee of the famous Apollo Theatre. Many well-known Black entertainers got their start there.

I could spend hours sharing stories about each of these land-marks. What fascinated me most, however, was the knot of five or six women gathered outside their houses every afternoon. Privately, I called them "The Women of West 124th Street." I knew most of them by name because I attended Sunday school with their kids at my church. Like my parents, these women had emigrated from the Carib-bean Islands in the early 1920's and worked hard to live the American dream. Their still noticeable West Indian accents and insular lifestyle distinguished them from other families in the community.

Let me share a bit more about this group. They were all married, slightly gray-haired, a tad past middle-age, and were raising their chil-dren during the 1950s while the Korean War was at its height. Most of their sons had gone off to war, and, to my recollection, thank God, all returned home safe.

Lilly Howard, short and rotund, took pride in her only son, Colbert. Mrs. Motley, with her smooth, Ebony-hued complexion and strong African facial features, always munched on something. She shooed her large brood of kids into the house while she continued to con-verse with the others. Mrs. Bellamy wore thick eyeglasses and never looked straight at anyone. I noticed she always held her head down while talking. Daisy Grant lived with her family in a small apartment building across the street from the others. She was the loudest and most verbose at the afternoon gathering.

"Hey there, Gracie," Lilly Howard would call to me as I passed. "How was school today?"

"Fine, thank you," I answered, not stopping even for a moment.

Ma had warned me to keep walking when I passed them, although I didn't know why. Curious by nature, I longed to linger with them to hear what they talked about, with such animation, every day. I also won-dered why none of their husbands was in the group. Since it was early in the afternoon, I guessed they hadn't arrived home from work yet.

One day, I got the answers to my questions. As I approached the group of women, I was surprised to see a man I knew among them. A minister at a local church, named Bishop Bates, was speaking to them in hushed tones, as he glanced around furtively. I couldn't hear what he said but noticed some of the women were happy and others quite upset.

"Yes. That's good," one exclaimed. "I'm a glad woman today."

Another remarked, "You have to be kidding. "How could I have missed it?"

"See you tomorrow, ladies," Bishop Bates chirped as he stepped in haste up the block and out of sight.

I was determined to discover what this was all about, so I called my dear Aunt Ermine, who always knew *everything*.

"Don't you know those old gals are a bunch of gamblers?" she asked.

Intrigued, I replied, "No, I had no idea."

"They're 'playing the numbers.' Bishop Bates is known as 'the numbers man.' Every day, the group waits for him to arrive with the news of which numbers they had bet on earlier that day had won. All desperately hope for a payoff when he comes."

I was shocked. "Do you mean they don't just gather to gossip and have fun?'

My aunt laughed uproariously. "You have a lot to learn, girl. Those women are harmless, but you'd be surprised to know what goes on around there."

"I see now why Ma told me to keep moving," I chuckled. "Ma always seems to know best."

After that, I still enjoyed passing those "Women of 124th Street." However, it was with a certain 'knowing,' I strode past them.

Our Church

My dad was the pastor of Ebenezer church at the time I grew up. When my siblings and I reflect on those days, we conclude those childhood experiences at our church could rival any Broadway show.

We called everyone at our church 'Brother' or 'Sister', as a mark of respect. The first person who comes to mind is Sis. Cora Kirkland, a tall, somewhat forceful woman, who was convinced she would become a famous opera singer someday. To prepare for her dream role, she insisted on being included on the program at special events at the church. I'll never forget one memorable occasion, to which she invited a reporter from a well-known newspaper. When announced, Sis. Kirkland made a grand appearance from behind a closed curtain. She regaled us for over half an hour in both German and Italian. We young people in the audience sat together in a single pew and covered our mouths to stifle the laughter that forced itself out.

Next day, the newspaper reported the following: "Mrs. Kirkland tended to stray away from the normal notes of her repertoire. In fact, her tones turned to shrieks as she struggled to reach the higher ranges."

That article remained in circulation among church members for quite some time.

Sis. Katherine Innis, who'd emigrated from the US Virgin Islands, preached her own sermon every Sunday, aloud in her pew, in unison with my dad's official sermon! Daddy wasn't a passive man, so I never could figure out why he allowed this to go on. Although her remarks were embarrassing and certainly out of place, I must admit they often caused ripples of laughter throughout the congregation. Here's one example:

During one of his messages, Daddy asked a rhetorical question, "Where is Heaven?"

As each person, silently, considered the answer, Sis. Innis took advantage of that poignant moment and blurted out, "Space!"

Every September, while our friends enjoyed themselves at Labor Day cookouts or at the beach, our church had a Fellowship service. The members of our "sister church" in Brooklyn joined us for the all-day event. In my opinion, the people from Brooklyn were even more hilarious than those in Harlem. Sis. Etheline Moses, for example, always wore a wide-brimmed straw hat which sloped to the side and covered her left eye. I chuckled when I saw her and wondered what her hidden eye looked like. Crossed? Opaque? I never ever found out.

One of the most humorous characters from the 'Brooklyn Brigade' was Sis. Marge Hancock, the organist. She certainly knew how to call attention to herself by the extraordinary jewelry and makeup she sported. Long false eyelashes, heavy face powder and rouge had been generously applied. As she pealed forth on the organ, her bosom rose and fell to the rhythm of the joyous music, along with her large gold earrings, and strands of pearls around her neck. Thinking back, she certainly was quite a distraction.

As you read forthcoming essays in this book, more characters from my beloved Ebenezer will come to life. I trust you will enjoy all of them as much as I've enjoyed telling their stories.

My Brownstone Home in Harlem

Ebenezer Church, Harlem, New York

Church Kitchen

Inez Hunte reigned in the kitchen at Ebenezer Church during my growing up years. I have no idea who appointed her but she was Queen of her domain for as long as I could remember. She deserves a lot of credit though because she really knew her job. When the feast was prepared, it was splendid, tasty, and served with mastery.

Everyone feared our large, ample bosomed, deep voiced Inez. She took her job seriously—too seriously in fact. One would have thought we were in Inez' own kitchen at home -- no imposters allowed. She barked orders at everyone but no one seemed offended. There was no point in arguing with her anyway. She didn't like kids in the kitchen either. She thought them pesky and underfoot. My siblings and I were the exceptions, since we were the pastor's children.

It always amazed me how deft Inez was at refashioning an ordinary job like cooking a meal into a major enterprise. For example, every Labor Day our church had an annual Fellowship Dinner when crowds of people attended and were fed downstairs in the Fellowship Hall. The Saturday preceding the event, the cooking staff gathered in the church kitchen to receive their orders from Inez.

My mom, the pastor's wife, was a member of the Ladies Aid auxiliary and readily joined the group in the kitchen. On one occasion she took me, age twelve, along with her. She cautioned me, however, to stay out of Inez' way. I heeded my mom's advice and sat in a corner, almost hidden. I was quiet and observed the ladies as they followed Inez' commands.

Earlier that week, Inez shopped at the wholesale market and ordered what she wanted. Meats, mountains of tomatoes, lettuce, sweet potatoes, carrots, dried peas and other vegetables, honeydew melons, cantaloupes, strawberries, a variety of seasonings and 25-lb. bags of rice, were delivered early that morning, like clockwork, to the church. Staff from a local bakery brought huge logs of vanilla cake, while ice cream, preserved in dry ice, arrived ready for the freezer.

By the time we got there, Inez had parceled out the hams and turkeys to individual ladies to be cooked at their homes and delivered Monday morning to the church. My mom was assigned to bake two of the turkeys. I was amazed at the size of the pots and pans that would be used to prepare the meal. Multi-gallon saucepans, skillets and bakeware were scrubbed, shined, and made ready.

Each of the women knew what her task would be: to peel, grate, cut, dice, slice, and season. They seemed to me like an army of bees working together in unison to get the big job done.

The most exciting part of the operation, for me, though was listening to the women tell their stories:

"I came here bright and early to enjoy a few hours of peace," Alberta Harding sighed and waved her grater in the air. "My husband wears me out. I can't do anything to please him. He grumbles about everything and it makes me sick."

"My new boyfriend asked me to marry him," Elouise Isaacs announced.

Spinster Claudine Jackson's face lit up like a Christmas tree. "Did you tell him, 'Yes?'"

"No, I didn't. As much as I'd like to get married, I'm not sure what kind of husband he'd be. He's lazy and just can't seem to keep a job."

"Then get rid of him." Claudine's finger made a slicing motion across her neck. "You don't need him to enjoy life. Please don't get stuck with him."

"I'm real tired of my two grown grandchildren in my house," Jenny Simmons confessed. "I'm hoping they'll soon move out."

"Please pray for my son, Elton," Kit Garrison almost whispered. "He was carted off to jail for shoplifting. I'm so upset about this."

"My daughter, Saundra, has been accepted into Harvard University and will attend there next Fall," Sylvia Wharton reported with pride. "She wants to be a doctor someday."

"Come closer," Miriam Harris beckoned with excitement. "I have some gossip to share."

The others huddled around her. "I'm glad Millie Davis isn't here today. She got into big trouble last week. Someone saw her hand in hand with her neighbor's husband as they left the Red Rooster Bar."

"You have to be kidding," Jenny said. Her eyes grew large with interest.

"There's more." Miriam lowered her voice and motioned the ladies closer. "The man's wife confronted Millie and a major row broke out right there on the street. The police were called and things settled down after that."

I giggled to myself but did not miss a word. I realized right away I had hit on something special. I would never have been allowed to hear older women talk like that about their private lives as I grew up. I was taught "children should be seen and not heard." But there I was, listening with full attention.

However, Inez must have heard my giggle. I had been caught listening.

"A kid is in our midst!" she yelled.

Embarrassed, my mom asked me to leave the kitchen and go outside to play. Ashamed at being caught, I scampered away.

Labor Day arrived, at last, and the much-awaited fellowship service. The women again gathered early on the appointed morning to cook the meal they'd set up. The service was in session in the sanctuary while heavenly aromas wafted upward from the basement below. I couldn't wait to dig my teeth in. After we sang the Doxology, we all made a beeline downstairs to enjoy the great feast.

Inez' team was transformed into an efficient wait staff wearing black dresses overlaid by white aprons. I couldn't believe it was the same crew I'd watched preparing the food in the kitchen.

Inez, it seemed, had forgiven me for eavesdropping since she greeted me with a smile. "Grace, did you get enough turkey?"

I nodded in the affirmative. "It tasted delicious."

"All right then, let me know if you want some more. I have some hidden away for my kitchen workers and the pastor's family to take home."

With a quick wink, and a rustle of her dress and apron, she hurried back to the kitchen control center. Sure enough, at the end of the day, Inez loaded down her workers and my mom with all the leftover food from the feast. We enjoyed it many days afterward.

There is nothing like the memory from one's childhood of a lively church kitchen.

My Three Aunts

I was born and raised in the Village of Harlem in New York City and came of age in the 1940's and 1950s. I grew up in a large family with several aunts and uncles. Three of my aunts made indelible impressions on me. Allow me to introduce each of them and share with you what I remember about them. Please note, we were not allowed to call our elders by their first names in those days and I always complied.

Aunt Dorothy

Aunt Dorothy was the oldest of my mom's siblings. She was warm and generous and I adored her. She loved her nieces and nephews dearly and we sometimes fondly called her 'Aunt D." She seemed to like that.

Shall we say though, Aunt Dorothy was "different?" I'll explain what I mean later on.

Looking back, I realize Aunt Dorothy was well ahead of her time. She had gifts and talents which might have been expressed beyond the confines of our community, had she been given opportunity. For example, she was a gourmet cook.

"Try this, Grace," she'd say as she offered me one of her fresh-baked pastries straight from her oven.

"Tastes delicious, Aunt D.," I would reply as it melted in my mouth.

During my younger years, it was Aunt Dorothy who introduced me to such delicacies as hearts of artichoke, liver paté, lemon soufflé, and Quiche Lorraine. How many ten year-olds, I ask you, even today, would know or be able to converse about those foods?

Long before the fitness craze came into being, Aunt Dorothy was doing what was called 'Calisthenics.' (Those of you of a certain age might remember this). Back in the '50s, Aunt D. donned white shorts and a white top. She created her own rhythm, kicked her legs, and twirled her arms, in an effort to stay trim and fit. She explained to me how important this is. "Exercise keeps you feeling good. We need it to stay in good health."

My Aunt Dorothy was also a classical singer. Her unmistakably clear soprano voice was fine-tuned by Mrs. Gilbert, her instructor, who gave concerts for her students annually.

If I closed my eyes now, I would see Aunt D., attired in a floor-length silk gown, elbow length gloves, tiara on her head. I would be transported to local sanctuaries, including St. Martin's Episcopal Church or Ebenezer Gospel Tabernacle, made available to Mrs. Gilbert for a Mozart or Handel's recital. I would see Aunt Dorothy appear at the appointed time either as soloist or part of a well-rehearsed trio or quartet. I would beam with pride at the end of the recital when they called her name.

"Miss Dorothy Morgan, please come forward and take a bow."

As flowers were presented to her, the thunderous applause from the audience confirmed their appreciation of the magnificent performance she gave.

One of my most cherished childhood memories is when Aunt D. took me downtown to New York City's Carnegie Hall to hear noted African American Soprano, Miss Marian Anderson, sing.

My aunt prepared me in advance, "Now Grace, after the concert you will meet Miss Anderson in person. Remember to keep your gloves on, curtsy, and shake her hand."

Sure enough, when the concert concluded, my dear aunt, with much determination, pushed her way backstage with me in tow. My young heart beat in anticipation. I did what she told me and was thrilled when Miss Anderson smiled at me and autographed my program. I held on to that program for many years after.

Aunt Dorothy was quite the eccentric. This is what I meant when I said earlier she was 'different.' Let me explain. For one thing, she cared less what others thought about her manner of dressing. In the wintertime, she wore three coats --all at the same time!

I once heard my mom ask her, "Dorothy, why do you need three coats?"

"They keep me warm so I'm wearing them," she retorted.

No one ever questioned her about this again.

"By the way, did I tell you I'm on my way to becoming a world class milliner?" she once asked when she visited our home. "I make all of my own hats now."

Only silence reigned as we looked at the outlandish hat she had on. It was puffed up high on her head and the fur seemed to have been extracted from a groundhog or a raccoon. When she appeared at our door in this crazy outfit, my siblings and I were forced to muffle our giggles. We dared not let our parents see or hear us laughing at her, no matter how hilarious she appeared. I suspect they, themselves, laughed uproariously when they were alone.

There was one more feature about Aunt Dorothy. She was always laden down with bags—sometimes two purses and three or four shopping bags at a time. The expression "bag lady" wasn't in vogue back then, but you, my readers, know what I mean.

"How do you manage all of those bags when you ride the buses?" I once ventured to ask.

"I make do," she replied. "Someone almost always gives me a seat if the bus is crowded.I sell the things in these bags, like greeting cards, hats, calendars, and canned goods. It's how I make extra money for myself."

This aunt rocked our family to its core when she reached age sixty-five.

"I'm getting married," she cheerfully announced one day at a family meeting she called.

Our mouths fell open in disbelief, since, to our knowledge, she had never dated or even had marriage on her mind.

"To whom?" my father asked.

"To a nice man whom I met recently."

Sensing we wanted more details, she continued. "Well he's ten years younger than I am, but that's okay, he's very mature."

"Is he as involved in the church as you are?" one of my uncles inquired.

"No, but he will be soon. I was conducting a religious street meeting when he passed by and saw me. He knelt down, accepted Christ and immediately proposed marriage. I've never been happier in my life."

Our concern grew stronger as Aunt Dorothy shared more information about her fiancé.

When my mom asked her where he lived and what work he did, she replied, "With relatives. He's been in the USA for several years, but he isn't legal. He will be though after we get married. He'll then be able to find work as well."

Several family members warned Aunt D. she was being taken for a ride by this man. However, convinced God had sent him to her, she accepted his proposal and heeded none of the family's advice. She went on to plan a huge wedding, at her own expense, complete with attendants, limousine, and fine dining.

Sadly, Aunt Dorothy lived in misery over the next several years. As predicted, the "happily ever after" she hoped for was only a fantasy. Her husband was abusive, but she chose to stay with him anyway. Ten years later, when he fell ill and passed away, she was free, at last, to live her happy, carefree life again.

Aunt Geri

Nearly everyone in our neighborhood knew Aunt Geri. She was stylish, humorous, and spoke Spanish fluently, having grown up in Panamá in Central America. She was the only one of my grandmother's children born in Jamaica, in the Caribbean. While expecting her third child, Grandma went back to Jamaica, her homeland, to visit her family. While there, Aunt Geri, was born. Grandma took her baby with her back to Panamá while still a young infant.

Although family gossip reported she had several boyfriends over the years, Aunt Geri never married.

"I'm a lifelong bachelorette," she often quipped. "I'm happy just the way I am."

Aunt Geri immigrated to New York as a young woman from Panamá but never travelled anywhere else after that. Strange, she seemed stuck within four square blocks in Harlem for the rest of her life. She never rented her own apartment either but simply occupied a room in various houses owned by family members. She lived in a room upstairs in our house for a number of years as well.

We could count on Aunt Geri, though, to be the life of any party. At family gatherings, she had us joking, laughing, and reminiscing. Despite this, I realized early on she was an insular and private person. She did not share much about herself, her past experiences, thoughts, or future plans.

"Would you someday like to have children?" I once recall asking her.

"Why is that important?" she answered, brushing me off.

I had the feeling that beneath the joviality, she really was unhappy. So much about her remained a mystery.

I discovered Aunt Geri wasn't generous either, although she pretended to be.

I clearly recall on my ninth birthday, she presented me with one-half of a cake she had made! She even iced it, but obviously, intentionally cut in half. It wasn't her birthday, but I guess she wanted to keep the other half for herself.

I was quite annoyed about it, but still told her, "Thank you," as my mother thought I should.

I am grateful to Aunt Geri, though, for rescuing me from a whipping another Aunt, named Lenora, was about to lay on me. I don't recall what she was upset about, but Aunt Geri rushed to the front door, opened it and said, "Run, Grace. Run as fast as you can."

Aunt Lenora chased after me, but of course, she was no match for a kid my age. She returned home, huffing and puffing, her mission aborted. Everyone laughed at her and told her she was silly.

Aunt Geri had a very morbid and superstitious side to her. She loved to attend funerals and look at dead people. She made it her business to be there whenever she saw a cortege entering Mickey's or Toppin's funeral home on Lenox Avenue. Most of the time she didn't even know the deceased!

She also dreamed a lot and put a negative spin on her dreams. If someone fell ill or passed away, she had already seen that in her dream. She believed if your right hand itched, money was coming your way. But if your left hand itched, money would leave you.

If I tried hard, I could pull from my memory bank many other "special" things about Aunt Geri.

Aunt Lenora

This aunt was in a category all by herself. Almost everyone disliked her because of her intractable temper and overbearing ways. If anyone disagreed with her, they paid a great price. Aunt Lenora was determined to win every argument.

"Don't try to over talk me," she'd yell. "You're no match for me."

To everyone's surprise, however, she met and married a nice man named Vincent. We never figured out what made him feel attracted to her. After they married, they never moved away from my grandparent's home. Perhaps Aunt Lenora knew Grandma and Grandpa were the only landlords who would put up with her awful ways.

Grandma operated a day nursery for many years that serviced several families in the neighborhood. The children's parents loved her and were happy she took care of their kids. One summer, my grandparents went on a cruise and left Aunt Lenora in charge of the nursery. On their return, Grandma quickly realized the awful mistake she had made. Not a single child was left in the nursery. Aunt Lenora's tantrums had scared all the parents away! It took Grandma a while to build up the nursery again.

Aunt Lenora had a smattering of musical talent. She played the piano and organ at my grandfather's church. My most notable recollection, however, was the music lessons she gave to my cousins and me on Saturday mornings at my grandparents' home. The word "torture" is an understatement of what we endured under her tutelage at the piano. She was strict, mean, and determined we should strike every note correctly. If we made a mistake, she used her well-sharpened pencil to rap our knuckles. She did this over and over until we got it right. Many a Saturday I fell into Uncle Vincent's consoling arms, crying, after a harsh session with Aunt Lenora. It was nice having someone nearby who seemed to understand. After some time, I could take it no longer and told my mom I wasn't going back to piano lessons. I know Aunt Lenora is the reason why I don't play piano today.

Uncle Vincent really tried hard to get along with his wife, Aunt Lenora. No one was surprised, however, when he asked for a brief meeting with family members. I was about twelve years old at the time but recall the occasion well.

"Lenora and I are separating and I'm moving out of town. She's become so unbearable, I have to go."

We were sad when he left. He was a great guy and we liked having him in our family. Nobody blamed him. We understood all too well. He returned a few years later when Grandpa passed away.

The funeral was a sad occasion for all of us. But Aunt Lenora put on a royal show to demonstrate her grief.

"Oh Papa! Papa!" she shrieked, then fainted in the middle of the funeral and had to be carried out.

We kids meant no disrespect to Grandpa, but could hardly contain our laughter as we witnessed her star performance. It was pure theatre!

I could go on and on with tales about these three aunts. You can tell each lived in a world of her own. I often wonder how they would have navigated life if they lived today in our time. Nevertheless, I learned a lot about life from each of them.

Church Picnic

Far in the distance, we could hear the jingling, popping, staccato rhythm of the tambourines, accompanying the fervent singing, as each of six buses arrived at the park:

"When the saints go marching in, when the saints go marching in,
"Oh Lord, I want to be in that number, when the saints go marching in!
"When they crown Him Lord of all, when they crown Him, Lord of all,
"Oh Lord, I want to be in that number, when they crown Him, Lord of all!"

The day of the annual Church Picnic had arrived, after months of planning. That July morning in 1958, was sweltering. Beads of perspiration rolled down my face. I felt as if I would collapse, as the heat and humidity merged with the merciless sun.

Daddy drove Ma and me to Sunken Meadow State Park, to be there when the buses arrived from Ebenezer Church. He made sure he was the first at the park every year. After all, he was the Pastor, and he was expected to be there to greet the people.

To get my mind off the heat, I thought about the beehive of activity that was our house earlier. The wonderful aroma of cooking and baking wafted from the kitchen throughout the rooms. We owned a four-story Brownstone house across from Mt. Morris Park, in Harlem, located uptown in New York City. Our family occupied the first two floors, while tenants lived upstairs. Ma awakened about 4:00 AM to get the food ready. I rolled out of bed an hour later to help her. Her hands moved with a familiar deftness as she made ham sandwiches with mayonnaise, tongue sandwiches with mustard, and codfish cakes. She also baked Jamaican patties, and coconut turnovers. My job was to wrap each sandwich and baked item in individual sheets of waxed paper. I also had to fill the heavy metal two-gallon jugs with the drinks we would have at the picnic. They had insulated linings, to keep the drinks cold. One of them contained Ma's favorite drink, West Indian ginger beer. I never knew why they called it "beer." Although it had a tangy, throat-tickling, taste, there wasn't a hint of alcohol near it!

"Ma," I asked, "how did you learn to cook and bake like this?"

"My mom-your grandma-taught me. It's a family tradition. What I've cooked so far are just the snacks, though. I'm getting ready to make our main meal now!"

In what seemed like no time at all, Ma was finished fixing our lunch. She had cooked fried chicken, string beans, and rice and peas with gravy. Potato salad, Cole slaw, and a lettuce and tomato salad completed the meal. It looked scrumptious. When we finished packing it all, we had six or seven picnic bags full. It seemed as if there was enough food to feed an army!

"I can't wait until we get there, so I can dig in," I declared.

Sunken Meadow State Park was located on Long Island, about fifty miles East of New York City. The two-hour journey by car seemed endless. However, the buses took about an hour longer to get there, since they weren't allowed to travel on the main highways.

As each bus rolled into the park, the passengers disembarked with their picnic bags and jugs in tow. Earlier that morning, most had walked to the church, since they only lived a few blocks away. They carried these items to the church, where they boarded the buses.

When the buses arrived, the kids and teenagers scampered ahead to secure unoccupied picnic tables. Earlier, my family had commandeered two tables for ourselves. Ma, first, covered them with old newspapers she'd brought along, then, spread multicolored tablecloths on top. She also brought a fly swatter, and real (not plastic), silverware for the meal. Now, we watched as others did the same. I smiled, having witnessed this ritual year after year.

Daddy greeted each one, as familiar faces emerged from the buses. "Welcome to Sunken Meadow Park."

My sister, Marilyn, and my brother, Luther, were among the first to get off.

"How was the bus ride?" I inquired.

Marilyn smiled, "It was great. We ate our snacks, played games, and sang our hearts out. I'm sure you heard us singing before you saw us."

"Brother Jones was in charge of our bus, though," Luther chimed in.

"As usual, he didn't stand for any nonsense. He reminded us in a stern voice, 'You are representatives of Ebenezer Church. You must be on your best behavior at the park,' "

"Did anyone answer him?" Ma asked, in a sarcastic tone.

Luther laughed. "We kids kept doing our thing, and the older people rolled their eyes."

Our church had a strict dress code back then. They believed women and girls should not wear pants at any time –not even to a picnic. They quoted the Bible verse which said, "Women should not wear men's clothing" (KJV: Deut. 22:5). Brother Jones, the head deacon, made it his business to enforce that edict. Each year, the morning of the picnic, he planted himself at the front doors of each bus as folks boarded, to ensure no one disobeyed.

Unbeknown to Brother Jones, this year, however, we teenaged girls hatched a plan.

"When we leave home, let's wear pedal pusher pants under our skirts. They are shorter than our skirts and won't be seen when we board the buses. When we get to the park, we'll take our skirts off, enjoy ourselves throughout the day, then put the skirts back on when it's time to go home. Brother Jones, 'the monitor' won't be able to do a thing about it."

We laughed, hugged each other in agreement, and swore ourselves to secrecy before the big day arrived.

Our plan worked. Peggy-Ann, Rita, Janet, Millicent, I and several others, gathered together, still wearing our skirts, headed to the playground.

"One -two-three go!" Someone yelled, as, in unison, we removed our skirts. We collapsed with laughter and high-fived each other – ecstatic we had pulled it off.

While we were at the playground, Ma and the other church ladies were busy setting out the food at their respective tables. They charged us we were to return for the grand feast at high noon.

It struck me funny, how, each woman wore a different version of the same outfit: a narrow-brimmed straw hat to keep the sun at bay; a cotton sundress WITH SLEEVES, (sleeveless dresses were also a sin for Christian women to wear back then); striped, ging-ham, or polkadot dresses, falling midway between the knees and ankles; (Ma always bought a brand-new dress for the occasion). Their outfits would not have been complete without a freshly ironed apron. Despite the heat, they wore brown, nylon stock-ings, with seams, attached to a girdle or garter belt beneath their dresses; open-toed shoes which were also open-backed, with one-inch heels. Some of their shoes were laced, and some had straps across the ankles.

"I chuckled to myself, *I guess Brother Jones is well pleased with their outfits.*

The ladies seemed happy as they chatted among themselves. They were all members of the church's Ladies Aid auxiliary, of which my Aunt Ermine was the President, and were serious in their commit-ment to it.

We wolfed down the delicious picnic food until we were stuffed.

However, we received strict warning from our parents, "No swim-ming in the pool or at the beach for one-half hour after lunch. If you do, you can get stomach cramps and die!"

We didn't know if this had happened to anyone before or if it was even true. But no one tried to find out either. We just obeyed.

One-half hour later, to the minute, a group of us kids headed for the changing rooms to don our swimming outfits. Sunken Meadow park had a great beach, so we all splashed in. The guys dunked the gals, while we feigned fear of drowning and screamed, "Stop! Stop!" It was wonderful fun for all.

"Oh-oh," Luther reminded, as a clock chimed somewhere in the distance.

"Sister Hunte said we should be back at the tables for dessert at three o'clock sharp. We'll get a tongue-lashing from her if we don't head back soon."

When we reached the tables, a long line had already formed. Sister Hunte was in charge of dessert at the picnic and had commanded the Ladies Aid members to form an assembly line. Each had a specific job. Some sliced the hug logs of vanilla cake, bought that morning at a neighborhood bakery in Harlem. Others loaded the cake slices onto paper plates. Ice cream, bought and preserved in large tubs filled with chunks of hot ice, was scooped out by several ladies, and placed on the cake-laden plates. Sister Hunte yelled at the crowd, "Let us know what flavor you want. Don't wait 'til you get to the table to think about it! And, by the way, only one flavor per person. Don't ask for both."

I whispered to Peggy-Ann, as we joined the line, "She makes that same speech every year."

My friend giggled, "She always buys the same two flavors anyway –Vanilla and Orange-Pineapple. What's there to think about? I'll bet those are the two flavors she likes best."

When Brother Smith joined the line, Sister Hunte asked if him if he was ready for his ice cream.

Brother Smith licked his lips and replied, "I'm ice cream, myself."

We collapsed with laughter.

After dessert, it was time for my favorite picnic activity. Daddy asked, "Who's ready for a rowboat ride?"

"Are we ready? You already know we're ready!"

The lake was calm, and sparkled in the late-afternoon sun, when Marilyn, Daddy, and I, boarded the rowboat. Several other boats and canoes, filled with laughing children, were there already. Daddy sat in the center, while my sister and I sat on either end. His strong, muscular, arms grabbed the oars and deftly guided us farther out on the lake. He pointed out various types of beautiful flowers and vegetation growing along the shoreline. Schools of brightly-colored fish swished by, while different species of birds flew low overhead.

"I think I spotted a Blue Jay just now, "I informed.

Marilyn pointed out a mother duck, with her brood of ducklings, walking behind her close to the water.

I broke out in song, "Row, row, row your boat, gently down the stream."

Marilyn chimed in, "Merrily, merrily, merrily, merrily, life is but a dream."

Daddy, the musical genius he was, shook his head with mock disapproval, "Not bad, but next time, perhaps you can stay in tune."

Our two-hour escapade on the lake came to an end too soon.

"What a great way to end our picnic," I remarked, as we disembarked. "I sure wish we could come this way more than once a year."

Marilyn reminded, "I'd better get my skirt back on. I may not be able to get back home if I don't!"

Ma and Luther had packed our things and taken them to the car already. Folks boarded the buses and bid fond farewell to each other.

"See you at church tomorrow, if you can make it out of bed!"

"I plan to be there, but, no doubt, I'll nod off during the preaching."

"The spirit is willing, but the flesh is weak."

When the last bus rolled down the road, Daddy followed close behind, then turned onto the highway.

Tent Meeting

I clearly remember going to tent meetings during my childhood summers. One mid-July evening in 1953 remains etched in my mind. The temperature sizzled at 98 degrees and the humidity, at 100 percent, made it even worse. But the weather didn't deter us folk from Harlem as we made the trek by subway to Brooklyn to attend opening night. After a sweltering two-hour ride on three different trains, we finally reached the Kingston and Throop Avenues Subway station. We emerged onto the street and walked the remaining block to the tent's location. As we arrived, people who lived in Brooklyn joined us. Some walked from home or rode buses to get there.

We kids were born in America, the children of immigrants from throughout the West Indies. However, most of our parents hailed from the island of Barbados. Despite being in the USA for several years, most maintained their strong Caribbean accents.

An enormous brown tent had been erected earlier that day on a large vacant lot at the corner of Thompkins and McDonough Streets. Several willing workers from area churches joined forces to make it happen. Thick sawdust was spread on the concrete floor. Lightbulbs were strung on sturdy electric cords and hung overhead throughout the tent. When all was done, they hoisted an old black upright piano onto a hastily constructed platform at the front of the tent. It sat poised to provide music for the service, accompanied by the many tambourines the sisters brought with them.

The air was charged with expectancy as we took our seats on, rickety, folding chairs, tightly packed together. Before long, a tent flap opened behind the platform. The dignitaries of the clergy appeared. Somber-faced, they looked and acted alike. Each man was dressed in a tight-fitting Sunday-best suit—either black, brown or gray—with matching tie. Each clutched a large worn Bible in his hand. As they found their places on the platform, they either kneeled or bowed their head, and breathed, a hasty, silent prayer.

At 7:00pm sharp, I recognized old Elder King as he walked to the rostrum. "Let's stand and give God praise!" His familiar scratchy voice bellowed in the night air. "Welcome to this year's tent meeting! We're going to have a time tonight and all the rest of this week!"

Leroy Boyce, a short, dark-skinned, rotund, young man, struck up chords on the piano. Maisie Welch, the appointed song leader, belted out the song, "I've Found a Friend in Jesus, He's Everything to Me." Leroy struggled to keep pace with her. The audience clapped while the ladies beat their tambourines in perfect rhythm. As some in the audience stood and waved their hands, the tent meeting roared into full swing!

By the third song, Sister Maria Babb danced her way to the front of the tent. Dressed in long white robes from head to foot, she swayed with the music, tapped her feet, and sang louder than anyone else:

"I am pressing, I am pressing toward the Glory Land!"

We kids stared at her in wonder. We dared not laugh under the watchful, ready-to-reprimand-instantly eyes of our parents.

Elder King then took the microphone from Maisie, "It's testimony time! We have a lot to do tonight, so make it short and sweet. If you testify, don't sing. If you sing, don't testify."

For the next half-hour, the saints stood, and in their lilting accents, with obedience, either sang or testified of the goodness of God in their lives. Some went into details perhaps should better have been left unsaid. Nevertheless, loud *Amens* echoed throughout the tent as they finished and sat down.

As if on cue, Brother Samuel Trotter, made his way down the side aisle and up to the platform. "Good evening, Saints. It's time to raise our offering. To rent this tent and keep these lights on costs real hard money. Tonight, I want 'waving money' and you can't wave no dime! Dig deep in your pockets and pocketbooks. Bring your best offering to the baskets up front. The ushers will guide you as Leroy gives us some real hot music to walk by."

The heat in the tent rose as the service wore on. Ushers provided us paper fans from a nearby funeral home. We fanned as we attempted to cool ourselves in the stifling summer air.

Just before the Evangelist was called, Bertine Brathwaite, came forward to sing. What would a tent meeting have been without a rendition from this notable soloist of tent-renowned fame? Bertine must have believed she was also an actress because she dramatized the words of the songs she chose to sing. She announced, "My song is entitled, 'It's Worth It.' Please pray for my voice since I have a slight cold."

Before she uttered a sound, however, one of Bertine's fans from her peanut gallery, of sorts, at the back of the tent, cried out, "Sing Berts!"

As if spurred on by this support, Bertine screeched in high-pitched tones, bowed herself down and wiped fake tears from her eyes:

"It's worth it! Saints, it's worth it!
It's worth my sighing, It's worth my crying,
it's worth my dying, to make Heaven, Heaven, Heaven my home!"

I muffled my laughter throughout her performance and tried to contain myself.

Charlie Walker, a tall, swarthy, handsome man, from Pennsylvania, was introduced as the Evangelist of the hour, amid loud cheers from the crowd. He had been a favorite preacher at tent meetings for years. That night the saints were not disappointed as he preached with power, under a rich anointing. Rev. Walker did not stay in the pulpit, but walked up and down the aisles, Bible in hand. His baritone voice penetrated as he beckoned folks to the altar. Crowds surged forward to re-dedicate their lives to Christ. Even as a child, I thoroughly enjoyed Rev. Walker's messages. I know, even now, they left a lasting impact on my spiritual development.

At the end of the three-hour service, we hugged, greeted each other, and vowed, "We don't plan on missing tomorrow night's service."

We weary travelers retraced our journey and caught the last train back to Harlem. When my siblings, parents, grandmother, and I finally arrived home, we collapsed in our beds, as sounds of the tent meeting still echoed in our ears.

Gypsy

When you read the title of my essay, GYPSY, you might have thought about an Indo-European Romani person who wanders in nomad groups in various parts of the world.

In truth, I am not speaking about a person at all, but, rather, about a language I spoke as a child. I am uncertain where Gypsy originated but I believe it's of Afro-Caribbean origin.

Although my parents were of similar cultural background, my mother's family spoke Gypsy while my father's did not. History indicates Gypsy is largely spoken by people from the Island of Jamaica. My maternal grandmother, Lydia, who hailed from Jamaica, spoke fluent Gypsy. My paternal grandmother, Clara, from Barbados, to my knowledge, knew nothing of Gypsy.

This language is only spoken, not written, and is passed down orally from one generation to another. One would be hard pressed, therefore, to find written information on how it originated and its prevalence.

In my family, the grownups spoke Gypsy to one another. They diverted from English whenever we kids were present. We dared not ask what was being said, nor were we invited to join the conversation. When plans were made and secrets shared, Gypsy was the order of the day.

Somewhere around the age of eight, I learned to decipher this family language. I listened with full attention and could soon guess what was being said. Every day in my room, I practiced speaking Gypsy in secret. After a while, I became fluent. It tickled me that my mother was unaware I was taking it all in. It was hard for me to contain myself as I listened to my relatives--mom, grandma, aunts and uncles-- speak to one another. I understood every word. It became clear also they spoke the language very rapidly.

I shared my secret with my brother and sister and asked if they'd like me to teach them Gypsy. To my delight, they were all in. After doing our homework, we went outside for Gypsy lessons on the front stoop. Soon, they were speaking it too. Our cover was blown, however, when our cousins came to visit. They learned the language from us, but, alas, were not careful to keep our secret hidden from our parents.

I don't recall if the older folk were happy about our new-found fluency in Gypsy or not. However, they started speaking to us in the language whenever they deemed it necessary.

For example, once in a department store, my mother spoke to me in Gypsy when the saleswoman behaved, with indifference, toward her. "Let's just walk away," she said in our family dialect, and we did.

Now, years later, my cousins and I, on occasion, still speak Gypsy. It comes in handy when strangers are within earshot and we want to discuss personal matters. Though I fear it is becoming a lost art, I'd still like to hold on to it as something valuable from my ancestors. I taught my kids, now adults, the language. They understand it but don't speak it much. I guess they are far too busy with their social media, cell phones, and other electronics to consider it important.

While preparing this essay, I did some research on Gypsy. As I suspected, I could find nothing on the subject. The closest language that appeared similar was Pig Latin.

Wikipedia defines Pig Latin as "a language in which words in English are altered, usually by adding a fabricated suffix or initial consonant of a word to the end of the word and adding a vocalic syllable to create such a suffix....The objective is to conceal the words from others not familiar with the rules. Pig Latin has rules that define how consonants and vowels are placed next to words."[2]

After all these years, I decided to decode my Gypsy language and came up with the following:

---

2   https://en.wikipedia.org+Pig_Latin+899788329

Definition of Gypsy

A language in which words in English are altered by adding a "g" in the middle of each word. Thus, the word's pronunciation is changed as follows: one-syllable words become two, and two-syllable words become four. The goal is to hide the words from those not familiar with the rules.

Gypsy Rules

The g is placed after each vowel and the vowel is repeated after the g. The subsequent letters of the word follow.

Below is a Gypsy De-coding Chart to help you pronounce the Gypsy language.

Have fun!

I'm glad I'm able to share my Gypsy language in this way. I hope you find it both fascinating and educational. Perhaps, someday, I can convince one of my grandchildren to learn our family language.

GYPSY DE-CODING CHART

1. You come here and sit down

English	Gypsy
You	Yo-gou
Come	Co-gome
Here	He-gere
And	A-gand
Sit	Si-git
Down	Do-gown

2. Read your Bible and pray

English	Gypsy
Read	Re-gead
Your	Yo-gour
Bible	Bi-gi- b-gle
And	A-gand
Pray	Pra-gay

Hot Comb

"Hold still, Grace," my grandmother cautioned as Mrs. Hume applied the hot comb to my hair. "Don't you want to look pretty tomorrow on Easter Sunday?"

I was seven and, at that point, I didn't care how I looked on Easter Sunday. This was torture. I squirmed and jumped from the heat of the hot comb. Mrs. Hume, our family hairdresser, put a towel around my neck and covered my ears so the hot comb and grease wouldn't burn me. I pulled my ears down almost to my shoulders, closed my eyes and prayed this ordeal would soon be over.

Thinking back over these many years, I smile at how connected we were with our families. My grandparent's house was the hub of all the action and the gathering place for many family celebrations. Nothing was ever discussed, planned, or celebrated without the input of our entire extended family. Even hairdressing involved all of us.

Every two weeks, on a Saturday morning, Mrs. Hume, a tall, slender, middle-aged woman, with tinted blue hair, dutifully arrived at Grandma's house with her bag full of straightening combs and curling irons. This was a daylong affair, since I and all my female relatives came to get our hair done. If I recall, there were between nine and twelve customers for Mrs. Hume on any given Saturday. She was a hospital nurse during the week. On weekends, my family guaranteed her some extra cash.

"Who's first today, Mrs. Wilson?" she'd ask on arrival.

Grandma, a true hostess, always served her a cup of coffee before she began. "Grace is first today. She got here early. I'll go last, as usual. We can chat a bit while you style my hair."

Back in the late 1940s and early 1950s, Black women embraced the credo of Madam C. J. Walker, the self-made, Black, female millionaire and entrepreneur. She espoused that a Black woman's hair is her crowning glory, and, if attended to, would take her far in her personal and business life. With that in mind, she created a line of hair products specifically for "colored women," as we were called then. Our hair is naturally quite thick and these products softened the strands, so it could be curled and styled into various beautiful hairdos.

When she arrived, Mrs. Hume would place her instruments on a lighted fire on Grandma's kitchen stove. While waiting for them to heat to the needed temperature, she parted and applied our favorite hair grease, *Dixie Peach,* throughout the strands of the freshly-washed hair. I can almost smell the perfumed, nearly spicy, scent of Dixie Peach even now.

As she worked on each person's head, Mrs. Hume's hands and fingers moved with deftness, creating the individual style desired.

"Did you go to hairdressing school?" Aunt Anita asked her.

"No, it all just came to me naturally. I watched a woman in my neighborhood style hair, and soon I could do it myself."

My mother told me later she was glad Mrs. Hume came to Grandma's house. Not only did she charge us less since she had so many heads to work on, but it also saved us having to wait forever in a beauty parlor.

I must admit when Mrs. Hume was finally finished with my hair that long-ago day, I looked totally transformed. When she handed me the mirror, I saw she had given me bangs at the front, and the rows of curls at the back and sides of my head I had requested.

"Wow!" I exclaimed with excitement. "I feel as if I could get dressed for church right now."

"Not so fast, Grace," Grandma chided. "You will have to wait until tomorrow. We will all sashay together into church, showing off our new hairdos and Easter outfits."

At the end of the day, with tired hands, Mrs. Hume gathered her hot combs to leave. When we girls and ladies told her how happy we were with our bouffants, updos, and waves, she beamed with great pride.

"Until next time," she confirmed, then slowly made her way to the bus stop.

Hold Still! Hot Combs & Curling Irons! Remember These?[3]

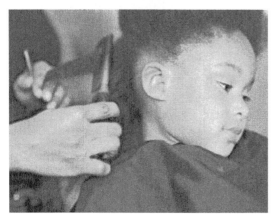
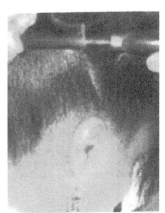

3   Photo Attributions on p. 473.

Origins

William Shakespeare in his play, *The Tempest*[4], said, "What's Past is Prologue." The idea is that history sets the context for the present, or, the past sets the stage for one's destiny. In other words, our history is a force in shaping our lives. If that is so, perhaps we should stop for a moment and consider that our ancestors taught us lessons, good and bad, about how to live today.

The following pieces relate true stories about connections of the past to the present. Several of them ask questions to ponder about why the past makes profound differences in our lives, current and future.

> *"For I know the plans I have for you,"* declares the LORD, *"plans to prosper you and not to harm you, plans to give you hope and a future."*
>
> Jeremiah 29:11 (NIV)

---

4   Shakespeare. 1611. <u>The Tempest,</u>

Why Am I Like This?

Janelle Burton, age forty, received the shock of her life when she learned she had siblings she never knew existed. She'd been adopted as an infant and was told about it at an early age. However, she knew nothing about her birth family.

Time and again, as she grew up, she'd plied her mother, Hope, with questions. "Who are they? Where are they? Do they even know I exist? Does my birth mom look like me?"

Hope, always with gentleness, reminded, "Your birth information is stored away and sealed in a vault, Dear. I'm sorry I can't answer your questions. Perhaps when you're grown, I'll help you find your family."

Janelle, an only child, in reality, was not unhappy, just spoiled. Growing up, her parents gave her privileges, such as parties, road trips, and games, that many of her friends didn't have. She knew her parents deeply loved her, as she did them.

As the years rolled on, Janelle began to have serious behavior problems. During her teen years, she became rebellious and difficult to manage both at home and at school.

"I don't like living here anymore!" she raged at her parents. "You're not my *real* family anyway."

As hurtful as her words were, her parents still nurtured and supported her and sought help through family counseling.

"If we could get more information about Janelle's birth family, we believe we can help her," they urged.

Desperate to get answers, Mrs. Burton began a quest to find her daughter's birth mom. Poring through the scanty information she had received at the time of Janelle's adoption, she was surprised she was able to locate her mother within a short time.

Her heart pounded as she dialed the number. She knew her telephone call was risky and the woman on the other end may not even want to talk to her. "Are you Sonia Blackwood?"

"Yes I am, who may I ask is calling?"

"I'm Hope Burton. We haven't met before but I think we have something in common. Did you give birth to a baby girl on October 28, 1977?"

The prolonged silence on the other end of the line gave her the answer. Then, the woman answered, "Yes, I did. How did you find me? What do you want?"

"I'm the woman who adopted your baby shortly after she was born. I'd like to come and talk to you if I may. I'm only seeking information I think you can give me."

Sonia agreed to meet with her. Hope made the trip to Sonia's home several hundred miles away. The women talked about the daughter they shared at a brief but emotional encounter.

"I had no choice but to give my baby up for adoption," Sonia, then age thirty-two, explained. "I was only sixteen and my mom told me I couldn't bring my child home."

Hope felt a deep sadness for Sonia upon hearing this. She pondered also what her own journey would have been had she and her husband not adopted Janelle.

"The nurses at the hospital where I gave birth told me not to even see or hold my baby. They said it wouldn't be good for me since I was giving her up for adoption. They didn't even allow me to give her a name."

"You never even saw her?" Hope gasped.

"No. I did what they told me, signed her away, and left her at the hospital."

"That must have been an awful time for you."

"Yes it was. But after a while, I put the whole thing behind me and tried to move on.

Gesturing toward a young child playing nearby, she said, "Thank God I had this little boy a few years later. His name is Donald. He's helped ease the pain of losing my first baby. They're the only two kids I ever had."

"You must have been shocked when I called you some time ago and told you I am the adopted mother of Janelle, your first baby."

Sonia nodded silently.

Hope shared with Sonia the problems with Janelle and asked her for information on her own family's background.

"My first baby's father left me soon after she was born. We haven't seen each other in years, so I can't tell you much about him. My son had a different dad, but he's not in his life at all."

Hope observed Sonia carefully as she talked. She appeared cold emotionally and seemed stuck in her surroundings. It was clear she hadn't done much with her life since Janelle was born. Hope was not invited into Sonia's house, so they sat talking in the yard outside. She saw the old, unrepaired building, Sonia called home, and the unkempt, crowded neighborhood. Sonia, with shaking hands, lit one cigarette after another. Her eyes were yellow and vacant. She admitted to Hope her struggle with drugs and alcohol. She said her sisters had similar problems.

Soon, an elderly woman came outside and stared at Hope briefly.

"Momma, this is the lady who adopted my first baby. She's here to visit me."

"I don't remember anything about that," the older woman replied. "I need you to get back in the house and start dinner."

When her mother went back inside, Sonia explained her mother had long-standing mental health issues and she was her caretaker. "Mama's been in and out of the hospital due to her problems. I and my sisters suffer from depression, too."

Thank God, I've had the privilege of raising Janelle. I think she'd have been in even worse shape if Sonia had decided to keep her, Hope said to herself.

"She's pretty," Sonia exclaimed as she glanced at the photos of Janelle that Hope showed her.

She didn't ask for many details about her daughter or express a desire to keep the pictures. She didn't seem to want future contact, so Hope didn't offer any personal information. Although she had obtained the information she wanted, she had the feeling, as she left, there was much more to Sonia's story.

Hope didn't let Janelle know about her meeting with Sonia until many years later. The counselors agreed, at the time, Janelle and Sonia had little to offer each other.

Around age thirty, Janelle, then living on her own, was very unhappy. She asked herself many questions, *why am I like this? why do I feel depressed? why do I enjoy the taste and smell of cigarettes so much? why am I always so angry? why am I attracted to street drugs?*

She had a hunch her birth family and her genes had something to do with her issues. She thought long and hard, then resolved to make contact with her birth mother in an effort to get answers. By then, Hope had told her of her visit years ago with Sonia.

Janelle wrote many letters and made phone calls to Sonia, without response. Her nagging questions continued.

"I guess it's not for me to find her," she told her boyfriend, Robert. "Maybe she's not even alive anymore." So, she gave up and put the matter to rest.

However, an unexplainable, badgering desire overtook Janelle just before her fortieth birthday. The quest to find her birth mother re-surfaced. By then, social media had become a phenomenon. "Why don't you search for her on the internet?"

Robert suggested.

Sure enough, Sonia's name popped up online and Janelle posted a request for contact. In less than a week, she received a long-awaited response—not from Sonia, herself, but from her younger brother, Donald. "How do you know my mother?" he asked. A photo of a man who resembled her, was displayed with the message.

Janelle collapsed on the sofa in floods of tears. This was just too good to be true.

After she collected herself, Janelle returned a message, "I'm your sister. Your mother is my mother too."

A few days later, Donald sent another message, "I never even knew you existed. My mom never told me about you. But she's con-firmed it now. Welcome to the family."

Janelle continued to reach out to Sonia without response. Thankfully, however, a cousin, Aisha, phoned her. She'd learned about Janelle through Donald.

"Sonia is my aunt—my deceased mother's sister. I confronted my aunt about her past and she admitted to me some deep secrets. I need to let you know my aunt not only gave birth to you and Donald, but to five other children as well!"

Janelle said nothing as she tried to absorb what Aisha told her.

"You were the oldest of Sonia's seven kids. She had four girls and three boys altogether. Each of the girls was placed for adoption immediately after birth but Sonia kept the boys."

Stunned, Janelle continued listening.

"Sonia also confessed that last year, two of the girls, separately, paid her a visit after searching for her. She didn't tell either of them the other existed. We now know about six of her kids. We're not sure of the whereabouts of the seventh one."

Aisha added, as she lowered her voice to a whisper, "To be honest, honey, I'm glad my aunt placed you girls for adoption. She must have realized it wouldn't have gone well for you. She never would have been able to give you the life you needed."

Janelle thanked Aisha and asked her to remain in touch. Right away, she tried to find her two younger sisters and it wasn't long before she did. Over the following year, the three of them talked to each other daily by phone and resolved to meet in person as soon as they could.

"I can't believe this is real," Denise, thirty-seven, said, tearfully, when they first made contact. "I'm thrilled we found each other. I wish we had met sooner."

"There's no doubt we're sisters," chirped Kamiah, twenty-seven, after they'd exchanged photos of each other. They all agreed they looked strikingly alike.

A year after they found each other, Aisha threw a party and invited the three sisters to attend. They all agreed to go. Janelle lived the farthest away and made Aisha promise her birth mother, Sonia, would be there. She desperately wanted to meet her and get some questions answered.

What do I say to her after almost forty years? She was both angry and excited as she pondered this. Her stomach was in knots that Sunday morning as she exited the airplane after the three-hour flight.

As her rented car reached Aisha's neighborhood, she could hear the music from the party long before she got there. Pulling up in front, she saw several folk standing outside smoking cigarettes and holding beer cans. The house was jam-packed with people of all ages and sizes. Everyone was grooving to the beat. Platters of food and bottles of liquor were everywhere. Janelle glanced quickly around and tried not to stare. She had never encountered a scenario like this before.

A tall, fair-skinned young man emerged from the kitchen. A short, middle-aged woman followed.

"Are you Janelle?" he asked.

"Yes, I am."

"I'm Donald, your brother. This here is Mama."

Janelle's heart sank. She looked nothing like the person she had pictured in her mind. Her eyes had a vacant look and her completely gray hair made her appear much older than her years. There was no doubt though she was her mom. She looked just like her—only an older version of herself. After forty years, mother and daughter were face to face at last. But the lack of warmth from the older woman made it clear she had no desire to bond with this her firstborn child.

Sonia stared at Janelle for a moment then gave her a thin smile. "Nice meeting you," she mumbled.

Janelle hugged her and followed her into the kitchen. "After so many years, I'm finally here."

Sonia didn't reply but stole furtive glances in her direction. Their conversation was sparse and rather superficial. Janelle had intended to ask about her birth dad but sensed she'd get nowhere. So, she didn't raise the subject. Her mother puffed constantly on cigarettes. Butts were everywhere. In the awkward silence, Janelle was unsure if her mom was happy to see her or not.

Janelle felt relieved when a woman about her own age appeared and greeted her warmly. "Hi. I'm Aisha. Glad you were able to make it."

Turning to Sonia, she said, "Janelle and I are going outside for some fresh air, Auntie."

"Okay."

Outside, Janelle got an earful. She listened, without comment, as her family's history tumbled from Aisha. What she learned was overwhelming.

"Sonia, your mom in the kitchen, lives alone in a rooming house. She's never married and suffers from depression. She's been in the hospital more than once for this condition. She's battled drugs most of her life. Thank God, you've not been here in the middle of it all."

Aisha said she knew nothing about Janelle's biological dad—neither his name nor his whereabouts.

"I like to keep tabs on all of the family," Aisha explained. "That's why I hold these parties from time to time. My grandmother, Sonia's mother, passed away recently. After she died, we all pretty much went our separate ways."

"You told me on the phone Sonia kept her three boys and didn't place them for adoption. I just met Donald, but where are the other two?"

"Jeffrey decided not to come today. He's sometimes strange-acting. He only lives across the street, but we sometimes don't see him for months. Anthony (we call him Tony), the youngest one, has been locked up in jail a few years."

"I'm excited I'll be meeting my two sisters today. I hope they come soon."

Before Aisha could reply, two young women approached them. They recognized each other from the photos they'd exchanged. Kamiah, Denise, Janelle and Aisha hugged each other and chatted together for quite a long time. Aisha then left them and went back inside.

"Did you meet Sonia, our birth mom? Did she tell you anything? What do you think?" they asked Janelle.

"I was disappointed at her response. I got no information from her. But I thank God my parents adopted me and loved me."

Kamiah added, "I believe God gave us a chance for a better life without her."

They all agreed but were grateful they'd found each other. They were saddened, however, there was no information about their other sister, Sonia's fourth daughter.

"One day we might find her," Denise said, hopefully. "But maybe not, who knows? After this, though, I think we need to leave Sonia alone. I have a feeling she'd like to keep us in her past."

Janelle concurred. "Somehow, now that I've met her, I no longer feel angry at her. I guess she made the decisions she made about us based on what she thought right at the time. I'm so glad we have each other and we can always remain in touch."

Janelle returned home after thanking Aisha for the invitation to visit. She experienced a range of emotions on the way, as she reflected on and processed what happened.

"Now I know the WHY of a lot of things," she exclaimed to her mom, Hope, shortly afterward. "I'm glad I found Sonia and my birth family. I plan to keep in touch with my sisters and Aisha. However, I want to tell you and Dad a great big Thank You. I didn't fully appreciate until now the wonderful life you gave me. God worked out His perfect plan for us by making us a family."

You're Not My Grandmother

Years ago, my daughter, age sixteen, gave birth to a beautiful baby girl, naming her Ebony Dawn. She decided to place her baby for adoption. Neither I nor her dad influenced her decision.

As tears flowed, she said, with determination, "I'm too young to be a mother. There's no way I can give my child the life she deserves. I'm still in school. I'm sure there's a mom and dad out there who'd love to adopt her. I know God will take care of her."

At her request, I helped my daughter find a maternity home where she could live until the baby came. While there, she was able to continue her education and make plans for her child's future. Efforts were made to include the baby's father in these plans, but he was unresponsive.

I was delighted to have been present in the delivery room when Ebony put in her appearance.

"You did a great job, I told my daughter. You really worked hard to bring your baby into this world."

"Thanks, Mom. I so wish I could keep her, but I can't. I guess Jeff and Julie will be here tomorrow."

As expected, next day Jeff and Julie Eastmond, the baby's adoptive parents, arrived at the hospital. I was so proud of my daughter as she handed Ebony to them. The joy on their faces, as they held and cuddled their new baby, was inexpressible. They had waited eighteen years for that moment.

They explained to us, "When the adoption is completed, her last name will be changed to Eastmond, like ours. But we'll stay in touch and send pictures as she grows."

My daughter and I said little as we drove back home. Each was lost in her own thoughts. I knew how painful the whole ordeal was for her as she left the hospital with empty arms. I marveled though at how mature she was throughout the process of giving her baby away. I felt a great emptiness inside as I left my newest granddaughter behind.

True to her word, over the years, Julie Eastmond gave us updates on how Ebony was doing. She sent photos of her various milestones, school activities, and family events. My daughter was happy to receive them and often declared, "I know I made the right decision by giving Ebony to the Eastmonds. They seem to be such a close-knit family. They give her everything and I think she's probably spoiled."

I always regarded Ebony as my granddaughter. I prayed for her daily, just as I prayed for my other grandkids, and wished her success in every area of her life. I hoped and believed I would see her again, if and when my daughter and the Eastmonds were ready for a reunion.

One day, I received a phone call from Julie. My heart raced with excitement.

"Jeff and I would like to bring Ebony to visit with your family. She's fourteen now, and is having a few emotional issues. She's seeing a counselor who advised it's probably due to having self-identity issues as an adopted child. The counselor thinks if Ebony could have a reunion with you all, this might help her."

"I'll speak to my daughter about this and get back to you."

At first, my daughter felt taken off guard by this. "I'm not sure I'm ready to see Ebony yet. This is so unexpected. I thought this might happen when she was much older. I really would prefer to keep that chapter of my life closed for now."

After a time, though, she agreed. "I guess if it will help Ebony figure out who she is, I'll let them come. I really want what's best for her."

The Eastmond family visited soon after, making the 400-mile trip to our town. We spent, what I thought, was a great weekend together. I was so pleased to observe that Ebony had grown into a lovely young teen—tall and with pretty facial features. She looked strikingly like my daughter. Though shy and rather reserved, I observed her eyeing her intently, as if trying to connect with her on some level. They spent the afternoon shopping together, while her parents, my husband, and I did lunch. We also worshipped together at our church next day before they returned home. I believed we all benefitted from the visit, and, of importance, birth daughter and birth mother got answers to questions they each had.

Over the next four years, The Eastmonds and our family bonded more closely. Julie told us during their visit she wanted us to have a closer relationship with them. "I'm glad Ebony has a family to which she can relate. Neither Jeff nor I have relatives who live nearby, and those who are near are emotionally distant."

My daughter, despite the visit, still did not want to share Ebony's existence with those outside of the family. So, she only maintained contact with her via text messages and occasional phone calls. This seemed to be fine with Ebony.

On one occasion, during a business trip to their town, my daughter paid a brief visit to the Eastmonds.

"I really enjoyed being there," she reported to us on her return. "Ebony was anxious for me to hear her play the trombone, which she plays in the school band. She really is good at it. I felt proud of her."

Ebony spent a Fourth of July holiday with us. She wanted to meet her cousins—my other grandchildren—for the first time. They were thrilled to meet her, and she seemed amazed and happy to have relatives her own age.

Julie kept me abreast of Ebony's progress in school and requested my input Into any major medical decisions they had to make. On one occasion, for example, Ebony had to be hospitalized with acute stomach symptoms. I was able to provide information and support and sent flowers to the hospital from our family.

When Ebony turned eighteen, she was ready for her High School graduation. Julie was excited to participate in all of the activities surrounding the senior year of high school. Ebony sent my daughter photos of her Prom dress and of the guy who was her escort, and she seemed glad to have been included.

We accepted the invitation to attend Ebony's graduation and six of us traveled to attend. We all felt thrilled as she stepped smartly to the stage to accept her diploma. Clad in navy blue cap and gown and high heeled shoes, she grinned and waved at us as we cheered loudly, "You go Ebony!"

I could hardly believe eighteen years had passed since I helped usher my tiny granddaughter into the world. Here she was, now bound for college!

Where has the time gone? I asked myself.

When I realized we were Ebony's only graduation guests, I felt even happier our family had attended. No other relatives or friends had come to help her celebrate such an important milestone! It then became clear how meaningful we were to the Eastmonds. I'm not sure if she received graduation cards and gifts from other family members, but I sure was glad we had taken ours. We joined with their neighbors in celebrating the graduation of their son and Ebony.

Little did I suspect on that graduation day, I would receive the shock of my life a few weeks later. A letter arrived from Ebony, addressed to my daughter and me. Here are some excerpts:

"Although it's difficult for me to bring up this subject, I feel that it's necessary to discuss this situation. From the first time I met you guys, up to graduation day, I feel like you guys think, since you put me up for adoption, you can just, automatically, have a say in what I can and can't do with my life."

Addressing me, specifically, she wrote:

"... I feel like you are being a little bit too involved in my life, for you to not be my real grandmother. This might sound harsh, but I've been waiting for the day to tell you how I feel. I have been always the one to just let things happen without saying how I feel. But that's going to change starting now. When I was little, I had a grandmother and her name was Susan. She was my best and closest grandmother. Without her, I wouldn't know what a loving and caring person was supposed to be, beside my mother Julie. I understand that you want to have a relationship with me, but I just can't call you my grandmother. I feel like I only had one and that was her. Just because she passed away, that will never change the way I loved her."

Ebony went on to address my daughter, her birth mother, saying:

"I understand that you had to put me up for adoption and now you want to be a part of my life, since you've missed a lot of my child-hood. You want the chance to make up some of the time you missed. But I just can't call you my 'Mom.' It just doesn't feel right. I know you gave me life, but the rest was the person who raised me to be who I am today. I would like to have a relationship with you, but we need to take baby steps. I hope you understand how I feel about this whole situation."

As I read and re-read the letter, I experienced a range of emotions. After the initial surprise, I felt deeply hurt and wept for quite a while. I then became angry. My daughter and I discussed our thoughts and feelings at length and raised the following questions:

What precipitated the letter? Did we miss some cues along the way about how Ebony really felt? How could she dare talk to us in such a disrespectful manner? For example, why did she repeatedly, refer to us as "you guys?" What role, if any, did either of her parents play, either wittingly or unwittingly, in how Ebony felt about us? Did they also share her feelings? Did they know the letter had been written and sent? Had her therapist encouraged her to write the letter? Why did Ebony hide her true feelings when we attended her graduation?

Of interest, my daughter felt differently about Ebony's letter than I. "I feel more hurt for you, Mom, than about what Ebony said. I know you regard her as your granddaughter, and I know it hurts you deeply to hear how she feels about you. As for me, it stings a little, since I tried to be supportive of her. But if she wants me out of her life, I'm okay with that. Julie raised her and really is her mother. Know-ing how Ebony really feels will help me close the door again on my past, which was opened when I didn't want it to be."

Here is the conclusion I came to about the letter:

I fully realize adopted children, at some point, must come to terms with the reality of their adoption. I also know they have the right to express their feelings around this sensitive and impactful issue in their lives. However, I don't feel, whatever anger they may have about what happened to them, their rage should be directed toward those who have tried to be helpful and supportive. I do feel both I and my daughter have been targeted unfairly by Ebony.

In my opinion, Ebony is in denial of the fact she is adopted and really doesn't want our family to be involved in her life anymore. Though this is painful, I'm willing to live with that reality.

Soon after, we asked Julie and Jeff if they had known about the letter before Ebony sent it. They said they did not. They were even horrified and embarrassed to learn about her feelings and that she had even mailed such a letter to us. I reassured them Ebony's letter didn't have to change our relationship with them. I strongly advised them to continue Ebony in therapy to help her sort out her issues.

My daughter and I responded to Ebony's letter by phone. We each approached her differently. She was gentle with Ebony and told her she still loved her and wished her well in her future. I was not unkind, as I spoke to Ebony, but I was firm in what I said. I told her the ball was in her court concerning my future involvement, if any, in her life. I reassured her I was open to future contact if that's what she wanted. However, I am also willing to distance myself if she prefers.

I told my daughter I believed when she wrote the letter, Ebony was immature and had not yet grasped the true meaning of "family." In the days and weeks that followed our receipt of Ebony's letter, I thought a lot about her and reflected on the wider implications. The following questions came to mind:

Am I Ebony's grandmother or am I not? How does one define family? Who are the members of one's family? Who decides? Must family members play an active role in one's life in order to be considered family? Can a blood relationship be changed?

I'm confident, in time, I'll receive some answers.

Postscript

We did not communicate with Ebony for several years after she sent the letter. Sadly, we never reconciled, although we stayed in touch with her parents.

At age twenty-one, Ebony passed away, suddenly, due to complications of an illness. The Eastmonds contacted us immediately, and we were shocked and saddened by the news. My daughter was deeply grieved at the loss of her daughter. I felt confounded and perplexed my granddaughter had left us.

We met with Jeff and Julie to comfort and support them, and help them plan Ebony's funeral. We sent tributes and acknowledgements and have continued to be in touch. We will always regard one another as family.

Should I Tell?

Carmen Santiago was my best friend from college days. We met on campus during my Freshman year and remained friends for many years thereafter. She was from New York City, as was I, and we got to know each other's family well.

Traditionally, on Sadie Hawkins Day on campus, the gals chased the guys, then took them to the Ice Cream Social after they caught them. Bob Williams, a handsome Sophomore, and new to the school, was chased and caught by Carmen. Their relationship blossomed and theirs became a match made in heaven. Bob and Carmen quickly became an "item" and were inseparable. I was happy for my friend, and liked Bob well enough. However, I felt a tad left out as their romance continued.

One day after classes, Carmen told me she had a secret she wanted to share with me. She said it had been on her mind to tell me and felt she could trust me. I listened carefully and was amazed by what I heard.

Her Mom, Martha Green, had become pregnant with Carmen at an early age. She never married Carmen's father, and they severed their relationship before Carmen was born. Some years later, Martha met and married Bo Green, who then became Carmen's stepfather.

Bo Green was many years younger than Martha and, according to Carmen, certainly didn't respect her. I had often wondered why Carmen referred to him as 'Mr. Green' instead of 'Dad' or 'Daddy'. I soon found out why.

Carmen told me, from the age of twelve years, Bo Green began to molest her. Desperate and frightened, she told her mom, Martha, what was going on. Martha chose to ignore the situation and did absolutely nothing to protect Carmen. At the young age of thirteen, Carmen found herself expecting Bo Green's child!

Martha took matters into her own hands. But instead of parting company, permanently, with Mr. Green, as Carmen expected, she took Carmen to a town several miles from home. They remained there until Carmen gave birth to a baby girl, whom she named Selena.

The baby was beautiful and Martha fell in love, immediately, with her new grandchild. She decided to take Selena home with her and continued to live with Bo Green. *After all, Bo is the baby's father,* she reasoned to herself.

Carmen was sent to live with her grandmother, Mrs. Washington, Martha's mother.

Everyone believed Martha when she told them Selena was her own baby. They watched her preen over and pamper the child.

Mrs. Washington and Martha charged Carmen, "Do not tell anyone the truth about Selena, and that you are her mother. Let us keep this a family secret forever."

Carmen told me when she saw Selena at family gatherings, she could never acknowledge she was her child. It made her feel so sad. She hated Mr. Green with a passion and avoided him, if possible.

Strange, Carmen said she bore no animosity toward Martha, her mother, and pitied her more than resented her. She regarded Martha as a victim of Bo Green who was powerless to do better. Carmen told me, over the years, her stepfather had found a girlfriend in the neighborhood, who bore him five children. Martha allowed the first of those children to move in with her family and she cared for him as if he was her own child. She continued to reason within herself, *I'm helping Bo take care of his children.*

Carmen went on to tell me, "Once, when Mr. Green was in a hateful mood toward my mom, he told Selena, who was about five years old at the time, that I, Carmen, am her birth mother. This news was very unsettling to her. But my mom chose to say nothing to Bo Green about this and remained silent on the issue."

"What did she say to Selena?"

"She told her not to talk about it and to maintain the family secret, just as she had warned me."

When Carmen told me her family's story, she said she didn't think she'd ever get married or have more children. She felt burdened by her past and, in her words, was 'tainted' for life.

When Bob Williams and Carmen began dating at college, I asked her, "Have you shared your story with him?"

"I have," she replied, with a happy smile. "He said it wasn't a big issue for him, and he still loves me. He promised to keep my secret."

Bob soon asked Carmen to marry him. "I can't believe my good fortune," she exclaimed, as we walked toward class one day. "It feels like a dream come true."

The week after graduation, Carmen and Bob tied the knot. I was asked to be a bridesmaid in the wedding and was pleased to fulfill the role. It was a beautiful summer ceremony, as I recall. Friends and family came from miles around. It was clear God had blessed and sealed their union.

Not long after, Carmen and Bob became parents of a handsome baby boy. Two years later, a pretty little girl arrived.

As time went on, I kept in touch with these friends, though not very often, since we lived many miles apart.

Years after our college days, Carmen and I re-connected. We met for lunch, in person, and caught up with each other. I was pleased to hear about her children.

"Selena is all grown up now and has become a doctor. She's also married and has kids of her own."

"What about your son and other daughter?"

"They've also done well and are living independently. Bob and I have a good relationship with them."

Carmen then leaned forward, lowered her voice, and said, "I've never told my other kids the truth about Selena. They think she is their aunt and don't know she is really their older sister. I prefer to keep it that way."

I was troubled when Carmen told me that. I didn't understand why she kept the truth from her children, who, by then, were young adults. Besides, Martha, her mother, Mrs. Washington, her grandmother, and

Bo Green, had all passed away. So, I wasn't sure why she still maintained her secret.

About six months after my lunch date with Carmen, her husband, Bob, phoned me with some terrible news. Carmen was desperately ill and, at the young age of 47, was dying.

A few weeks later, my long-time friend, Carmen, transitioned from this earth and went to be with her heavenly Father. I could not contain my sorrow. Bob and the children were devastated – overwhelmed with grief at her passing.

I was unable to make it to her homegoing service but kept in touch with Bob and their two children.

I was overjoyed a few years later when he called and informed me he was getting married again. I attended the lovely wedding, and it was clear he and his new wife, Toni, were happy. His children were there, but I noticed Selena was not.

Later, I asked Bob about her. "Unfortunately, we've become estranged. We haven't seen or heard from Selena for a long time."

I told Bob, "I believe if Carmen were alive, she would be upset if Selena became estranged from you and her younger brother and sister."

He was dumbfounded. "I had no idea you knew Carmen's secret."

"I've known since our college days. Have you finally told your son and daughter the truth?"

"No, and I don't plan to. Carmen took her secret to her grave, and I will do the same."

Years passed. Then I received a phone call from Bob's' daughter-in-law, Reba, his son's wife. She asked me if I could do them a favor and talk to their kids about Carmen, their grandmother, whom they had never met.

"I've heard so many wonderful things about Carmen. I'm sorry she passed away before I married her son. I'd like the children to get an understanding of who she was. You knew her a long time."

"I'd be thrilled to tell them about my friend, Carmen," I told her. "But what about Bob, their grandfather? Has he told them much about her?"

"My father-in-law is much older now and has lost most of his memory. At this point, he remembers little about the past."

Not long after, Reba and her family passed through my hometown while on vacation. They came to my home, and I shared about my old friend, Carmen. In fact, I created a scrapbook for them, with pictures of their grandmother. They were thrilled to receive it and felt happy to learn more of their family's story.

When they left, however, I felt guilty I had kept a part of the story hidden from them. I always believed they had the right to know the truth. I also thought, perhaps knowing the facts might help them reconcile with Selena.

I pondered, for a long time, what course of action, if any, I should take.

Should I tell them? Should I leave "Well enough" alone?

Finally, I came to a decision. I determined not to raise the issue with them. However, if asked, I would reveal the truth to them as I knew it. I would not remain silent.

I thought, *Perhaps, one day they might ask.*

A Blast from the Past

Margaret Griffin saw the old fashioned, red and white striped, airmail envelope right away as she extracted her mail from the mailbox. It was wrinkled, slightly soiled, and yellow from age. It had obviously come from far away.

I don't recognize the handwriting or the name on the envelope, she noted.

The stamp and postmark on the letter told her it had come from Trinidad, an island in the Caribbean. Margaret smiled briefly, remembering. Growing up, her mother, Dora, had shared many stories with her about Trinidad, the land of her birth. Margaret, now age fifty, born in New York, had never visited Trinidad. She was certain she knew a lot about it, however.

Margaret's heart beat wildly and her hands shook uncontrollably as she read and re-read the contents of the letter. *Is this a joke? Is this a scam?*

As she contemplated what the writer told her, various emotions washed over her—surprise, disbelief, then rage and sadness.

"Dear daughter,

I know you will be greatly surprised when you read this letter. I felt compelled to contact you before I pass on from this life. I am gravely ill from cancer and cannot hold on to this secret any longer. You are my only child, conceived from a brief relationship with your mother, now Mrs. Dora Griffin. We were both mere children at the time—she was sixteen and I was seventeen. We really believed we were in love.

We wanted to get married when we discovered you were on the way. My family, however, flatly opposed the idea of marriage and we were forced to go our separate ways. Your mom was sent to New York to live with relatives and give birth to you. I remained in Trinidad. We parted, tearfully, and I continued with my schooling. I eventually married and became a teacher here. My wife and I had no children and she has passed away.

I am now retired, and, as I reflect on my life, I have many regrets. My greatest remorse is that I wasn't involved in your life as you were growing up, and that you were not in mine. You may be surprised to know, however, that your mother's sister, your aunt Agnes, who still lives here in Trinidad, has kept me informed about you over the years. I beamed with pride when she shared with me your accomplishments.

I am fairly certain you knew nothing about me until now. Your mother made me promise not to reach out to you. She also asked Aunt Agnes not to share with you anything about me. At this stage, however, you are free to confirm what I've said in this letter with your mother.

I know I'm a stranger to you, but my deepest desire is to meet you in person. We have a lot to talk about. I have property and an inheritance that belong to you, and I want you to learn about this before I am gone.

By means of this letter, therefore, I am inviting you to come to Trinidad. Please come as soon as possible. Forgive me for not being the father I should have been. Please respond quickly.

Sincerely,
John Crawford."

Margaret sat for a long time with the letter in her hand. Tears flowed as, somehow, she knew in her heart its contents were true. But she had many unanswered questions. *Who am I? Who is David Griffin, the man who I was so sure was my father, until now? Why did my parents keep this from me? Should I go to Trinidad? Should I answer the letter or simply 'let sleeping dogs lie'?*

It felt as if a wound had been opened. Margaret felt greatly deceived by this and decided to confront her mother. "Is John Crawford my father? Is what this man said in the letter, true?"

Dora folded her arms, pursed her lips, and replied, crisply, "I suppose it is if he said so."

Margaret struggled to control her rage. It was clear Dora had no intention of discussing the matter further with her. The issue was closed forever.

A few weeks later, Margaret boarded a Trinidad-bound airplane, determined to put the puzzle pieces together, if she could.

How could I have missed the cues throughout my life? How could I have been Margaret Crawford, and not Margaret Griffin, for fifty years and not have known it?"

John Crawford met Margaret at his home in Port-of-Spain, Trinidad's capital city. Dressed in his Sunday-best clothing, he had a nice lunch prepared for her.

"We meet at last," he greeted her warmly, with outstretched hand.

"I contacted Aunt Agnes before I traveled here," Margaret told him. "She confirmed what you told me in the letter and encouraged me to make the trip. My mom said little to me about it."

Margaret looked closely at the old man. She saw a resemblance to herself and decided to listen carefully to his story. She wanted to sort out the truth.

"Life is strange," he declared. "I never thought I'd ever meet you in my lifetime. But I'm so glad you came."

Margaret and her newly found father talked for several hours, sharing about their respective life's experience. Both lamented their meeting hadn't happened years sooner.

True to his word in the letter, John gave Margaret the legal papers for his property and all his assets. They met with his attorney concerning this before she returned to New York.

Margaret stayed with Aunt Agnes for a few days after her visit with John Crawford. Her aunt showed her around Port-of-Spain and helped her sort out the intense and deeply emotional exchange she had with John.

"I'm glad he was honest with me and didn't hold back the truth."

"Truth, somehow, always comes to the light," her aunt declared.

Margaret watched the shimmering waves hit the shore, as she sat alone in the moonlight at her aunt's seaside home. She was headed back home next morning.

I know I'll always be somewhat resentful toward my mom, and toward David, my stepfather, she thought to herself. *I still love them, though, and am thankful for the good life they gave me. I'm a big girl now, and I must accept life as I find it.*

Overwhelmed

I, Nadiah, always wondered about the other half of my family. Who was my Dad? Who were his family members? My dad passed away when I was about four years old. So, I didn't really know him, and I didn't know my family on his side. My brother and I moved in with my grandparents when we were two years old, and we lived with them five years. After that, we moved in with our mom.

All my life I've had two parents, which were my grandparents. So, I've always had a mom and a dad in my life. Having your grandpa as the father figure in your life is amazing because you get extra spoiled! My grandpa did and still does an amazing job at being my father figure. Growing up, I referred to my grandparents as my parents. I called them "Mommy" and "Daddy" because they were really all I knew. I didn't really know about my actual mom and dad.

When I was seven years old, my brother and I moved from my grandparents to live with my mom. We slowly started to learn more about our dad, who neither of us remembered. My mom told us so many amazing stories about him and the sweet, genuine, loveable, fun, joyful, strong, and wholehearted person he was. Hearing and listening to all the stories about him made me feel like something was missing. It made me feel a little broken inside because this remarkable person is gone and everybody else got to enjoy his presence and light except me.

I began to ask my mom questions about my dad's side of the family. But she never really said much about them because they weren't really very fond of us. Three years after returning to live with my mom, I met one of my aunts on my dad's side for the first time –well, the first time that I remember. She told me how much I resemble my dad and shared some stories about him as well.

Fast-forward four years, I was now 14 years old. My dad's birthday is September 11th, and his side of the family celebrates his birthday every year. So, on September 8, 2019, they reached out to my mom and invited my brother and me to celebrate our dad's birthday with them. The party was held at Dave n 'Busters. Once we got there, we looked for them for about ten minutes. We walked past them three times because we didn't recognize them! Then, my mom saw my dad's brother. She told us that was our other family. My brother and I, along with my best friend, who tagged along for moral support, walked up to them, and told them who we were. They all just stood there in disbelief. They couldn't believe how tall we were and how much we favor our dad. It was almost as if someone had cast a spell on all of them. They stood there and looked stuck!

After the "spell" wore off, one by one they came over, hugged, and admired us. They kept telling us how much we looked like our father.

I quickly began to feel overwhelmed because I couldn't believe I was actually meeting them, and they all looked like the photos of my dad. It was a lot to take in. I kept thinking to myself, "They've missed out on my whole life so far. They had the opportunity to be a part of it and didn't take it. Now they're all smiling in my face and telling me they've missed me."

I began to grow even more overwhelmed and confused, so my best friend took me and sat me at a table. My two sisters on my dad's side came up to me and introduced themselves as I sat there in awe. I look so much like them, and they look so much like my dad. I then began to feel overwhelmed again.

I ran into the restroom, and my best friend and my mom followed me. I threw my back against the wall and slid down, as tears flowed down my cheeks.

"What's wrong?" my mom asked me.

I couldn't answer her because my words were stuck. She began to name ways I could possibly be feeling and got to "Overwhelmed."

I shook my head, "Yes."

She began to comfort me. Then my two sisters come into the restroom. When they saw me crying, they started crying. Once I saw them crying, I dried my tears and walked out of the restroom. My two sisters followed me, pulled me aside, and asked if I was okay. They apologized for not being a part of my life all those years and expressed how they wanted to grow a relationship with me.

About ten minutes later, everyone went outside to do a balloon release on behalf of my dad and take pictures. My sisters and I exchanged telephone numbers and shared a few things about ourselves. Soon after, we all parted ways.

That was probably the first time I've ever felt so overwhelmed. I never want to feel so overwhelmed again. I still miss my dad to this day.

My sisters and I text and check on each other from time to time. I do hope to grow even closer to them, and my dad's name will forever live on.

Nadiah Jem Victoria McCain and Grace Allman Burke, Co-Authors

Section B: Summer Days

Journeys

We take many kinds of journeys in life. Some are for pure pleasure, like jaunts or junkets, that may only last a few days. Others are more permanent and relocate the traveler in far flung places. Such are the journeys immigrants make when they leave their native countries to live in new locales. A third type of journey is abstract, such as the journey from youth to maturity, or even metaphysical, like a journey through time.

The Essays in this Section take the reader on four different journeys. Each provides insight into the traveler, as well as the destination. Please enjoy and learn from all of them!

> *"For we walk by faith, not by sight."*
>
> II Corinthians 5::7 (NKJV)

Solo in Europe

Around 1970, my best friend and I, young and adventurous, decided to take a trip to Europe. We had never been over there but had heard and read about the great capitals – London, Paris, Rome, etc. and wanted to see them for ourselves.

After months of getting ready, purchasing airline tickets, and attending to other pre-travel essentials, our excitement increased even more. Then, boom! my friend decided to back out from the trip, citing lack of enough funds. I could hardly believe what she told me, and my disappointment was palpable. Thoughts of money lost on already-bought travel items, and the shattered dream of going to far-flung places, crashed in on me.

When I called Fran, my travel agent, however, she had a whole different take on my dilemma. "Why would you let someone's problem prevent you from having a good time?"

"But I can't go by myself!

"Why not?"

"It's too risky for a girl, especially a Black girl like me, traveling that far alone. I know no one over there."

"Listen, Girl, in my opinion, it would be a mistake not to go. I've been to Europe on several occasions, and I can put you in touch with many of my friends and clients who live there. You only need to get used to the idea of traveling on your own, meeting new people, and you'll have a great time."

I knew I was already somewhat of a risk-taker, and thought about Fran's advice. Before long, I called her back and told her I was ready to go.

I must admit I had a few butterflies in my stomach when I entered the departure lounge that morning. I got there early and noticed the room was filled with Caucasian people, probably returning home to Europe after an American vacation. No one glanced my way, but that was okay, since we were complete strangers to each other, anyway. As I walked over to the concession stand, however, I saw an African American young lady, of my approximate age, nearby. We nodded politely at each other but didn't speak right away. We passed each other again as we circled the lounge, and, that time I decided to make her acquaintance.

"Hi, my name is Grace. I'm assuming you're traveling over to London, also."

"Yes I am. I'm Cheryl and this will be my first time in Europe. In addition to London, I'll be visiting Amsterdam in Holland, Paris, France, and Denmark's capital, Copenhagen."

I couldn't believe what she told me and my good fortune in meeting her. I knew God had smiled on me in placing me with a travel companion. I learned we were going to many of the same places, including London, Copenhagen, and Paris, and she was, like I was, a nurse going on vacation. She also knew one of my closest friends and lived in the same apartment building as she!

We sat together on the airplane, laughed, and exchanged stories, and found out we had a lot of similar interests. We decided we would hook up as much as possible on the trip, as travel buddies.

London

Cheryl had friends with whom she was staying in London –that land of castles and tea-drinkers – while I had booked a hotel. So, we went our separate ways that first night, but met for breakfast next morning, and were joined at the hip after that. What was great about having a travel pal like Cheryl was we were both flexible and had no hang-ups about times to eat or our own personal routines. We just let happen what would happen and were always on the move.

Our main mode of travel during our five-day escapade there, was the Underground, which was much cleaner and organized than our own subway system in New York. We visited as many of the major tourist sites for which London was famous as we could.

A riverboat ride on the Thames River to Hampton Court Palace, southwest of London was a treat. It was both interesting and exciting to be taken back many centuries to the yesterdays of British royalty.

Spending money in pounds and pence, rather than in dollars and cents, was different. A day shopping at famous Harrods, London's luxury department store on Brompton Street, was lovely. We got our exercise as we walked on the High Streets afterward.

An Underground ride took us to Piccadilly Circus and Trafalgar Square, near Southwest London's famous Soho area. Knowing about the love for live theatre and entertainment by Londoners, encouraged Cheryl and me to take in a play while there. The acting was fantastic.

Buckingham Palace and the Changing of the Guard was a must. So was a visit to London Bridge and the Tower of London where we viewed the famous Crown Jewels.

Cheryl's London friends, of Caribbean descent, invited me one day to join them at their home for dinner. It was wonderful to meet Black people and to notice the incorporation of Jamaican culture into their adopted British life. The food was tasty and delicious.

"Isn't this a great change from what we're getting in the restaurants here?" Cheryl asked.

I laughed out loud. Cheryl already knew, although I was enjoying the trip to its utmost, I was turned off from British fare. "The food here is tasteless, to me," I said. "It has no seasoning, and every dish is topped by a large fried egg. I couldn't believe it when they served fish and French fries (they call it fish and chips) on newspaper, instead of on a plate."

Our hosts laughed, "It was something we had to get used to also when we first came here. However, several years later, we've assimilated. Our kids are real Brits, you know."

While loving the scenes of London, both Cheryl and I were anxious to get on with our trip to other places on our respective European itineraries. Next stop—France.

Paris, City of Lights

Cheryl and I had booked our London to Paris trip on different flights. So, we waited in the Paris airport's Arrival Hall until our respective flights arrived. Neither of us had planned a set itinerary for our time in Paris, so we consulted our travel brochures to give us direction. We agreed to meet next day at the Champs- Élysées.

Fran, my travel agent, reserved a room for me at a hotel run by a Vietnamese family. It became my home away from home, as they seemed determined to look after me while there. I suppose a young Black woman, running the streets of Paris, alone, was not seen very often. I also was surprised to hear Vietnamese people fluent in the French language. Although the family spoke English also, I was happy to practice my old high school French, which was taught by unforgettable Madame Leclerc. In Paris, my past three-year study of the French language, really paid off.

In a blink and a nod, the two-mile, eight-minute Métro ride from my hotel took me to meet Cheryl next morning at our agreed destination. It was a bright sunny day and my hotel parents advised me to wear comfortable walking shoes for the full day ahead.

My memory of the Métro, their equivalent of London's Underground, and our Subway, is of its colorful vaulted stations in Art Deco style. I also remember the long hikes down the stairways to the trains, that left me breathless on many occasions.

At the Champs-Élysées, the famous boulevard, lined with luxury shops, theatres, and gardens, Cheryl and I had coffee and croissants in one of the sidewalk cafés. Our first stop was the Arc de Triomphe, the massive arch commissioned by Napoleon Bonaparte in the eighteen-hundreds. We took a brief elevator ride to the observation area where we got a sweeping view of Paris.

We determined to take in two more sites, popular with tourists, on that first day. They were Notre Dame Cathedral and the Eiffel Tower. We marveled at the cathedral's French Gothic architecture and its location on Île de la Cité, an island on the Seine River, in the center of Paris! We were only able to view a miniscule amount of the magnificent collection of famous art works while there, before we moved on.

We ate dinner at a wonderful French restaurant before visiting the famous Eiffel Tower. "Now this is eating!" I exclaimed to Cheryl, as we sampled the appetizing food. We brought home memories of lamb, roasted potatoes, and a mixed vegetable dish of eggplant and zucchini. Of course, the proverbial bottle of fine French wine accompanied the meal. As we ended our main course, we sampled various cheeses from a tray offered. For dessert, we had a variety of tartes and other sweets, and cups of strong French coffee.

We were stuffed as we left the restaurant, but still went to our last port of call for the day, a night-time visit to the amazing Eiffel Tower. The latticed iron work of this one thousand-foot iconic symbol of Paris was just as it was pictured in books and magazines the world over. We took the Lift (Elevator) to the top, where we had a magnificent, three-hundred and sixty-degree view of Paris, the City of Lights. Cheryl and I were two young women filled with both wanderlust and wonderment. We could only utter the words, "This is amazing!" at the sight.

On our third and final day in Paris, we decided to spend our entire time at the Louvre Museum. One day there was simply not enough to view it all, but there were two famous women we were determined to see there: the Mona Lisa and Venus de Milo.

Instead of wandering around on our own, we took a guided tour of the famous museum. When we got to Mona Lisa, the famous painting by the Italian artist, Leonardo da Vinci, we learned she was still shrouded in mystery. The woman in the portrait, sat with folded hands, wearing her famous smile which people come to look for. By contrast, the ancient marble Greek statue, Venus de Milo, stood in stark display with both of her arms missing. It is believed they had been deliberately broken off many years ago.

Our visit to the Louvre ended with a leisurely walk through the famous Tuileries Gardens, immediately opposite the museum. Lovely coiffed landscapes lined the pathways and made for great relaxation as we came to the end of our time in Paris.

Copenhagen

I was filled with anticipation as I contemplated my two-week stay in Copenhagen. I was invited to visit and stay with Gina, my long-time friend and classmate. After a whirlwind romance, she moved there to live with Olaf, her Danish husband. She had written to tell me, before I made the trip, of all the exciting things we would do together as we toured around the city. Cheryl, meanwhile, was bound for the Amsterdam leg of her journey, but would meet me in Copenhagen a week later.

As I deplaned at the airport in Copenhagen, I looked in vain for Gina, who promised to meet me on arrival. When over an hour had passed and there was no sign of her, I tried to use the telephone to call her. Little did I know the telephone system was far different than that in the United States, and, worse, the telephone operator who answered did not speak English! I was a little lost girl in Europe! Finally, a gentleman who spoke a little English, and saw me walking alone, offered to help me. Thankfully, he was able to call Gina and she answered the phone.

Gina's voice was low and muffled – not cheerful as I was expecting. She did not welcome me to Copenhagen, but explained she was ill and could not accommodate me at all.

"My mom is on her way over from New York right now to take care of me," she said. "I have to let her use our spare bedroom. You'll have to stay in a hotel and be on your own while you are here."

I cannot explain the feeling of rejection I experienced. My heart fell to my shoes, as I realized the enormity of my situation. I was already there in a foreign country, knowing only my friend, who told me, "Don't come. Make it by yourself!"

Tears flowed as I contemplated my next step. Thank God for Fran, my travel agent, however. I pulled out the list of people she gave me in each country of my itinerary, whom she said could help me if I needed assistance. I contacted a woman who had a home with rooms for rent to visitors and she allowed me to stay there two nights.

"What am I to do the rest of my scheduled time here in Copenhagen after the two nights at this home are up?" I asked myself.

God had helped me thus far, so I had confidence, despite the situation, He would open another door. I reviewed Fran's list again and saw the names of two of her personal friends, Dave and Veronica, who lived and worked in the city. I called them and explained my dilemma.

"What are you doing over there, anyway?" Veronica asked, as if she'd known me for years. "Pack your bags and get here at once by taxi. We have plenty of room for you."

I felt as if a miracle had happened for me. I stayed the two days, as agreed, with my landlady, then went by taxicab to Dave and Veronica's residence. My eyes opened wide as I viewed their home and situation. Here were two Black folks, who had embraced the Danish culture and were working and living their lives in comfort, far away from their home in the USA. They welcomed me with open arms, showed me to my room, and there I stayed until my fourteen-day tryst in Denmark was over.

At first, I assumed my hosts were a married couple. However, they soon made it clear theirs was a platonic relationship and they lived together merely for convenience. Dave was gay and was a well-known dancer and dance instructor there. Veronica was straight and worked in a night club as a singer. He occupied the downstairs area of their spacious, well- furnished home, while she occupied upstairs. My room was on the second floor. Veronica cooked daily and had not forgotten the spicy southern recipes she had been raised on. I soon was introduced to their eclectic mix of friends, most of whom were Black ex-patriates from America – all frustrated with the racial situation back home. Dave took me to his dance studio, while Veronica insisted I visit one night with her at the club. The two of them treated me well, as if I were a long-lost sister who had come over to visit with them.

Still concerned about my friend, Gina, and against both Veronica's and Dave's recommendations, I decided to call her. They thought she'd done me wrong, regardless of how sick she was, and that, at least, her husband might have been concerned for my welfare. After all, I had been invited to be her house guest! They viewed the situation in racial terms, as White people not caring about Blacks.

When I reached Gina by telephone a week after I arrived, her mother had come and gone back to America. Her husband was working, and she was left alone to recuperate from her illness. She asked me to come over to visit her and I did. Her home was disheveled, and she looked sad and dejected. I really felt sorry for her. A brief glance in her kitchen cupboard revealed very few groceries there. I knew then what I had to do and why God sent me there ahead of Cheryl's arrival.

I asked Gina where the nearest grocery store was and I set out, walking, to find it. Although I couldn't speak Danish, I recognized the foods I wanted to buy. The grocer helped me as I pointed to what I wanted. I returned to Gina's apartment with my arms full. After ensuring her comfort, I set about to cook the couple a meal. I fried chicken, cooked mashed potatoes, green vegetables, and salad, with rolls to go with it. When Olaf, her husband, arrived home, his eyes grew as big as saucers when he saw the meal I had prepared. He wolfed it down in seconds, as if he hadn't eaten in quite some time.

"I'm sorry we couldn't accommodate you," said Gina. "I hope we'll still remain friends."

I never quite figured out what was happening with that couple while there, but we did renew our friendship several years later.

One positive thing Gina had done before my arrival, was arranged for me to visit Rigshospitalet, one of the largest and most highly specialized hospitals in Denmark. As a newly trained midwife, at the time, I wanted to experience what maternity care was like in that country.

I was extremely impressed by my visit with the midwives. I soon recognized the laboring mother was treated as queen! The maternity suites and the midwives' uniforms were spotlessly white. Very few drugs were used and babies were born into a pleasant and compassionate environment. I was amazed to discover health care, even highly specialized care, was completely free of cost in Denmark.

I was introduced to and warmly welcomed by the main physicians in the department. I was glad I had visited and gained a new perspective on my chosen profession.

Cheryl arrived in Copenhagen the second week of my stay. I returned to life as a tourist and really enjoyed myself there. Veronica and Dave extended their hospitality to Cheryl, and, on several occasions, she shared meals with us. She loved their humor and unusual lifestyle.

A day spent shopping on Strøget, Copenhagen's famous one-mile walking street, was truly a delight. The shopkeepers were welcoming and not at all hostile toward us. One piece I still have from that long-ago shopping mecca, is a delicate blue and white vintage bowl, made of Danish china, that adorns my buffet cabinet. I was glad I could mail my purchases back home from there without having to lug them with me throughout my time in Europe.

As we wandered along, we sampled Smørrebrød, Copenhagen's popular open-faced sandwiches. They were delicious and made from a variety of ingredients. Mine was roast beef and pickle, while Cheryl's was made of herring and shrimp. They were piled high on mountains of lettuce, radishes, and other chilled vegetables.

Before ending our day, we paid a visit to the Little Mermaid. The small bronze statue sits quietly on a rock by the waterside in Copenhagen. Over one hundred years old, it is an iconic symbol of Denmark.

A highlight of my time in Scandinavia, was a train ride aboard a ferry travelling to Gothenburg (they call it Göteborg), Sweden. Again, a classmate of mine had invited me for an overnight visit when she heard about my pending visit to the region. Her husband, a Swede, and former exchange student at her home in the USA, and with whom she had fallen in love, like Gina's husband had taken her back to his country to live.

"Are you going to find yourself abandoned again over there?" asked Dave, with sarcasm. "We won't be there to help you out if you do."

"No, I made sure I called my friends, and they'll be waiting for me at the train station in Gothenburg."

Sweden

I marveled as the train, without difficulty, boarded the ferry with passengers still seated, for the two-hour trip to Malmo, Sweden. On arrival, it just as easily exited the ferry and traveled on its way down the train tracks to onward destination points. I breathed a sigh of relief when I saw my hosts, a few hours later, waiting for me at the station. They seemed genuinely glad to see me. Their children had snow-white hair, as did most of the children I saw in Scandinavia while there.

My day in Gothenburg, located some three hundred miles from Stockholm, the capital, was spent on the water with my friends who were avid water-skiiers. The sea and waterways surrounding Gothenburg, on Sweden's west coast, beckoned families to have fun that late-July afternoon. I sat in their rented boat as Betty and Lars, her husband, skillfully navigated the white-capped waves. After an evening's meal and relaxation later at their home, I wended my way back to Copenhagen next day the same way I had come.

Veronica and Dave were sorry when it was time for me to leave. In fact, Veronica, approximately the same size as I, insisted I leave with her a quantity of my clothing. She declared Danish women are small and thin, and don't have the buxom shapes African American women have. She said if I left my dresses with her, she wouldn't have to make alterations to them as she has to with those she buys over there. With some reluctance, I left them with her. I was extremely grateful though, for their warm hospitality.

My trip to Europe, solo, is yet indelible in my mind. Despite the discouraging and disappointing situation at the beginning of my Denmark experience, I still had lots of fun, both with old and new-found friends. I was able to make something beautiful of an ugly situation.

When I left Europe, I planned to go again, perhaps to other countries, with other friends someday. Cheryl and I remained friends for several years.

Touchdown in Tel Aviv

For many years, my husband and I talked about making a pilgrimage to Israel, in the Holy Land, and were confident one day we'd go. Sure enough, in the year 2000, our long-time wish came true.

How excited we were the day we joined our pastor and one-hundred and forty other parishioners on the life-changing journey. After a twelve-hour non-stop flight from Newark, New Jersey, the huge jetliner touched down in Tel-Aviv-Jaffa on Israel's Mediterranean coastline.

We received a warm welcome to that ancient biblical land from Ami, our Tour Guide, and Rafi, our Bus Driver. They were trained and knowledgeable, and, right away, initiated us into the wonders and intricacies of Israel. There was no time to waste and so much to experience during our ten-day sojourn there.

Interspersed with sightseeing and educational activities, the most memorable parts of our itinerary were, for me, the spiritual experiences I encountered at the holy sites I had read about in the Bible since childhood.

Mt. Carmel came alive as I stood where Elijah, The Prophet, called down fire from heaven and consumed the altar sacrifice. He proved Jehovah was the only true God.

One warm, sunny morning, we sat on the grassy hillside on the *Mount of Beatitudes.* I recalled Jesus, by a miracle, multiplied the loaves and fishes for the multitude gathered.

The *Jordan River,* was a highlight as we, along with other pilgrims, were baptized there. That experience gave credence to the words of the old Spiritual:

Jordan River is chilly and cold, Chills the body but not the soul![5]

---

5   Negro Spiritual. *Jordan River.* Author Unknown. Public Domain.

I'll never forget our dip in the *Dead Sea,* which has mineral-rich healing properties. Because of its heavy salt content, we were able to float, face up, without fear of drowning. *Lot's Wife* is said to have been turned into a Pillar of Salt at that location.

I experienced a range of emotions as we arrived on the outskirts of *Jerusalem.* Viewing the Holy City from the *Mount of Olives* was truly breathtaking. I completely lost it when we entered the *Garden of Gethsemane.* My tears flowed as I sat among the ancient olive trees and contemplated the betrayal and agony of our Lord. I found myself softly humming the words of that poignant hymn:

> *Lest I forget Gethsemane, lest I forget thine agony*
> *Lest I forget thy love to me, lead me to Calvary.*[6]

I could go on and on about our other visits: to *Caesarea,* the town where the Christian gospel was first preached to the Gentiles; I could talk about *Capernaum, Nazareth, Bethlehem, and Jericho.* At the *Sea of Galilee,* we had a delightful meal called *Peter's Fish Fry.* Each of these places had its own special significance. I was stunned into silence, however, when I saw *Golgotha – the place of a Skull,* and *Calvary.*

I felt overwhelmed with joy as we worshipped in the *Garden Tomb* where Jesus was betrayed, crucified, and resurrected. The words of William Reed Newell sprang to life:

> *Mercy there was great and grace was free;*
> *Pardon there was multiplied to me;*
> *There my burdened soul found liberty—at Calvary*[7]

---

6   Hussey. 1921. Lest I Forget. Public Domain.
7   Newell. 1895. At Calvary. Public Domain.

The Empty Tomb: He is Risen!

Our final holy site call was to the place of prayer, the *Western Wall*, also known as the *Wailing Wall*. What a privilege it was to place the prayers, given to me by friends back home, into the crevices of the Wall. As I offered up my own prayers, I believed, by His miracle-working power, God would answer theirs.

Though weary and foot-sore, I enjoyed our visits to many archeological digs throughout Israel. I was fascinated by the remnants of ancient places, unearthed and honored: Among them, *Beit She'an*, a Roman city; *Qumran*-the site of the Dead Sea Scrolls' discovery; and *Masada*, a place of fortitude and courage. I will long remember the heart-rending *Holocaust Museum*, where six million murdered Jews are memorialized.

Archeological Excavations. Ancient Israel Ruins.

Our meals in the Holy Land were scrumptious☐ popular Falafel Sandwiches, Hummus, and Shawarma, were savored. These were eaten with a wide variety of fruit and vegetables.

What a surprise it was for us, while out shopping on the famous Ben Yehuda Street in Jerusalem, to find a McDonald's fast-food Restaurant!

We were delighted to visit the Four Quarters of the Old City of Jerusalem: Christian, Armenian, Muslim, and Jewish, which divide its inhabitants by culture, religion, and history.

"What an amazing time we had in Israel," I remarked, as we winged our way home.

"Yes," my husband agreed. "New knowledge, new insights, and spiritual awakening."

We join others in praying for the peace of Jerusalem.

In Search of My Panamá Roots:

From the time I was a child, I heard about Panamá. For me, "Panamá," conjures up a place of mystery, a confluence of cultures, and a mixture of languages.

"One can hear both Spanish and English spoken in Panamá," I once read in my history book, "as well as several tribal tongues which the indigenous Indian tribes there speak."

So, you might wonder, "Why is Panamá of interest to me? Why would that country, sandwiched between Costa Rica in Central America, and Colombia in South America, fascinate me?"

My answer is simple. Panamá is the land of my mother's birth. My mom and most of her siblings were born there in an area called the Panamá Canal Zone. For many years, that section of Panamá was owned and operated by the United States government, and the flag of the United States flew proudly over it. The Americans were granted ownership of that fifty-mile region by the government of Panamá, because they spearheaded and controlled the building of the Panamá Canal.

In the early twentieth century, around 1905, my grandparents left their island home in Jamaica and joined several other young people from throughout the islands of the West Indies, who were traveling to Panamá. They were responding to the call for workers to build the Canal.

Luther Morgan   *Lydia Morgan*

Their children were born during their twenty-year sojourn there and became infused into the culture, language, and lifestyle of Panamá.

In my grandparents' time, life in Panamá was extremely difficult. Living conditions for the migrant workers were less than optimal. An area was carved out for them in a northern province called Colón. A positive outcome was the formation of small communities in Colón, where families were able to maintain their island culture, socialize, and worship together. My mom and her family lived in Colón for many years. My grandfather became pastor of a church he founded there called The Christian Mission of Panamá.

My family was not destined to remain in Panamá, however. When the Canal was completed, they faced three major choices:

- Remain in Panamá, accepting it as their permanent home.
- Return to their original home in Jamaica, reconnecting with family and friends or
- Immigrate to the USA to benefit from the economic opportunities which beckoned.

My mother's parents chose the latter, departing with their children from their beloved Panamá to make a new life for themselves in the USA. My mom was fifteen years old at the time.

After a five-day voyage aboard the ship Aconcagua, the weary travelers sailed into Ellis Island in New York City on New Year's Day, 1925. They made their way to Harlem, a village in upper Manhattan, and began a new life there.

WILSON FAMILY ARRIVES IN NEW YORK JANUARY 1, 1925 ABOARD SHIP SS ACONCAGUA FROM PANAMÁ.

I was born in New York City many years after my mother arrived on American shores. While growing up, I came to realize Panamá had made an indelible impression on my family.

Grandma spun endless tales about her life in Panamá although she had left there so long before. "Yellow Fever ripped through the country like a whirlwind. But US Surgeon General, William Gorgas, was able to wipe it out in a fairly short time."

Her favorite stories were about the canal builders from the West Indies.

"Those were the real heroes of Panamá. Getting the Canal constructed was a massive operation. Sadly, many died from injuries on the job. But they finally finished it after ten long years."

Ma captivated me as she recalled the exciting annual Carnevale. "The entire nation of Panamá came to a standstill. Everyone participated."

She'd close her eyes and I could tell she was seeing it vividly replayed in her mind's eye. She spoke of her family standing with the crowds, watching the marching bands as they passed. Sometimes she would sing for me, "Mi Pollera, mi Pollera, mi Pollera Colorada," a favorite tune sung as dancing ladies, clad in colorful, traditional dresses, called *polleras,* passed by.

POLLERA, PANAMÁ NATIONAL DRESS[8]

---

8   Traje Tipico Panameña : Panamá.

What fascinated me most, however, was the ease with which my family members conversed in both Spanish and English. They were fully bilingual. Later when I went to college and enrolled in my first Spanish class, I realized how much I learned from them by simply listening to their conversations, and I became fluent in the language myself.

Fast forward to 2006. By then, my parents, grandparents, aunts, and uncles, had all passed away. However, my sister and I, and a few cousins of our generation, decided it was time to make our pilgrimage to Panamá. We wanted to explore and experience the land of our parents' birth. I, especially, longed to visit Colón, to find out if any of our family roots remained.

Eighty-one years after our ancestors arrived in the USA from Panamá, eight of us returned to Panamá. We called ourselves, "Ocho Primos"—"Eight Cousins". Many of our parents' stories came alive for us as we visited places where they lived. The trip was both exciting and nostalgic. We wished we'd gone there years earlier, and, perhaps, taken some of our elders with us.

We flew out of JFK airport in New York and landed in the busy capital, Panamá City, in the wee hours of the morning. Immediately immersed in the Spanish language, which flowed over and all around us, we decided to speak to each other throughout the trip, using our Spanish names. That made it oh such fun!

"You are now Ernesto," I told Ernest, as he laughed heartily.

"Who am I?" asked Alice with a wink.

"You are Alicia, for as long as we're on the trip."

"I already know I'm Esparanza," my cousin, Hope, declared.

"I like Marilena. It sounds exciting," said Marilyn.

Carol was all right being called Carolina. "It makes me feel elegant."

"Elena is my new name forever, I'm never going back to Lena," my cousin advised us.

"My name is already a Spanish name," said Dolores. "So, I don't need to change it." We still used a twick of an accent when we called her by name, though.

"My Spanish teacher called me Graciela," I told them. "So, I'll keep that one. You can call me Grace when we get back home."

During our week-long journey to Panamá, the sights and sounds were exhilarating. The cuisine was 'sabrosa'– delicious, to say the least! Our hotel served us breakfast every morning before we hit the streets shopping. We sampled Panamanian tortillas, made from corn dough and topped with white cheese or eggs. We also were introduced to Carimañolas, a popular breakfast dish there. We learned it's a fritter, made from yuca or cassava, stuffed with cheese and ground beef, then fried.

The main shopping items we sought were the beautiful gold fil-igree earrings, and other fine jewelry, for which Panamá is famous.

"I'll take you to the stores where we locals shop," Zoraida told me in Spanish. She was the gracious sister of my Panamanian friend, Hilda, back home in Texas. Hilda had asked her to be our shopping guide while in Panamá City and she willingly complied.

The earrings and bracelets at the shops to which Zoraida took us were amazing. The prices were also far less than those at stores designed for tourists. Together, we brought a treasure trove back home.

"We'd like to try Sancocho de Galina—your national dish," I said to Zoraida, later. "We've heard so much about it. Can you recommend a restaurant?"

The restaurant to which Zoraida took us was the real thing, serv-ing authentic Panamanian dishes. The national dish, light chicken soup cooked with a variety of local vegetables, was flavorsome and filling. Zoraida suggested we try Ropa Vieja, another popular dish—a beef stew– next time.

By far, our two most memorable experiences while there, were sailing through the Panamá Canal, and my long-anticipated visit to Colón.

The five-hour Canal tour was exciting. We sailed aboard the Ship Pacific Queen, and navigated the locks, which connect the deep waters of the Atlantic Ocean to the deep waters of the Pacific. While there, I reflected on Grandma's stories of long ago and of the brave Caribbean workers who built the canal.

To my surprise, while sailing, I ran into a colleague of mine, a doc-tor with whom I worked in Texas!

"What are you doing here?" we asked each other.

We chatted a while, then moved on.

Marcus Bryan and his sister, Clara, escorted us on our road trip to Colon. My friend, Delna, in Dallas, asked her two siblings to keep in touch with us while in Panamá. We rented a car and began our fif-ty-mile trip from Panama City. After a brief stop for souvenirs in La Zona Libre de Colón, a huge, enclosed, tax-free shopping area on the outskirts of the city of Colon, we finally reached our destination.

I must say I was quite disappointed when I viewed the unkempt, impoverished, and, obviously, underserved city. I later learned, during my family's sojourn there, Colón had been a well-kept, thriving town. Later, however, it was dubbed, "The City that Panamá forgot."

Still, I was overcome with emotion and exclaimed to my sister, Marilena, "This is why we came to Panamá. This is where Ma grew up."

COLÓN, PANAMÁ, CIRCA 1915.

We had little information or clues about whom or what we were looking for in Colón. We only had names of family members who lived there previously or with whom our forebears had lost connection. Marcus, however, was quite familiar with Colón. So, by word of mouth and a few telephone calls, Voilà! We located Mrs. Cox, age ninety. This spritely lady, who spoke only English, was born in Panamá and lived with her granddaughters, who spoke only Spanish! Somehow, they communicated quite well with each other, and welcomed us warmly into their home.

"I'm so glad to meet you all," she said. "It's such a pity my departed husband is not here to talk with you. He knew all the names of family members who left Panamá years ago."

Mrs. Cox was a storehouse of information and filled in many information gaps for us. She shared about her life in Colón after our relatives migrated to the USA.

"Meeting you has made my journey to Panamá so worthwhile," I told her. "Colón, in particular, is where I've always wanted to come. This has truly been a family reunion."

On our final day in Panamá, we eight cousins relaxed and reflected on our time spent in the place of our origins. We all agreed it had brought us full circle and had been an adventure of a lifetime.

Welcome to Paradise

I perked up, groggy, after our eight-hour non-stop flight from Dallas.

"Welcome to Paradise!" the captain's voice boomed with sheer excitement over the airplane's loudspeaker. By the end of our eight-day stay in Hawaii, I fully understood the captain's meaning. It was truly a sojourn in Paradise.

My husband, Neville, loved to visit tropical climes, but up to that point, his experience was limited to jaunts through the Caribbean islands. After my insistence we try someplace new, he agreed to a Hawaiian vacation. The occasion was celebration of his retirement after a forty-five-year engineering career.

It was early September 2003. We arrived late one Sunday afternoon in Honolulu, the state capital, on the island of O'ahu and were greeted by a delightful delegation of local goodwill ambassadors. They warmly welcomed us to the Aloha State and gave us brightly colored floral garlands, called leis, to wear around our necks.

There was no time to linger in O'ahu, however. The regal Norwegian Star, our cruise ship, and home away from home, awaited us at the port. We were due to set sail that same evening—the start of our discovery of enchanting secrets of the islands.

HAWAII, 2003

I could talk forever about our many wonderful experiences as we spent a day in each of five Islands. Hilo, the lush town on Big Island, thrilled us with its waterfalls and volcanoes. Beautiful Maui, displayed thousands of acres of macadamia nut and papaya orchards. We will never forget our scenic boat ride on the Wailua River in charming Kaua'i. A wonderful group of troubadours serenaded us as a brilliant golden sun slowly descended and gave way to a magnificent starlit sky.

When we returned to O'ahu, we went on a delightful shopping spree, then lounged on famous Waikiki Beach.

The most fascinating cruise stop, for me, by far, was a day spent on Fanning Island, an unspoiled hideaway in the Republic of Kiribati. We visited on the third day of our itinerary. Nothing prepared us for what we experienced. We were transported back in time, perhaps several hundred years, when we met the people of the Island.

Our cruise liner was too large to enter the harbor, and so, remained at sea on the outskirts. We boarded small tenders which took us to the island proper.

Unlike the other islands visited, Kiribati is not part of the United States of America. Therefore, as foreigners, we were subjected to immigration clearance procedures. Once our passports were stamped, we were permitted to enter the island.

Soon, we could hear clear melodious voices of the local people, as they welcomed us in song. Men, women, and children, clad in grass skirts, sang and danced. They wore necklaces and bracelets made from shells, and wreaths on their heads.

FANNING ISLAND, KIRBATI, MEN'S WELCOME DANCE

Fanning Island is a nine by six-mile area, one of thirty-three islands, which comprise the Republic of Kiribati, in the Pacific Ocean. These islands are located on the edges of the Equator.

Our cruise liner designated our stop in Fanning Island "a day of rest and relaxation." By agreement with the islanders, we were free to roam as far as we wanted or spend a day, at leisure, at the beach. A carved-out lagoon had been designated for our swimming pleasure. On that day, we were surprised there were no other visitors on the island but ourselves!

Neville and I wandered freely and came upon a large open-air market. It was a beehive of activity. We bought woven straw baskets and a few carvings, sold by native women. Shy but friendly, nearly naked, dark-haired, olive-complexioned, children darted in and around the stalls under the watchful eyes of their mothers. The kids observed us closely as we made our purchases.

The road to the beach was comprised of thick vegetation of coconut palm trees, native bushes, and shaggy running vines. The rich, fertile soil produced a variety of fruit and vegetables such as pineapples, bananas, and breadfruit. Houses, built on wooden platforms, intrigued us. Their windows were without glass and their roofs thatched.

At the water's edge, we came upon the delicious barbeque our ship provided. Later, we dipped in the warm crystal-clear water that beckoned us. Before nightfall, we re-boarded our ship and continued our journey to the next island.

Our visit to Paradise would not have been complete without a stop at Pearl Harbor, site of the US Naval Base of the US Pacific Fleet during World War II. We were taken by bus to that historic location on our last day in Hawaii. On the way, we toured downtown Honolulu, viewed historic statues, and the State Capitol Building.

On arrival at Pearl Harbor, we joined hundreds of visitors, like ourselves, from all over the world. We were shown a documentary film, which refreshed our memories of what we had learned years ago in our history books about this site. We then took a US Navy shuttle boat to the USS Arizona Memorial. A feeling of sadness overcame us as we reflected on the nearly two thousand sailors who perished aboard the Ship USS Arizona. It exploded and sank when Pearl Harbor was attacked by Japanese forces.

As we walked around, we gazed in awe at military history on display. We saw several outdoor exhibits, related to submarine warfare. Also, relics of US airplanes and battleships.

When we departed Pearl Harbor, our tour bus took us directly to the airport for our trip back home. We had reached the end of our Hawaiian sojourn and were sad it was over.

As our jetliner winged us homeward, we whispered to each other, "Aloha, one day we will return to Paradise."

Family Ties

"**B**lessed be the tie that binds,"[9] says an old hymn by John Faw-sett.

We are all born into families as part of God's divine purpose. Some of us were born into small, nuclear families, some into huge, extended ones. Some people become family via adoption, and these families are no less important or loving toward its members than are biological families.

I've found that people, for the most part, cherish their family members. However, some don't define "family" as blood relations, necessarily. They might describe friends, colleagues, or neighbors, as family, and keep genetic relatives at a distance. In this section, I've provided a Welcome and Farewell to a family member, as well as six Essays exploring family relationships of people I knew. All have given me insight into what family truly means. Perhaps you, the reader, have your own definition.

> *"And now these three remain: faith, hope and love. But the greatest of these is love."*
>
> I Corinthians 13: 13 (NIV)

---

9   Faucett, 1782 Hymnary.org. Blessed Be the Tie that Binds. (Public Domain).

Welcome and Farewell

Welcome

A Tribute to My Granddaughter Sarah Javonne Davis

Dear Sarah,

I watched you scream your way into this world on a cold January day in Abilene, Texas.

> "Go light the world, Sarah," Jesus told you as you left heaven. "That will be your job until I call you back home to be with me."

You didn't know then how long it would be, so you did your job well for the twenty-one years He gave you. You were, indeed, a beautiful light that came down from heaven as a gift to all of us.

At the moment of your birth, your tiny hands grasped tight to life as you breathed your first breath. We were all amazed at how strong you were and how happy you seemed. You, God's awesome creation, squirmed, kicked, blinked, and smiled, as you met us, your new family. Tears of unspeakable joy rolled down as each of us, in our own way, thanked God for sending you, a healthy baby, to us.

Sarah, I saw the profound love your parents, Jackie and Joseph, immediately had for you, their long-awaited daughter. The indescribable pure joy expressed on their faces said it all. You knew right away how they felt as they held, fed, cuddled, and stared at you with absolute wonder. You snuggled close and let the warmth of their love embrace and enfold you.

You grew up, Sarah, in a wonderful, godly home. Your parents spared nothing to make you happy, and experience all that parents could possibly give their child. In response, you became a sensitive, caring, fun-loving young woman. In so many ways you let them know they had done a great job.

As you crossed from childhood into adulthood, it was nearing the time for you to say goodbye. Neither we, you, or your parents, knew you were going, since everyone had big plans for your future. But your work on earth was done, Sarah. God wanted you back with Him and His angels. You are now at peace with Jesus, with your beloved Grandma, and with many who've gone before.

Your parents, Joseph and Jackie, will never ever forget you. When you arrived, you opened the door for so many blessings and experiences God wanted them to have. Neither will we or the rest of your family forget you. So, "So long for now," Sarah. We'll meet again someday around God's heavenly throne.

Lovingly, Grandma Grace and Grandpa Neville

Farewell

"When the Gates Swung Open, You Walked on In"

My child Sarah, there is not a day or an hour that passes that I don't think about your smile and the fun times we had together, as Mother and Daughter. I never would have thought I would have to say, "farewell" to you.

I think about you in the silence and middle of the night and wonder if you are okay. I know you are because you are dancing in the Hands of Jesus. You are enjoying your new life with Jesus. There is no more pain, no sorrow, no more labor, or suffering. The Trumpet sounded and the Gates were opened just for you.

Your Wings were ready for you to fly. But your Dad and I were not ready to let you leave. You were and are my last shining light.

The Gates swung open and you walked in, knowing Jesus had promised you a home over there. I can feel your presence just the same. I know you are far, yet so very near. The things we felt deeply are the hardest to let go of. But I know God needed you to come back to Him.

I knew, and God knew, you were tired, weak, and worn. There is a place in my heart no one else could ever fill. That part is you. I am left with the other one-fourth to keep in memory of you.

My Child, "So long for now," we will not say, "Goodbye." You left on the Evening Train to Glory.

You were twenty-one years and two months, but still my Baby. Your work is done here, so wear your Crown with a smile, although life is not the same without you. God sounded the Trumpet, the Gates swung open, you took your Crown, and walked on in.

**In Loving Memory of Sarah Javonne Davis
January 28, 1999 to April 21, 2020
Your Mother, Jacqueline Davis
Jacqueline Davis and Grace Allman Burke, Co-Authors**

Hyacinth and Joe

In 2009, I visited my cousin, Hyacinth, at her home in New York City. I went to help her celebrate her birthday at the tender age of one hundred and six. I was amazed to discover her mental faculties were still intact and her keen sense of humor had not faded.

She shared with us memories from her one hundredth birthday celebration, six years prior. "My church family brought a huge birthday cake, flowers, a golden tiara for my head, and served me Communion. They read a Proclamation from the Mayor of New York City, declaring that day *Hyacinth Haywood Lemba Day,* if you please!"

Isabella, Hyacinth's only surviving daughter, herself, age seventy-eight, beamed with pride. "Mama is a miracle to us all."

I was intrigued as I spoke with Hyacinth –a person of such advanced age – whose memory was so sharp. With her permission, I wrote with passion, as she reminisced about highlights of her life. Here is Cousin Hyacinth's story.

Early Life

Hyacinth was born on the Caribbean island of Jamaica in 1903 to Rosalind and Thomas Haywood. She was the firstborn of their seven children. Her parents took her as an infant, first, to Costa Rica in Central America, for a short time, then to Panamá where she grew up.

Youth

In November 1928, keen-witted and feisty Hyacinth, age twenty-five, left Panamá aboard the Ship SS Cristobal. She was headed for America, seeking a new life for herself.

She bade her parents a sad goodbye, not sure if she'd ever see them again. "I'll write to you often, she tried to reassure, "I'll always be thinking about you. Maybe someday you'll join me in America."

Hyacinth's parents both passed away in Panamá, however, before they could be reunited with their daughter.

Travelling alone had been a daunting experience for Hyacinth. Her shipmates were largely comprised of family groups, which kept to themselves. The single men on board were naughty and aggressive. Young and innocent, she had not encountered such behavior before. But she trusted God to make her journey safe, and He did.

On arrival in New York, Aunt Matilda, who lived with her family uptown in Harlem, warmly welcomed her into her household. "You can stay here with us forever, if you like, Hyacinth. This will always be your home."

"Thanks Aunt Matt. That makes me feel so good. I'll look for a job, then see what happens next."

New York was breathtaking to Hyacinth. The lights, the sights, the sounds filled her with joy and hope as she anticipated her future.

A New Acquaintance

Hyacinth found work in a factory downtown. Her wages were small, yet she managed to give some to Aunt Matt for her upkeep, and save some to send back to Panamá to her parents. Somehow, though, she felt lonely and unhappy. She longed to meet people and taste the good life of New York.

One evening after work, while riding the subway home, Hyacinth noticed a short, handsome, very dark-skinned guy eyeing her. They exited the train at the same stop and he ventured to talk with her.

"You look like a fine young lady," he began, "You're pretty and I'd like to get to know you."

"You're a stranger," she replied. "Who are you anyway?"

"I'm Joe. I'm from the Belgian Congo in Africa."

Hyacinth enjoyed hearing his thick accent as they walked and talked for quite some time. Their chemistry was instant and thus began their passionate love affair.

Joe told Hyacinth the story of his childhood and why he was in America.

"I was born in 1899 when Belgium ruled the Congo. My parents were Unguma and Victoria Lemba. Life was very tough at that time, as violence and racial segregation were meted out to my people by the colonials. As soon as I could, I got passage on a ship that was headed for America. I heard America was a free land and I could find good fortune living here. I came here four years ago."

Hyacinth plied Joe with questions. "Where do you live and what kind of work do you do?"

"I rent a room in a boarding house downtown. I'm a construction worker on different projects."

"What are you doing here in Harlem?"

Joe was amused by Hyacinth's inquiries, but told her what she wanted to know.

"To be honest, I'm very lonely. On weekends, I find myself in Harlem where there are lots of immigrants. I visit local clubs and restaurants where I feel more at home. Besides, the food up here is so much better."

A few weeks after their first meeting, Hyacinth brought Joe home to meet Aunt Matt. "This is Joe, my new boyfriend."

Aunt Matt was polite to Joe but disapproved of him right away. "I think you're rushing into this relationship too fast, Hyacinth," she advised her, later. "You need to get to know him more. Does he go to church? Does he have ambition?"

"Joe is everything I've dreamed about, Aunt Matt. We're planning to move in together soon."

Aunt Matt was heartbroken. "Okay, my dear. You're grown and I can't stand in your way. I hope you won't be sorry later for what you're doing."

There was one thing about Joe which Hyacinth knew she could never let Aunt Matt know—he was a heavy drinker. He loved his beer and liquor whenever they went out. She reasoned, however, once they moved in together, he would slow down his drinking.

One Plus One Make Three

The couple found a room in Harlem on Eighth Avenue, not far from the Apollo Theatre. She imagined in her mind the good times they would have attending the shows there. Before long, however, Hyacinth found herself with child. This was not how she had planned it but was happy when her new baby girl arrived. She named her Isabella. Before she could return to work though, she was expecting again. Another girl, Glendine, came.

Sadly, Joe's drinking got worse and he began to drift. He missed days from work, arrived home late at night, and there was less and less money for the household. Joe and Hyacinth's arguments became more frequent, as well as his verbal outbursts, aimed at Hyacinth and the girls. In the midst this, however, a third baby girl put in her appearance. Hyacinth named her Jo Ella, after her father, Joseph. She finally married Joe, hoping this might help settle him down.

Nothing seemed to work though. It became crystal clear to Hyacinth she faced a hard life ahead of her if something did not change. She had lost her husband to alcohol and struggled to maintain a life for herself and her three little girls. She was forced to accept Welfare assistance from the government, and Joe became an absentee dad. He blew in and out of the home and in and out of their lives over the next few years, until Hyacinth had enough.

"I need you to get your things and leave," she told him. "I and your daughters can't take this any longer. Try to get yourself some help."

Joe left without a word, although, from time to time, they heard from him.

Single Again

Hyacinth still visited Aunt Matt, who always was kind to her. There was always food on the table for herself and the girls, and Aunt matt never questioned her about Joe.

One sad day, Hyacinth received the shattering news: Joe was found dead in a downtown area of Skid Row. She and the girls buried him with little fanfare in a popular cemetery in the Bronx.

"He was still your father," she told them. "He may not have been a good one, but, deep inside, he loved you and I loved him."

Hyacinth, still strong and healthy, determined to be the rock of her family. She returned to work, found a church, and became a useful member of her community.

Sad News Again

Hyacinth's is a story of overcoming and survival. She wanted to be there for her girls as they navigated their road in life. Sadly, however, they got caught up with the wrong crowd during their later teen years. Isabella, a single mom, struggled to raise her son, Joey. Glendine, like her dad, loved the taste of alcohol, and Jo Ella got mixed up with drugs.

Hyacinth was elated when Glendine got married to Saul. Although he was of a different religious faith, a Black Muslim, she hoped he could help Glendine curb her drinking. As it turned out, Saul spent most of his time in the Nation of Islam and ignored his wife's problem. Glendine could no longer work and drank throughout most days. Five years into their marriage, Glendine died of Cirrhosis of the liver, a devastating complication of alcoholism.

Nearly a year after Glendine's passing, Hyacinth, again, was hit by a bombshell. Her youngest daughter, Jo Ella, died alone from an overdose of heroin, in an abandoned building in Harlem.

"I don't know how I survived," she later told her cousin. "Those were really dark days. I couldn't believe I'd lost two of my children. Jo Ella was only eighteen. I wish I had been there to hold her hand."

Several years after her daughters' deaths, Hyacinth, the matriarch, again faced family tragedy. Joey, Isabella's son, her only grandson, was shot and killed. He had joined a gang and a member of an opposing one murdered him.

Despite these horrible misfortunes, Hyacinth kept going, not letting life's reversals hinder her. In her later years, she expressed sadness, not bitterness, about the loss of Joe and her other family members. "We just have to keep on going," she always said, "until God calls us home."

In 2013, I got the news from Isabella that her mom, Hyacinth Lemba, had passed away peacefully at the ripe old age of one hundred and ten. I felt despondent when I heard from Isabella, yet joyful, I had known her mom.

The Day after Christmas

D ecember 26, 2004 was indeed a memorable day for my family. It was a day most adults will recall -- the day of the huge earthquake in the Indian Ocean, which, in turn, spawned the great Tsunami. On that day, an undersea earthquake triggered a series of devastating tsunamis along the landmasses bordering the Indian Ocean.

The result was overwhelming. Whole communities were lost, inundated by waves rising one hundred feet in height! An estimated 230,000 people in fourteen countries were killed. It was, in fact, one of the deadliest natural disasters in recorded history.

Indonesia was the hardest-hit country, followed by Sri Lanka, India, and Thailand. The plight of those countries prompted a massive global response. Calculations showed a total of fourteen billion dollars in humanitarian aid were donated to that region.

I am in no way, shape, or form, making light of the horror that befell our neighbors on the other side of the world that day. I am using the word, Tsunami, here, figuratively. My family experienced a tsunami of sorts when, on that same day, Nehemiah and Nadiah, my beautiful twin grandchildren, put in their appearance. Since they arrived, our family has not been the same. We have been encountering mini tsunamis since.

We had hoped the twins would have given us a special blessing by arriving on Christmas Day. The Lord, however, had something else in mind. I believe He wanted us to finish our traditional family celebration, stuff ourselves with scrumptious holiday fare, open our presents, then be ready to receive our remarkable babies.

After our friends and family went home, I fell into bed, exhausted. However, at 6:00am that Sunday morning, I was awakened by the shrill ringing of the telephone.

"It's time for the babies, Mummy, my daughter, Jhanna, advised, with urgency in her voice. "We're on our way to the hospital. Please come right away and meet us there."

Jhanna was scheduled to have a Cesarean Section. Since I'm a Certified Nurse-Midwife, she wanted me to be with her in the operating room. Her husband, Nehemiah, whom everyone called "Popcorn," was squeamish about anything medical, and asked me to take his place at the delivery. I promised them I would.

I arrived at the hospital as the staff was wheeling my daughter into surgery. I gave her a reassuring hug as they prepared for the big event. I was thrilled when I saw Gary, a nurse-anesthetist and colleague of mine, involved in her care.

"I'll be administering the anesthesia," he advised.

"Gary, I'm so glad you are here."

In what seemed like record time, a boy, my grandson, Nehemiah Joshua Xavier, emerged, weighing five pounds, six ounces—not bad for a twin infant who arrived one month early. One minute later, a girl, Nadiah Jem Victoria, appeared. She weighed a mere four pounds and one ounce. However, as tiny as she was, she screamed loudly for all the world to hear.

I was thrilled to hold and introduce my spanking new grandchildren, one by one, to Jhanna, their mom. She wept with joy upon seeing them.

"They're beautiful," she said, as she reached out a hand and stroked each of them on the cheek. They seemed to nod their little heads in acceptance of the compliment.

Popcorn, Nehemiah, Sr., beamed with pride at his newborn babies. After being the dad of two girls already, he was elated to have a son, at last.

When I saw the active movements of my fourth and fifth grandchildren, I was so grateful they were healthy and normal. I anointed each with oil on their foreheads and prayed for them, "Dear Lord, thank you so much for granting us a safe delivery of Jhanna and her babies. I pray the world will be kind to them and their journey will be prosperous. In Jesus' name, Amen."

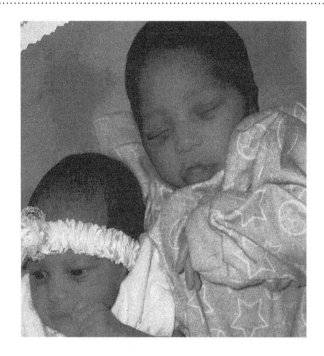

Twin Treasures (Womb Mates), 2004

Three days later, mom, dad, and the babies left the hospital to begin their new life as a family. They seemed ready to face life and all it would bring their way.

As of this writing, the twins are thriving, making names for themselves, are sports enthusiasts, love the Lord, are popular at the high school they attend, and will turn sixteen years old – on the day after Christmas.

Two to Tango

Not all babies arrive on planet earth alone. Sometimes the Lord sends them down in pairs. Perhaps He knew they would do better as a marvelous duet, singing through life together. Maybe He told them, "Dance for the world to see! It takes two to Tango!"

When I was growing up, I was always fascinated by twins– and there were many in my community. Take for instance Carl and Clive, who later made major contributions to society. Clive became a world-renowned kidney and liver transplant surgeon, while Carl became a celebrated Judge. He advocated for the poor in New York City.

I can't forget Maude and Mamie, who attended my church. I knew them as older twins, identical in appearance and nature. They excelled at cooking and baking and each had a jolly personality. Mamie, herself, was blessed with twin daughters, but her girls were fraternal twins and not at all alike in personality. Lenora, the older, was thin and tall and worked for years overseas as a nurse in foreign service. Gloria, short, lighter in skin tone and freckled faced, was a teacher, then became a high school principal.

My mother ran a day nursery when I was a young girl. You guessed it! A pair of twin girls was there. Lois and Yvonne, fully grown and now, married with their own families, are my dear friends to this day.

During my career as a nurse-midwife, it was my privilege to bring several babies into the world. Early in my career, I delivered three sets of twins. These babies were born before the days of sonograms, so no one knew twins were expected.

Harry and Larry's mom barely made it to the hospital before they arrived. They were her eleventh and twelfth children, and I was on hand to help them as they howled and screamed their grand entrances. Despite having an already large family, their mom was quite happy and exclaimed how blessed she was God had given her these babies.

My joy at the birth of one set of twins turned to astonishment, then sadness, however, when their mom announced she would not be taking her babies home with her.

"I'm placing those babies for adoption!" she yelled as the baby girls emerged. Adding a few curse words, she continued, "I came here to this hospital to have one baby, and I'm sure not leaving here with two!"

Sure enough, a few days later, she walked out of the hospital without her pretty baby girls and was never heard from again.

"Good luck in your lives," she mumbled, and gave them a fleeting glance as she left.

How I wished I could have taken them. But it was not possible for me to do so at the time. I felt relieved when I later learned the babies had found a nice home.

When I was a student nurse-midwife, I did research on twins. I was surprised to learn Black women have the highest rate of twins of all ethnic groups in this country. A more recent study at the University of Texas at Austin confirmed this fact and cited 36.8 twin births per 1000.[10]

An even more astounding revelation is that twin births in the Caribbean and Africa far exceed those in Asia and in predominantly Caucasian countries. Digging further, I learned this phenomenon originates in Nigeria, West Africa.[11]

I was amazed to learn the rate of twin births there is about four times higher than in the rest of the world. In the small town of Igbo-Ora in that country, an average of 45 to 50 sets of twins per live births are recorded. The people there have celebrated this situation over many generations and regard twins as special gifts from God. While it is clear genetic factors are at work, diet has also been pinpointed as a factor.

Years ago, when I got married, it was my secret desire to be a mother of twins. Well, I never gave birth to twins, but I learned you

---

10   University of Texas. 2019. *The Twin Project.*
11   BBC World Service. 2001. *The Land of Twins.*

should still be careful what you wish for. Little did I know, in the strangest way, my wish would come true. I was thrilled when my oldest daughter called me sixteen years ago and told me she and her husband were expecting twins. More exciting, a later sonogram revealed they were having a boy and a girl! It was my greatest pleasure, also, to have been present at their birth.

Sadly, when my grand-twins were still very young, their dad passed away. My daughter was left with the task of raising not only the twins, but also her two older children. My husband and I stepped in and became surrogate parents of our twin grandbabies. We raised them full-time in our home over the subsequent five years. We had both retired by then and it wasn't an easy job. But God gave us the strength and courage.

You'll be pleased to know our grand- twins are living again with their mom, are doing very well and attending high school.

I still maintain my fascination with twins, and pause whenever I hear unusual stories about them. Remember, it takes two to Two to Tango!

McCain Twins, That Was Then

McCain Twins, This Is Now

Angry Kin
(We All Have Them)

I have three relatives, Kristen, Wanda, and Leona, who demonstrate, by their behavior, they are bitter and most unhappy. Maybe angry is a better word to describe them. I've been trying to figure out for a long time why they are like this. But it is clear none of them enjoys being with people, and, certainly, not with their kinfolk. Maybe they never developed adequate social skills, or, perhaps, they are just plain meanspirited. Whatever the reasons, no one in our family is comfortable when they are around.

Brilliant intellectually, raised in two-parent, middle class homes, all these women reaped the benefits of a sound education and better than average job opportunities. Leona, 75, and Kristen, 55, are both Attorneys. Wanda, age 60, is a Systems Engineer. Collectively, they've earned degrees from top US universities. Two are married, with adult children, and one is single.

I grew up with the belief that family is everything and we should always be all about family. I still believe this. However, I've come to realize not everyone shares this belief. Many people are of the opinion blood ties are far less important than the bonds one creates with friends and those within their social circles. These three relatives demonstrate they are far more comfortable with "outsiders" than with family. Their message to kinfolk, both covert and outward, seems to be, "Keep out! My door is closed to you."

Perhaps we'll understand better why these women behave so negatively toward family when we take a glimpse at their stories.

Wanda

Wanda was born in the Caribbean and immigrated with her family to New York during her middle childhood years. She seemed happy and outgoing, and eagerly absorbed her lessons in the local public schools, under the watchful and encouraging eyes of her grandmother. She was accepted into all the colleges and universities to which she applied and graduated with honors from the one she chose to attend in another State.

Wanda did not enjoy a good relationship with her Black college roommate and spent little time with her. Although inwardly supportive of the university's Black Students Organization's objectives, she did not associate with them, choosing rather to hang out with White students, whom she deemed more socially acceptable. She never dated throughout her four years of college and believed it was because both Black and White male students found her unattractive.

Determined to find her place within a good profession, Wanda entered a Master's program immediately after college and completed it successfully. During graduate school, she met an African student, who was personable, fun to be with, and who appeared to love her dearly. She accepted his marriage proposal and asked her mother to help her plan her wedding.

When Wanda returned to New York for the wedding, an ugly side of her personality reared its head. She was haughty, in general, toward her wedding guests, and especially toward those who were African American. She ignored family members, while she laughed and joked with guests who were White. She argued, publicly, with her mother, who served as wedding coordinator, and was rude and hostile to her future in-laws. The groom appeared to be quite embarrassed by Wanda's behavior. The guests left the wedding, puzzled, about Wanda's conduct.

Kristen

Born the second of three girls, Kristen, early on, had many friends. Her mom, a Registered Nurse, and her dad, a popular Musician in the area in which they lived, spared nothing in providing their daughters a wonderful home environment. They lived in a large house in the sub-urbs and attended schools of high academic caliber. Kristen was very athletic and was privileged to play tennis, basketball, as well as violin, while growing up.

Of the three relatives I describe in this piece, my relationship with Kristen is the most problematic. Although I am several years older, she never treated me with respect. I noticed over the years, what-ever subject was under discussion when I was around her, she became argumentative and took an opposing view from mine. On one occa-sion, I asked Kristen why she was hostile toward me, and she flatly denied there was a problem. This left me feeling frustrated and dis-connected from her.

I hadn't heard from Kristen in several years and learned through the grapevine she had cut me off completely. I was told she didn't trust me and believed me to be manipulative and calculating. I was shocked to hear this and inquired how she had come to this conclu-sion. I was told she had become angry at me over an incident which had occurred years ago, and, in my opinion, was quite trite. Upon hearing this, I became upset because Kristen had not discussed her feelings about the situation with me, nor had she given me the oppor-tunity to defend myself. I believe, Kristen, even as an attorney, does not seem to understand there are always two sides to every story.

Recently, I felt inspired to call Kristen, to renew our relationship. Her hostility toward me was palpable.

"Why are you calling me?" she asked.

"I just wanted to reach out to you and let you know I love you. We are family, you know."

"I'm asking you not to call me again. I believe you have a motive for doing so."

"No, Kristen. I thought we could mend our relationship and move on."

"That's not what I want to do."

Thereupon, she ended the conversation by hanging up the phone.

I felt saddened and puzzled by her stance. It was clear she wanted me to leave her alone.

Leona

Leona, the oldest of my three kinfolk described here, has been angry for a long time. Born in Jamaica, and the daughter of a school Principal, she had the privilege of attending private schools there. She was resentful of her family's move to the USA and was even angrier at her parent's decision to live with extended family on arrival in New York. Although relatives attempted to make her feel welcomed, she was sullen, moody, and appeared to be preoccupied.

As she grew into adulthood, Leona often spoke of her loyalty to her native Jamaica. She made it clear that, to her, the USA was only a place from which to obtain favors, such as the chance to gain a higher education, and other opportunities she would not have gotten otherwise. Her behavior usually reflected the question, "What's in it for me?"

For example, when she became engaged to be married, she sold her car without first informing her fiancé of her plans to do so. During a later conversation when he referred to "our car," her response was, "What car? 'My car' has already been sold. If you want 'us' to have a car, it's up to you to buy one for 'us.' "

Of above-average intelligence, Leona successfully completed a Law degree and landed a job in a prestigious law firm. On the rare occasion she attended a family function, she upstaged conversations and put down people whom she considered inferior to herself. She boasted of her successes in "beating the system" and the ways she outsmarted those in positions above her.

Leona rules her household, controls her husband, and dominates her two adult unmarried sons.

Discussion

I have struggled with the questions, why are my kinfolk so hostile, isolated, and unloving? how should I relate to these relatives who are near to me by blood, but far away by relationship?

Here are my conclusions as I looked more in-depth at their behaviors.

First, I believe, although their paths were different, my angry female kinfolk have certain commonalities. Somewhere along the road, something changed profoundly in each of their lives, which caused them to morph from friendly, outgoing girls, to angry, cynical women. Perhaps they were victims of racism, assault, or violence. Perhaps people or situations hurt them so deeply, they continue to hurt people by their actions or words. Whatever changed for each of them, it was so devastating, they deny, and continue to deny, there is a problem. Consequently, they have not sought help to resolve it.

Second, although some of my other family members have given up on these relatives, and believe, as adults, they should be left alone, I, on the other hand, affirm "love conquers all." Therefore, I must find a way to love them, anyway.

Finally, I turned to the Word of God for answers. The Bible confirmed for me love is, indeed, the right way. As a Christian, I must love unconditionally. I am called to love anyway, despite what people may do to me. Jesus said in Luke 4:18 we have been "sent to heal the brokenhearted"[12] and "to set at liberty them that are bruised.[13] "I am asking God to show me how to help heal and restore my three relatives.

I am also required to forgive. Colossians 3:13 says, "make allowance for each other's faults, and forgive anyone who offends you. Remember, the Lord forgave you, so you must forgive others."[14]

I am determined to pray for my kinfolk and believe that real change is yet to come.

---

12   Luke 4:18. King James Version (KJV).
13   Ditto.
14   Col. 3:13. New Living Translation (NLT).

Cassie's Children

Cassie Duncan, wistful and frightened, couldn't believe she'd boarded a railroad train to New York City. A young woman, age eighteen, she had never left the rural fields of her native Georgia. In 1925 in the USA, people's financial situations were extra hard. Little did Cassie know she was joining thousands of black people from throughout the South in a movement called "The Great Migration." Their goal: to improve their economic plight by heading North.

"I wonder why Mama chose me to go to New York?" she pondered as she gazed at the passing landscape. "There were fifteen of us kids. I know we were a handful for Mama. But why me?"

After twenty tiresome hours, the train roared into Pennsylvania Station. Cassie looked out of the window at the crowds in wide-eyed disbelief. People with handbags and luggage of all shapes and sizes hurried up and down the platform in several different directions. She arrived in late November and folks huddled in large overcoats to protect themselves from the biting cold.

"New York, New York," the Pullman porter shouted. "Last stop. Everybody off."

The young man who sat next to her, woke up and stretched. "Are we here at last?" He spoke with a deep southern drawl. "Hope my people are here to meet me as they said they would. Need any help with your bag?"

"Thank you. I do," Cassie replied. "My aunt should be here for me. She left for New York about two years ago. I'll be staying with her."

Earlier, while they munched on the food they'd brought with them, the young man told Cassie a bit about himself. "Name's John – John Ramsey. Born in Savannah but lived in Albany most of my life. Got tired, so I'm headed for the great New York. At twenty-five, it's time for a man to move on."

Cassie, short and rotund, had giggled to herself as she admired this tall, handsome stranger. "My name is Cassidy, Cassie for short. That's what everyone calls me. Born and bred in Savannah. I plan to work and send money to my Mama back home."

When the train came to a halt, John and Cassie alighted. Before they said goodbye, John copied Cassie's aunt's address from the paper she clutched in her hand, then disappeared into the crowd.

"Is that you, Cassie?" she heard behind her. "Cassie turned to see her aunt coming toward her, her face wreathed in smiles.

"Aunt Cassidy! I'm here in New York at last!" (She was named Cassidy after this aunt).

After a long embrace, her aunt steered her toward the subway for the ride uptown to Harlem where she lived. Cassie then began her long and remarkable life in the heart of New York City.

Things were hard for Cassie over the next few years. For starters, she'd never learned to read or write. Her family back home was large and needed everyone to work to provide income. She had to stop going to school as a young child in order to work and help out. At the age of seven, she began to pick cotton in the fields near home. Now, here in New York, it was hard to get a job without those basic skills. With great determination, however, Cassie found work as a live-in domestic servant.

About a year later, on one of her days off, she returned home to Aunt Cassidy. Her aunt, a wonderful cook, had prepared a mouth-watering meal for the two of them. Halfway through their dinner, there came a knock at the door.

"I'll get it," exclaimed Cassie, as she walked toward the entryway. To her amazement, she saw a man with a familiar face. John, her seatmate on the train from down South, stood there in front of her!

"I'm glad I found you and I don't want to lose you again," he blurted out.

"Come in. It's good to see you, also. What have you been doing since you came to New York?"

Not long afterward, with Aunt Cassidy's blessing, Cassie and John got married at a neighborhood church. They set up house in a tiny apartment in the projects and looked forward to a joyful life together. They both worked hard and did their best to make it despite tough times.

"I love being called 'Mrs. Ramsey,' Cassie confessed to Aunt Cassidy one day, as she stared at her plain yellow wedding band.

"Sounds good," replied her aunt. "I hope you'll always be happy."

Little did Aunt Cassidy know what struggles lay down the road for her niece.

Soon, Cassie found herself expecting their first child and gave birth to a pretty little girl whom she named Elizabeth, after her mother back in Georgia. John beamed with pride and spoiled Elizabeth to the fullest. Following Elizabeth, Cassie produced a steady stream of children, year after year, just as her mother had. Within ten years of their arrival in New York City, the Ramsey family had seven people to feed: Cassie, John, Elizabeth, Rosie, Barbara, Doris, and, finally a boy named John Jr, whom they called Johnny.

"We can't stay here in the projects," John declared one day. There are way too many of us. We need a larger place."

Cassie hated to leave the neighbors she had come to know as dear friends. But she agreed with John. Indeed, the stress of raising so many young children in such limited quarters wore on both.

"Go ahead and look for someplace else," she conceded.

John was a go-getter. He found a three-bedroom apartment in a six-story walk-up tenement a few blocks away. Cassie felt discouraged as she surveyed the neighborhood. Although the new apartment provided a lot more room, the area proved not to be a nice one in which to raise a young family. The streets were littered with trash. Men hung out on street corners playing checkers throughout the day. Children roamed the streets, not attending school. Women, for the most part, were stay-at-home moms. Bars were in abundance. Alcohol was a big problem and Illicit drugs had crept in.

"I've got to work hard to keep our kids on track," Cassie promised herself. She kept that pledge by learning hairdressing. She didn't attend school for it but soon caught on. In no time, customers were

coming to her home, along with their little girls, to get their hair done. Her earnings, along with John's, kept the family afloat.

Alas, however, the neighborhood blight spread its long tentacles, and, little by little, engulfed Cassie's family. John, her cherished husband, began to drink and often returned home extremely late at night. Their arguments over this escalated and began to affect the children, who were then pre-teens.

One night, John didn't come home at all. Cassie, speechless, and sick with despair, couldn't sleep at all. He had never done this before. The next morning, she and the children branched out and searched for him throughout the neighborhood. Somehow, however, she knew deep inside no harm had befallen him. He simply had chosen not to come home. A few days later, John appeared and announced to his family his plan to move out. "I've found a new 'wife' and a new life," he told them.

Cassie and the children screamed and cried and begged him not to go. "Daddy! Daddy! Why? Don't you love us anymore? Please don't leave us."

John, deaf to their pleas, packed his belongings into two shopping bags and walked slowly down the stairs. The family sat in stunned disbelief for a long time. Cassie wept as the enormity of the situation gripped her. She couldn't believe her husband would be so uncaring. *How could he leave me with full responsibility for the kids? What evil has invaded his heart? Doesn't he love me anymore?*

Cassie found out John had moved to another part of the city with his new "family." He never supported her or the children, financially, after that. He never visited them again. No Christmas or birthday gifts were ever received. He had chosen to simply disappear.

It was 1943, and World War II was raging when John walked out on his family. Rationing of food and limited resources were the norm. Cassie prayed and asked God to have mercy on them during this awful time. She did not want to apply for public assistance, but she had no choice. She had to keep a roof over their heads and food on the table. The few dollars she earned from hairdressing were a blessing but certainly nowhere enough to sustain them.

After John left, sadly, the family spiraled downward. The kids became angry and rebellious. Some even blamed their mother for their dad's departure. The older ones were out of control. They went to school when they chose to and there were frequent visits from the truant officer. At the tender age of fifteen, Elizabeth, the oldest, became pregnant.

"Lord, another mouth to feed!" cried Cassie when she learned the news. She felt as if she and her children were at war.

Over the next several years, as her kids became teenagers, then young adults, Cassie struggled to keep her family intact. She joined a church and became active. Still quite attractive and now age thirty-eight, she caught the eye of a gentleman named Jacob. Cassie felt strongly drawn to Jacob and wondered about a future for the two of them. Jacob soon proposed marriage. However, Cassie explained she and John, her husband, had never divorced. She explained to him that a few years earlier, she had found John and asked him for a divorce, but he had refused.

Although disappointed, Jacob told Cassie they could still be a couple since John had walked out on her. Jacob moved in with the family and became the children's stepfather. None of them liked him, however, and resented his presence. Besides, by then three grandchildren were added to the Ramsey household. The three older girls dropped out of school and each became a teen mother. Cassie felt obligated to help her daughters care for their children and encouraged them to remain at home.

Elizabeth, twenty, and Rosie, nineteen, smoked marijuana, and worked on odd jobs. Cassie was distraught upon learning Barbara, age eighteen, had turned to heroin. For weeks at a time she went missing as she fed her addiction. On several occasions, the police arrested her for drug possession, while her mother, Cassie, raised her child. Thank God, Doris and Johnny remained in school and graduated with their high school diplomas.

Amid all of this, in 1948, Cassie, aged thirty-nine, herself became pregnant. She delivered another boy and named him Peter. A year later, a baby girl arrived whom they named Sylvie. The last two additions brought the total number of occupants of that apartment to twelve! As Peter and Sylvie grew, the rivalry between them and Willie's grandchildren became untenable. Though Jacob, loved his children, he could no longer stand the tension in the household or the family's continued animosity toward him. So, he moved out. He supported his own two children from time to time, but soon faded out of the picture.......as could have been predicted.

One sad day, in 1954, word reached the family that Barbara, age twenty-one, had been found dead from a heroin overdose in lower Manhattan. Cassie's greatest fear had been realized. She had prayed she never would have to bury any of her children. But life now seemed to mock her, and death stared her straight in the face. She became sick with grief.

After the funeral, Johnny joined the Army and became independent. Doris moved in with her boyfriend on the other side of town and started her own family. Cassie, then, had two older daughters, three grandchildren, and two young children of her own, to raise. Her friends marveled at how she continued on. What extra strength had God given her to keep moving despite her situation?

Cassie's story had many twists and turns ahead, however. Life still did not prove easy for her.

Rosie returned home one day with some very disturbing news. "Mother, I've been diagnosed with advanced brain cancer." Cassie struggled to understand.

"Those terrible headaches I've been having made me go to the doctor. He told me l have only a few weeks to live."

Cassie burst into tears and wept out of control. "First Barbara. Now Rosie. Is God taking back all of my kids?"

Two months later, Rosie passed away in Cassie's arms. She was twenty-eight years old. Cassie sank into a deep depression and attended the funeral in a daze. Elizabeth, then twenty--nine, resented the responsibility which fell to her of caring for her own son, her niece and nephew, and her younger sister and brother. In her mind, her mother had this duty, not herself. Except for her son, she didn't treat the children well. In fact, she abused them and barely gave them enough to eat. Unfortunately, they missed the love Willie would have given them had she been well enough to care for them.

When Cassie recuperated, she tried to pick up with the children where she left off. Elizabeth handed them off to her and returned to the street and her drug-taking ways. She soon graduated to heroin. Although Cassie tried hard not to face it, she knew the same fate that had befallen Barbara, could happen to Elizabeth. The 1960s streets in New York were mean and unforgiving. Drug dealers cared less about people. Their only desire was to make money in whatever ways they could.

Elizabeth deteriorated in no time. When she grew tired and weary, she returned home to Cassie. Her mother's heart bled to see her beautiful firstborn baby in that condition. But by then, "Mr. Heroin" had taken over her life. She tried more than once to come off the drug. She attended a clinic that gave her Methadone, a heroin substitute, but to no avail. She died of an overdose in a hospital Emergency Room where she was taken. She had just turned thirty-three.

Johnny and Doris came home to support their mom as she tried to make sense of her third child's death. They arranged for Cassie to spend a few weeks in a convalescent home where she received much needed counseling and therapy.

"Mother, you're like a cat with nine lives," Doris told her when she was discharged home. "I'm glad you're better, though."

By then, at age fifty-three, and with greater insight into her family's trials and tribulations, Cassie tried hard to steer Peter, 14, and Sylvie, 12, along with her three teenage grandchildren, in the right direction. Perhaps she underestimated the breadth of the task though. A single older woman, raising five teenagers, proved no match for the street, which was still there with its wretched environment. When they were almost finished high school, Sylvie and Peter fell prey. Sylvie delivered her first child at age sixteen, while Peter dropped out of school and began using methamphetamines. Her two granddaughters (Elizabeth's and Rosie's daughters), became teenage mothers and did not finish school.

There was a bright light in Cassie's situation, however: her grandson (Barbara's boy), despite the odds, graduated from high school and went on to college. This was much to his grandmother's delight. He was the first in their family to attend college-.

When Cassie became a great-grandmother at age fifty-eight, there were then four generations residing in her household.

Peter didn't last long in the street. He followed his two sisters in death from a drug overdose. He was at twenty years old. His mother, Cassie, fainted at his funeral. Jacob, his father, attended, and afterward told Cassie how much he regretted not having been active in his children's lives. Cassie did not respond to him.

Sylvie, Cassie's youngest child, tried to raise her son with her mother's help. She found a job in a factory and, at first, seemed determined to provide the best she could for her child. She attended church with Cassie and became involved with the youth department. Cassie was happy and Sylvie seemed stable.

Once again, however, Cassie's hopes for her child were dashed. Sylvie met a guy who introduced her to methamphetamines. Despite the deaths of her siblings, she decided to try the drugs anyway and became hooked. By the time she reached her early thirties, she had plummeted deep into the drug culture and was injecting the drugs intravenously. At that time, the HIV AIDs epidemic started and was in full swing. With regret, Sylvie contracted the virus, which soon took her life. She left behind a sixteen-year-old son whom her older brother, Johnny, took to live with him and his family.

That time, Cassie refused to attend the funeral. "I can't do it again! I can't take it anymore!" she wailed to her two remaining children, Doris and Johnny. "Five of my kids are gone! You take over for me and see that Sylvie gets a good burial."

Family and friends comforted her as she contemplated the deaths of her children. She often asked herself if coming to New York long ago had been the right thing to do.

Yet, Cassie's story of great resilience has a wonderful ending. Johnny and Doris and their families took great care of her in her later years. Her three grandchildren continued to live with her and made sure her needs were met.

Looking back over her years in New York City, Cassie concluded, "All that happened to me was part of God's plan for my life. I still remember my kids who passed on and love them so much. I don't regret anything."

Cassie was mentally sharp, loved God, and was very thankful until the end.

Cassidy Ramsey went home to be with her Lord at the ripe age of ninety-nine years, surrounded by her remaining family.

Three Tough Gals

Front Story

When I grew up in New York years ago, Caroline, Willie Mae, and Mabel fascinated me. They were larger than life, fearless, unstoppable, older women, who cared not what others thought about them and were forthright in all they did.

Each arrived in New York as a young woman during the 1920's. All three settled uptown in the neighborhood of Harlem. Most likely, at the time they arrived, none of them was aware of two powerful, concurrent events going on: The Great Migration – the movement of thousands of Black people from the South and the Caribbean to Northern USA States; and The Harlem Renaissance– the heyday of the African American cultural and entertainment experience.

Mabel and Caroline emigrated from the West Indies, while Willie Mae relocated from the South. Maybe the times in which they lived contributed to these women being indomitable. It was the interval between two World Wars, money was scarce, and life itself was tough. Perhaps though, their spirited personalities compelled them to leave home in the first place to seek a better life elsewhere.

To my knowledge, none of these women knew each other. However, because of time, location, and events, such as weddings or funerals, they very well may have crossed one another's paths.

They shared many similarities. For example, each one's husband had a passive personality and allowed his wife to be in charge. I often wondered what kind of glue kept those marriages intact. Also of interest to me, each had a large sum of money at her disposal. More about that later.

Although all these women have now passed away, they left an indelible mark on those whose lives intersected with theirs. As you can tell, their doings are still in my memory bank, though many years have come and gone.

When I first met these gals, I was in my mid-teens. Because of my friendship with each of their granddaughters, I was privy to some of their personal lives. I learned a lot about them whenever I stopped by to visit these grandmothers along with my friends. After a dutiful greeting, I faded into the background and feigned unawareness of what was going on. Truth was, I observed everything– especially what the grandmas said and did. They were bossy and loud, with take-charge attitudes.

None of them worked outside the home, but each ran the household finances. Money was an area of frequent disagreement between them and their spouses. I was never quite sure why this was so, since my friends said their grandmothers each kept a private "stash" of cash, unknown to their husbands. It was also rumored at least two of them "played the numbers" to add to their personal resources.

All the women spoke harsh words to their husbands. I noticed though, their spouses remained silent and never questioned any action taken by their wives, no matter how outrageous it might have been. They knew any protest would have been shut down forthwith.

Now that you, my readers, have been introduced to my older women friends, I'll share some snippets from their individual lives, as I observed them. I'll note the lessons I learned from knowing each of them.

Mabel

Mabel was in a class by herself. Though not gorgeous, she was attractive and knew how to dress in the latest fashions. She also could out talk anyone-anytime. Her husband, Leon, was smitten by her when they first met and soon married her to chase his loneliness. Not long after, he regretted his rush down the aisle, but thought it was his duty to stick with her. Over the years they grew distant from one another and their relationship became a loveless one. Leon was a taxi driver and relished his interactions with people throughout the day. He dreaded going home at night to Mabel.

Leon had a daughter with another lady long before he married Mabel. That child, when grown, had a daughter named Cynthia, who was very close to Leon, her grandfather. Mabel accepted Cynthia as her granddaughter. Cynthia, and I went to elementary school together and we developed a long-standing friendship. She often invited me along whenever she visited Leon and Mabel.

Mabel and Leon, together, had a son and a daughter. Both of them were grown by the time I met Cynthia. Their son was married and lived elsewhere. But their daughter still lived at home. Mabel doted on both of her children.

Over the years, although homely and very overweight, the daughter proved to be a talented singer. Mabel paid for voice lessons to help boost her career. When an undocumented immigrant, desperate to remain in the USA, came to Mabel's notice, she struck a deal with him. For a fee, she arranged for him to marry her daughter to legally stay in America. Mabel gave the couple a lavish, second-to-none wedding.

I was a guest at the wedding, and I heard Mabel boast, "This is the wedding of the year! Thank God, I can afford it!"

Mabel's son became a high-level government official. However, it all came crashing down a few years into his career. He was arrested and plead guilty to a charge of tax fraud. Although his mother conscripted the best legal help she could find, none of Mabel's efforts could prevent him from being sentenced to years in the Federal penitentiary.

I'm told, in the courtroom, she shouted to the judge, "They lied on my son!"

She was forthwith escorted outside.

Mabel was quite active in her church and always spoke about her religious devotion. Her denomination allowed women to preach and enter ministry. Before long, because of her gift of gab, she rose to the rank of "Evangelist" and was sent to preach at various churches. Although she had no ministerial training, she soon convinced her superiors to ordain her. True to form, at a ceremony which the town's mayor attended, the title of "Reverend" was conferred on Mabel. She was then installed as pastor of a small congregation in Brooklyn.

Sundays were a relief from Mabel's aggressive behavior for her family members. None of them attended church with her and worshipped elsewhere. Mabel dominated her own parishioners as she saw fit. However, she never learned how to drive and demanded Leon take her to her own church every Sunday before he went to his.

One Sunday, Leon arrived at his church with a black eye. "My wife beat me up," he told the pastor, with tears in his eyes. "We had a terrible argument on our way to her church. When we got there, she reached over and punched me hard in my face. After that, she picked up her Bible and marched into her church like a saint. She never even looked back at me."

"What do you plan to do about this?" the pastor asked.

"I guess I'll go get her later and take her home."

After a while, Mabel became bored with her pastoral duties and sought to expand her scope. She soon announced she had become a missionary to Africa. She made her own contacts and arrangements and flew solo to a small West African territory. By all reports, the people there welcomed her. She made several such visits, and, to her credit, collected clothing and food staples for those in need. She shipped them in barrels and arranged for them to reach their destination to coincide with her arrival.

During Mabel's forays to Africa, Leon enjoyed seasons of peace and quiet in his home. He admitted to friends and family, "She can stay over there as long as she likes. If she never comes back, it's all right with me!"

Leon could never have foreseen what happened on one of Mabel's trips to the Motherland. Little did he know it would impact his life forever. On a visit to an orphanage, Mabel noticed a certain little girl who sat alone. By some maneuver, she was able to bring the child back home to the USA with her! Leon had not been consulted nor had her other family members. Everyone was shocked when she deplaned with the little girl in tow. Soon after, the mayor pulled strings on her behalf, and Mabel officially adopted the shy little seven-year-old.

The child became her pride and joy. She took her everywhere and showed her off to everyone. "This is my little African Princess I rescued from an orphanage and now she's mine!"

I was never quite certain how the little girl really felt. She seldom smiled and always seemed unsettled. I wondered if she missed her life back in Africa, or if she simply did not like Mabel. Whatever the case, I suspected her unhappiness ran deep.

Caroline

Caroline was tall, bosomy, and had a not-a-step-nearer attitude. Even though she had no real estate background, she owned several properties around Harlem. Somehow, within twenty years of her arrival in New York, she was able to attain a much higher than average, comfortable lifestyle. In the mid 1950's, she moved her family across the East River to a large home in a nice neighborhood in Queens. This occurred when few "Colored People," as we were called then, could afford to do so. Despite the long commute, Siebert, Caroline's husband, sought daily respite from his wife's carping personality, and continued to work downtown in New York's Garment District.

Caroline's youngest granddaughter, Janice, and I were Sunday school buddies. She and her siblings were living with their grandparents when we first met.

Caroline attended a different church than Seibert. However, she insisted the children go to church with her.

Janice's dad, Caroline's only son, married a girl when only in his late teens, against his mother's wishes. By Caroline's estimation, the girl he married was from a lower-class family and not worthy of being her daughter-in-law. Her animosity toward the girl was palpable and became a wedge between them. Although the young couple struggled financially, they kept their distance from Caroline. Their children were born in rapid succession and soon they were the parents of five, including a set of twins. Janice was their youngest child.

When Janice was nine years old, her mom suddenly absconded to parts unknown. Her heartbroken dad was left to care for their brood all by himself. In a note she left for him, his wife told him she was never coming back, and she never did.

"You sure made a dumb decision, boy," was Caroline's refrain. "I warned you not to marry her."

After a while, with great reluctance, he asked Caroline to help take care of the kids in her home. After fuming about his request, Caroline agreed. Her husband, Siebert, was not asked for input.

Caroline laid down the law. "They'll have to follow my rules. I don't stand for foolishness."

The kids did not want to move to their grandmother's house. However, they were given no choice. Angry, frustrated, and confused, they tumbled one day into Caroline's abode which became their permanent home for years afterward. Caroline became their guardian, and Siebert, their grandfather, became their saving grace.

Janice frequently invited me to visit. Whenever I did, Caroline amazed me all over again. She ruled with an iron hand and her home was always in chaos. Not only did the grandchildren live there, but also Janice's two unmarried aunts. The younger one was handicapped and received little education. Although fully grown, she behaved like a young child and accompanied her mother, Caroline, everywhere. The other daughter was a mortician. Caroline helped her purchase a funeral home and appointed herself its chief marketing officer, of sorts.

One day, while I was visiting, Caroline answered the telephone. The family of a deceased person was on the line.

"You need to call the funeral home, not my house!" she screeched. "That's the public line, this is private!"

I'm uncertain how much business was lost by her daughter, the funeral home's proprietor, due to Caroline's crass behavior.

Siebert was no less immune from Caroline's wrath. I witnessed one such verbal assault.

"What do you care what I do with my money?" she shouted, right in front of me. "You take care of your business and I'll take care of mine!"

Embarrassed, Siebert beat a hasty retreat outside.

Caroline shouted after him, "Make sure you don't touch my rose bushes while you're out there! I have to put some of them on the altar of my church on Sunday."

It was remarkable to me how Caroline spoke with such reverence and devotion to God but acted quite the opposite at home. Janice and her siblings longed for the day when they would be free of their grandmother's tyranny. The scars she embedded on them ran deep. Much later, Janice shared with me the sad and brutal lesson she learned: "Caregiving without love isn't caregiving at all."

Willie Mae

Willie Mae had been a schoolteacher in the South, following her graduation from a Historically Black College. She married a minister and had a daughter. Later, she found out her parson- husband was a bigamist. He never told her he had married before, nor that he had not divorced his first wife, before marrying her. When Willie Mae discovered his dirty little secret, she had the marriage annulled, forthwith, and, with her young daughter, left for New York. Upon their arrival, she was determined to find a new husband who could provide for them.

One night, Willie Mae went to a dance at a local nightclub and met a handsome dude from Trinidad, named Bentley. He was of mixed African and Portuguese extraction and his smooth olive complexion and curly black hair made him stand out from the crowd. Willie Mae became flirtatious and made no bones about her interest in him. They left the dance together, resolved to "get to know each other better."

Fascinated by Bentley, Willie Mae extracted many secrets from him during their whirlwind courtship. Heretofore, Bentley had been careful to keep his private life hidden, and lived, unobserved, in the community. His most classified revelation to Willie Mae was that he, like her, had been married before. He confessed, further, he had a family back in Trinidad. He never explained why he left his wife and kids behind, ending all contact with them. He took a job as a galley cook on a seafaring vessel and traveled to many parts of the world. His former life became a closed book and he wanted to keep it that way. None of his former family was aware he had settled in America!

When Bentley showed Willie Mae his divorce papers, she married him without fanfare before a Justice of the Peace. Bentley's apartment was a treasure trove of artifacts from the ports at which his ship docked. Willie Mae enjoyed hearing about his wonderful experiences. He proved to be a great stepfather to her daughter, and he got along with all her grandchildren. My friend, Harriet, whom I met in high school, was his favorite.

Harriet told me Bentley went to work every day, but his line of employment remained a mystery. She knew from Willie Mae, her grandmother, he had lots of money which he saved over the years. I think this was true because I found out his money financed all the weddings, christenings, vacations, and other occasions celebrated by Willie Mae's family.

"I need a thousand dollars to help my daughter put a down payment on a house," I once heard Willie Mae tell her husband.

"All right, Dear," came the mumbled reply. "I'll let you have it next Monday."

"Make sure you bring all of it in cash. I don't trust anything but greenbacks!"

I was a bridesmaid in Harriet's wedding. Bentley paid for the whole affair and Willie Mae spared nothing for her granddaughter's big day. Due to his wife's insatiable greed, I'm uncertain how much of Bentley's money was left when he passed away.

I was asked to be godmother when Harriet's baby was Christened at Willie Mae's church. She was Chairman of the Willing Workers Usher Board and she put on a grand performance. Dressed in a starched white uniform, a nurse's cap, and a large white handkerchief pinned to her shoulder, she gave orders to the members of her team.

When the baby and parents arrived, Willie Mae cried out in a loud voice, "Oh thank God they're here!" and collapsed into a pew. The ushers fanned her and administered smelling salts until she revived.

Later that day, when Willie Mae gave a Christening party at her home, I was dumbfounded to realize she had prepared two separate meals. In the kitchen where I was serving, in hushed tones, she declared, "The big meal in here is for family only. Everyone out in the living room will just get snacks."

Harriet told me her grandmother had a private money stash, separate from Bentley's money. She said it was safe in a secret bank account. Harriet found out the night Bentley and Willie Mae's apartment caught on fire, however, that this was not so.

"Please let me get my money, first!" Willie Mae shrieked when the firemen arrived to evacuate them. "I have it all in cash. Some bills are under the bed. Some are in the closet. I sewed some cash into the hem of my window curtains!"

All her loot was lost in the fire. They watched in horror as their apartment building burned to the ground. Their choice was either to save the cash or save themselves. Harriet told me thousands of dollars vanished before their eyes. Thank God, Bentley's money was safe in the bank and, over time, they were able to rebuild their lives.

After almost fifty years of marriage to Willie Mae, Bentley lost his battle with cancer. Willie Mae was left a grief-stricken widow. As fate would have it, a year after he passed away, Bentley's two adult children showed up on Willie Mae's doorstep. They had been searching for their dad for years, without success. Willie Mae was happy to fill in the missing pieces about Bentley for them and they became close friends.

Takeaway

What did I learn from my experiences with Willie Mae, Caroline, and Mabel? As I reflected, some lessons were good, and some were not so good. True, they all were examples of independent, fearless women, determined to get what they could out of life. Despite the odds, they got further ahead than most of their peers.

On the other hand, in my opinion, they were self-centered, outrageous, and bereft of human warmth. Money seemed to dominate their lives. As the Scriptures say, "The love of money is the root of all evil."[15]

The money to which these women had access, did not make them well-adjusted, generous people. While each gave to others in her own way, their marriages and their lives, in general, were superficial, and without genuine affection.

From each of them I received a close-up of how a woman's choices and actions can influence the outcome of her life and the lives of those in her circle. That influence can be for good or detrimental.

15 I Pet. 6:10 (King James Version).

Section C: Autumn Leaves

Unexpected Opportunities

I've discovered that, in life, unexpected opportunities come our way. When they do, we have a choice to explore and accept them, or, ignore them, perhaps not wanting to interrupt our routines.

Sometimes we've been praying for something to happen, then, suddenly, a door opens, we walk through it, and receive the thing we've been asking for.

At other times, fate deals a cruel blow and we feel all hopes are dashed. Then, without warning, someone steps up to the plate, and lifts us out of the dilemma in which we find ourselves.

The next five essays shine a light on how situations can change – sometimes without warning– and alter, with significance, the trajectory of our life.

> *"And this same God who takes care of me will supply all your needs from his glorious riches, which have been given to us in Christ Jesus."*
>
> Philippians 4:19 . Holy Bible. New Living Translation.

A Fortuitous Phone Call

The telephone in my home rang briskly one late-March afternoon. It happened years ago, but I remember it as if it were yesterday. When I answered, a woman called me by my name in an official-sounding voice.

Puzzled, I asked, "Who is this and how can I help you?"

"I am the Chief Nursing Officer of an international organization. We are headquartered in Washington, DC."

"How did you get my name?'

"A friend of yours sent me your resumé. You are the exact person I'm looking for to work for us."

Intrigued, I asked, "Can you tell me more?"

"We send consultants all over the world to advise on health matters. Our special region of focus, however, is Latin America and the Caribbean."

I remained quiet for a while as I contemplated what she told me.

With a tinge of impatience, she pressed, "Are you interested?"

"You've piqued my interest. But I need more details. I'd like to know the who, when, where, why, and how."

"Can you fly to our headquarters here in Washington fairly soon-- like within a few days? We'll pay for your air fare and hotel room. The interview will probably last a full day."

It sounded exciting, but I wanted to discuss her proposal with my family, before I committed.

"I think I can come early next week. I need to check my work schedule and speak to my manager though. May I get back to you tomorrow?"

My dad, who was a cautious, slow-to-decide person, surprised me with his response when I discussed the phone call with my parents. "I think you have nothing to lose by going for the interview. A great opportunity may be looming ahead."

My mom agreed, with a twinkle in her eye, "I think you should give it a try. You're twenty-nine years old– you're young, single, and free."

I tried to keep an open mind as I flew to DC. I was put through a day-long series of grueling interviews with various levels of people within the organization. At the end, however, I could envision myself transported to a brand- new world, working with interesting people.

I accepted the offer of a two-year assignment as Nursing Advisor in the Eastern Caribbean. There followed a flurry of activities, including a security clearance, resigning from my job, and packing and shipping my belongings. I enjoyed several farewell parties and was bursting with fervor as my new life lay ahead.

As I winged my way back to Washington DC, then on to Caracas, Venezuela for orientation, I could not believe how my life had changed in the space of a few short weeks!

I smile today when I remember that time in my life. What began as a two- year foreign tour, continued thirteen more years, for a total of fifteen! I returned to the good old USA having had amazing experiences, personal, spiritual, and professional, just as my dad predicted I might. I made lifelong friends among the people of the islands as well. Here are some striking examples of what I experienced:

Just as I was about to return home at the end of my two-year tour of duty, I met a handsome dude, who became my husband shortly thereafter. I remained in my job position and settled there, indefinitely. When we finally returned home at the end of fifteen years, my husband and I introduced our three school-aged children to life in 1980s America. For them, the change from Caribbean life was radical.

On the spiritual level, on one of my work assignments in the tiny, remote Island of Dominica, Jesus met me in my hotel room and blessed me with a life-changing experience. I received, from Him, the Baptism in the Holy Spirit. I had been asking Him for this new dimension, as described in the scriptures in the Book of Acts.[16] Since I received it, I have never been the same.

---

16   Acts 19: 1-6. King James Version.

While I knelt in prayer, Jesus walked into the room. I felt His Divine presence and His wonderful hands touched me on my forehead. Immediately, I fell backwards, flat on my back on the floor. I felt something rumbling on the inside, and my lips began to move. I spoke chattering words, at first, then a heavenly language burst forth.

Without a shadow of a doubt, I knew what I was experiencing. *"This is it! This is what I've been asking God for!"* I exclaimed out loud.

For three continuous hours, I lay there on the floor, and spoke in my heavenly language. My heart was full of praise and thanksgiving. I could not wait to share what had happened to me with everyone. I preached the gospel to all whom I met. I told them Jesus wants to live in their lives and work out the plans He has for them. My prayer life changed and I became an intercessor. I re-dedicated my life to His service. I, then, understood why He had orchestrated my sojourn in the Islands.

Professionally speaking, my work in the Caribbean allowed me to impact mother and infant care at the highest levels of government. As part of a team of colleagues and senior health officials, I helped craft policies and procedures to improve the health of women and prevent infant deaths.

I also taught nurses and midwives throughout the islands, the science and art of birthing babies; prevention of childhood illness; and contraceptive techniques. I had the privilege, also, of serving as Visiting Advisor to the Regional University. These teaching opportunities prepared me well for my future faculty positions at colleges and universities when I returned to the USA.

Yes, life often brings unexpected opportunities, and I'm sure glad I seized that one.

Apartment 2B

Gilda Graham, a tall, attractive, forty-ish, single woman, was happy with her life. She had accomplished most of what she set out to do since graduation from college some twenty years earlier. Now at the top of her game in a successful marketing career, she toyed with the idea of a foray into local politics.

Gilda lived in a fashionable section of Southwest Washington, D.C., to which she relocated from New York City right after college. She loved her adopted city, that teemed with history and diverse cultures. She found a wonderful church. Her apartment was one of two on the top floor of a vintage three-story brick building which had no elevator.

"This daily walk up and down stairs gives me the exercise I need to help me maintain a healthy lifestyle," she once told a friend.

One day, weary from a hectic workday, Gilda arrived home, envisioning a hot cup of tea and a quiet evening. As she navigated the stairs upward toward her apartment, the door to Apartment 2B suddenly opened. Startled, she saw her elderly neighbor in the doorway.

"Good evening, Ms. Graham." He addressed her with a slight bow.

She wondered how he knew her name and what he wanted. "Good evening, Sir," she replied.

She had never had a conversation with him before, nor, in fact, with any of her other neighbors. Most were urban professionals who lived active lives. A nod or a mumbled "Good morning" was the extent of their communication. Gilda preferred it that way and enjoyed the sense of anonymity.

"Please don't think me rude. My name is Carter Simpson and I'd very much like to speak with you. Won't you come inside for a moment?"

Gilda hesitated while studying his face intently. Although he was a virtual stranger, she decided to take a chance and enter his apartment.

She took a seat on the living room sofa, glanced around, and was impressed with what she saw. The surroundings were immaculate. Her neighbor had tasteful furnishings and beautiful décor. Mr. Simpson was dressed in a well-made linen suit and sported a cravat at his neck. His full head of silver hair was neat and combed to one side. Gilda sensed her neighbor was no ordinary person and, no doubt, had lived an interesting life.

"I've prepared some tea for us. Won't you have a cup? To set your mind at ease, I'm eighty years old and I am not out to harm you."

The china tea set was elegant and the steaming tea inviting. Gilda accepted. Still puzzled, she sat silent, curious about what he had to say.

Carter Simpson's words tumbled out. "Let me tell you a bit about myself. I'm a retired physician and a widower. My wife passed away five years ago. Because we were childless, I have no heirs and it's been difficult living here alone. You may be surprised to know, Ms. Graham, I've admired you over the years since I lost my wife. I decided it was time I approached you."

Gilda leaned forward, hoping he'd soon get to the point.

"Let me let you know right away, I'd like to marry you. Will you agree to be my wife?"

Gilda's heart pounded as she stared at this stranger with bewilderment. "Your wife? We don't even know each other!"

"I know it sounds preposterous, Ms. Graham, but perhaps I know you better than you think. You're a religious woman and I've observed you leaving on Sundays for church. Of greater importance, however, is my perception of your respectable style and demeanor as you go in and out every day. It's obvious you've been brought up well and your life values are strong. I would be honored to be your husband."

Truth was, Gilda always wanted to be married. She had dated many guys over the years, but, somehow, none of those relationships led to a walk down the aisle. Never in her wildest dreams, however, had she imagined life with an elderly man like Carter Simpson. She'd have to think long and hard about his proposal. But at this moment, her thoughts raced with pros and cons.

Carter observed her, sensing what she was thinking. But he waited until she replied.

"Mr. Simpson," she began, "I can see you are quite serious. But your proposal is so sudden. There are many questions to be answered and issues to explore."

"You're right, Ms. Graham. I'd be disappointed if you didn't feel that way. Please take your time, then get back to me with your decision. At this point in my life, I'm seeking companionship and a safe person in which to endow my fortune."

Shaken, Gilda stood and started toward the door.

"Ms. Graham, there are two more things you should know about me and I hope these won't be deal-breakers in your decision. If so, I'll understand."

Sensing a bombshell coming, Gilda stopped in her tracks and waited for him to continue.

He lowered his voice to a whisper. "First, I need to let you know, I'm impotent. Because of this, if you respond "yes" to my proposal, ours would be an open marriage. You're still a young woman and it would be unconscionable of me to demand your total faithfulness. You would be free to date younger men and find satisfaction elsewhere. My only request would be that you would show discretion. I just wouldn't want to know the details."

Gilda did not comment on this, but looked straight at him. "You said there was something more."

"Yes. You also need to know I've long-since departed from organized religion. However, if we were to marry, you'd be most welcomed to continue to practice your faith."

Gilda's feet felt like lead as she trudged up to her apartment. Her thoughts were a strange mixture of confusion and excitement.

Aloud, she said, *"I can't believe what I just heard--I've been proposed to by someone I don't even know. This must be a dream from which I'll soon awaken."*

The sun sank slowly. She collapsed on her bed, but could think of nothing else.

I was one of Gilda's friends among whom she sought wise counsel. Early the next morning, after her meeting with Carter Simpson, she called and we discussed the situation at length.

"He's handsome, intelligent, well- educated, and apparently rich," she told me. "These are all ideals I've wanted in a husband. But our forty-year age difference scares me."

I asked my friend some hard questions. "How would your social life change? What kind of intimacy would you share with him? What are his religious beliefs? You're a devout Christian."

At first blush, it seemed to me a breathtaking and unexpected opportunity had come her way. Digging deeper, however, I thought better. I was candid with her about my reservations. I reassured her though, as a friend, I would be there for her, whatever she decided.

One month later, Gilda phoned me again. She sounded light-hearted and free.

"I told Carter 'No'," she exclaimed. "I prayed hard and asked the Lord for guidance. I spoke to my family and other friends as well."

"What played into your decision?"

"I was really tempted to take the plunge and marry Carter. He has many attractive assets. But when I pictured myself as Carter's wife, reality hit me. I realized a life with him is not what I want. First and foremost, my walk with God would be deeply compromised. Also, I know I'd be much happier and feel more compatible with a younger man. I hope someday to say 'Yes' to someone. But not to my neighbor in Apartment 2B."

Happy Birthday to Me

Years have passed but this memory still makes me smile. I awakened one day, and excitement welled up. *"Today is my day."*

My birthday arrived. I took the day off from work and kept my vow to myself that my birthday would always be a personal day for me to do whatever I enjoyed.

I felt a tad guilty not being at work during our busiest season, but only a little. My enthusiasm about my day overcame any guilt I had.

"God gave each of us one day of the year in which we can do what we want," I argued with me to encourage myself. *"So today I'm going to relax and enjoy myself."*

Living in New York City offered several choices. I lay in bed, contemplating the hours ahead, then a thought came to me.

"I think I'll visit my two elderly aunts today. I always have such fun with them. I'll surprise them and their laughter will help make my day."

Aunt Dorothy, my mother's older sister, lived alone in a huge apartment in lower Harlem. Tall and slender, she was very attractive in her younger days. A somewhat feisty gal , she knew her way around town. Now, age eighty, and only slightly gray-haired, she had slowed down a lot, spending her days, for the most part, reading and watching television, especially the news broadcasts.

My father's younger sister, Aunt Ermine, lived in upper Harlem in a five-story walk-up apartment. Her son and daughter-in-law who lived with her, both were worked during the day, so she spent her days alone until they returned home. Aged ninety, and crippled from arthritis, my aunt could only leave home in an emergency. Thank God, though, her mind, was still sharp. She kept on top of things and never complained.

I visited my neighborhood florist and bought my aunts some special bouquets —mauve tulips for Aunt Dorothy and red roses for Aunt Ermine.

Aunt Dorothy was my first stop. I rode up the ancient elevator to the sixth floor to her apartment, which was almost hidden away in a corner. Whenever I visited her, I enjoyed looking out of the large picture windows that provided an expansive view of the street below.

How surprised she was to see me standing at her door.

"Today's my birthday," I explained. "So, I came to spend the morning with you."

I could see small teardrops well up in the corners of her eyes as she, with happiness, invited me in. She Ooed and Ahhed over the flowers while she found a vase and put some water in it for her bouquet. We laughed and reminisced over the next few hours.

"You were too small to remember this….," she reflected. Or, "Let me tell you what happened to so and so…."

I couldn't recall a time when my aunt seemed as animated and joyful as she appeared that day.

Glancing at my watch, I noticed noon had passed.

"Are you leaving so soon?" she asked, as I stood, saying goodbye.

"I'm heading for Aunt Ermine's house," I explained. "She doesn't know I'm coming either."

"Have fun and tell her I send my regards."

The twenty-minute drive to my aunt's street was easy, but the walk up the four flights of stairs to her apartment took all my breath away. Huffing and puffing, I knocked on the door and waited.

"What on earth brings you here?" she inquired with a twinkle in her eye. "I'm so glad to see you."

Aunt Ermine, a wonderful cook, loved to entertain her family whenever we visited. I knew though if I had told her I was coming, she would have rolled her wheelchair to the kitchen and sat preparing a virtual feast for me.

"Today's my birthday and I get to do whatever I want today. I decided to visit you so we could enjoy each other's company."

I extended the flowers to her. "These are for you."

"Roses for me?" she exclaimed and sent me to retrieve a beautiful vase.

The afternoon sped by as I shared memories with this older aunt. Her stories travelled far back to her childhood. I even learned some things about our family as well as some family secrets as she spoke.

When I returned home that evening, how blessed and enriched I felt. My visits that day were also unexpected opportunities for my aging aunts to feel special.

"*Happy birthday to me,*" I crooned. "*Happy birthday to me.*"

Where Are they Now?

Ruby Neal gave birth to five beautiful daughters. They were olive skinned, had curly black hair, and each had a lovely smile. The girls were like stair steps — each one being two years older than the other. She named the first Ruby, after herself, then Ivy, Erika, Carlotta, after her husband, Carlton, and Jocelyn.

Ruby, a stay- at- home mom, was fierce in her protection of her girls. They were seldom allowed to venture away from home without a sister in tow. In fact, even as teenagers, they moved around together with their mom right beside them. At church, they sat together—all in one row.

Carlton loved his daughters and worked hard to support them. He spent most of his time at the small grocery store he owned and really was not happy with the way his wife raised his girls. In fact, this issue caused his relationship with Ruby to be strained.

I grew up with these girls, and, if my memory serves me well, age-wise, I was between Carlotta and Jocelyn, the two youngest. Those were the ones to whom I related most.

There was always an air of mystery and aloofness about this family. Although my parents knew their parents well, I don't recall our families ever visiting one another at our respective homes.

The girls were quite talented, especially in music and art. Jocelyn was accepted into a special high school art academy. Ruby was gifted in languages and landed her first job after graduation as a Spanish Interpreter. They all had great voices and, early on, formed a singing group called "The Neals." You guessed it, though, Mama Ruby was right there playing the piano whenever and wherever they sang.

I often wondered how they really felt about being together all the time. I pondered if any would break away and set out on her own.

There was another strange thing about these siblings. They always dressed alike. Stranger still, their clothing was never in the latest fashion. Back in the 1960's, when we grew up, most of us girls wore colorful chemise dresses with crinolines underneath to make our skirts extra wide and poufy. The Neals, on the other hand, wore straight skirts and plain blouses that made them look much older than they really were.

While, as teenagers, we girls giggled at boys and vied for their attention, the Neals were not allowed to date or even hang out with males our age. What amazed me most was these restrictions seemed to be all right with them. They always smiled and made superficial conversation.

The people who knew them well, began to notice this family undergoing a gradual change, and no one thought it was for the better. For example, one day at church Mama Ruby announced she had received a special call from God. He had directed her and the girls to travel full-time around the USA on a gospel music circuit. She said she had to obey this call. This meant the four older girls, then working, had to quit their jobs and follow her. Although Jocelyn had a promising career ahead of her, she was forced to drop out from the art academy.

As expected, their father, Carlton, disagreed with this plan and distanced himself from it. But the girls, dutiful to their mother, complied with what she wanted, and soon were on their way. Over the course of a few years, they travelled, months at a time, gave concerts, and even made a few recordings.

While they traveled, Carlton continued to operate the grocery store to put food on the table. He allowed his wife to do as she pleased and decided not to get into conflict with her over it. He felt powerless over the situation.

Following one of their trips, Ruby and her daughters returned home and made a shocking discovery. Carlton had died alone at home from a heart attack. His death had a profound effect on them. The true source of their livelihood was gone and rumor had it they were in dire financial straits.

The Neals, then, spiraled downward and made strange decisions. For example, they withdrew their membership at the church and asked that no one call them.

When members of their large, extended family tried to visit them on several occasions, they were met with angry rebuffs.

"Who asked you to come here? We told you visits are by invitation only."

"We are concerned about you. Please let us in, at least to pray for you."

"Go away! God is taking care of us. We won't allow any devils into our home."

It was clear, the sisters, then in their twenties and thirties, along with their mother, had deteriorated psychologically. Sadly, some of them were seen in the neighborhood at night, disheveled, and begging for food.

The neighbors called the local authorities when mounds of trash from their house piled up and spilled out onto the street. Their utility services had also been disconnected. Social Services removed the family from their home, and took all of them to a psychiatric hospital for evaluation and treatment.

The saddest part of this family's story was told by a relative as follows:

One day, a nurse took the sisters outdoors for fresh air on the grounds of the hospital. One of them noticed a security gate had been left ajar, by accident. She motioned to her siblings, and, as if on cue, they bolted and ran outside into the street. All of them escaped. They took the unexpected opportunity to abscond. Great efforts were made by authorities to find them. Family members joined the search but they were not found and never were heard from again. Ruby, their mother, who, by that time, was bedridden and in an advanced state of dementia, was left behind.

Now, many years later, the mystery surrounding this family remains unsolved. Troubling questions still are asked by those who knew them:

"What really happened to this family?"

"Was there anything anyone, or group of individuals, could have done to help them?"

"Should their dad have been more forceful and authoritative?

"Did their church fail them in any way?"

What about their extended family? Should they have done more?

No one seems to have answers.

My question is, "Where are they now?"

The Ring

The sun shone bright and glorious that warm spring morning in Los Angeles. I had flown from Dallas the day before and was headed to my niece's wedding. After arriving early at the Country Club, I wandered around the grounds, briefly enjoying the lovely, blue hydrangeas in full bloom planted near towering Cypress Fir trees.

I was directed to the bride's dressing room as I entered the foyer, where my niece, Diedre, prepared for the ceremony. I stood and stared at her for a moment. I was in awe of how beautiful she was. She was dressed in an A-line floor-length gown, made of embroidered white Nigerian lace, complete with a grand cathedral train. A tiara, nestled in her ebony curls, sparkled in the sun's rays coming through the window. Her lovely bridesmaids were all there, as well as her mom, who was looking after every detail.

"Aunt Grace," she greeted me as her face lit up with a smile. Stretching her hands toward me, we embraced. "I'm so glad you're here. I always feel better when you're around. I know you'll help calm the butterflies flitting around in my stomach."

Before I could answer, her sister, Kay, rushed into the room. In near- panic, she blurted out, "The ring's gone! No one knows what happened to the wedding ring."

"Kay, is this your idea of a joke?" I knew my tone sounded irritated. "What do you mean, 'the ring's gone'? "

"I'm not joking," she replied. "Maurice said when he opened his dresser drawer to retrieve the ring, the ring box was empty, and the ring was nowhere to be found. He searched everywhere."

We all were speechless. The silence in the room was deafening. It was clear, with only twenty minutes to go before the ceremony, there was no way the ring could be replaced. I looked at Diedre and could see tears gathered in the corners of her eyes.

Crestfallen, she sat down and held her head in her hands. "This has spoiled my big day," she moaned. "How could this have happened? Somebody stole my ring!"

I felt so sorry for her. My mind raced with questions. *What can be done? How can we proceed with the wedding ceremony without the ring?*

I prayed and asked the Lord to give me an answer.

Suddenly, a solution came to me. *What about my ring?*

"I've got a ring!" I offered. "Try it on, Diedre." I handed her my own wedding band. "See if it fits."

Her face broke out into smiles when she tried it on, and it fit like a glove. "You're a lifesaver, Aunt Grace."

Everyone in the room clapped and cheered.

The wedding rites went on without a hitch and none of the guests suspected the ring was borrowed. When all the festivities were over, my niece returned my ring and thanked me profusely. Her husband promised to buy his bride a new one. I felt so gratified to have lent a hand…or a ring…to aid this couple's dream.

Just so you know, the ring was never found. Maurice and Diedre had their suspicions, but, to this day, it remains a mystery what became of the missing ring.

Once Upon an Island

The pear-shaped island of Barbados is situated far easterly along the chain of islands in the Caribbean Sea. Its climate is mild most of the year, its people fiercely loyal to their homeland – "De Rock," as they call it.

English is the official language. But it is spoken with a strong, rapid, clipped accent, with traces of words and phrases from Britain, and a few African words thrown in. Most "Bajans," as they call themselves, in addition, speak a dialect which most outsiders would find difficult to understand. This dialect is laced with humorous expressions and colorful symbolisms which can be quite entertaining to listen to.

My father and his siblings were born in Barbados, which is fondly known as "Bimshire" or "Bim." They lived there until adulthood, when they immigrated, individually, to the United States. As do most immigrants, they brought with them their dialect, food and recipes, customs, and rules for living as well.

When I was born in New York City, I was surrounded by my Bajan aunts and uncles. I heard about De Rock, Bim, and Bimshire throughout my childhood. Thus, I was submerged into a culture external to the wider American culture. My task and that of my siblings was to navigate both cultures, sorting and sifting, and arriving at a harmonious blend, that would become our own, by the time we reached adulthood.

I visited Barbados for the first time at age twenty-one, with my Aunt E. It was a fascinating time of connecting with my roots. I returned several times afterward.

I was fortunate to move to Barbados, years later, to work for an international organization. What was intended to have been a two-year stint, evolved into a fifteen-year stay. I returned home to New

York with my Bajan husband, and three kids in tow –chock full of wonderful, enduring memories.

Five essays comprise this section, providing you, the reader, with glimpses and insights into life on "De Rock." Perhaps, one day you'll go there, inspired by these narratives, and experience Bajan life for yourself.

> *"Let them give glory to the Lord and declare His praise in the islands."*
>
> Holy Bible. Isaiah 42:12 . King James Version (KJV).

Holiday in Bimshire

"**A**ren't you ready yet?" I chided my younger sister, Marilyn, the morning of our departure for Bimshire.

"I'm hurrying," came the reply. "I have a few more of my favorite things to put in my suitcase."

Bimshire? Where is that? you might ask. It's an affectionate name for the Island of Barbados in the Eastern Caribbean. It's the land of my forebears, who were carried there several generations ago from the mighty continent of Africa. I had heard of Bimshire all my life, and I soon would experience this place of my roots, in person.

The long, tiresome flight on the British Air Carrier propeller plane was exhausting. But the anticipation of landing in "Bim" filled me with excitement and kept me wide awake.

Four hours into the flight, I recovered from my traumatic experience in the departure lounge of LaGuardia Airport, our takeoff point, in New York.

Eight of us, led by my fearsome Aunt E., comprised the group that banded together to travel. My sister and I were the only ones among them who were born in America. The others were women at midlife, or in their senior years —all returning home to their native Barbados, for the first time, after many years away.

Included were a singer, a piano teacher, a church organist, a secretary, and two domestic workers. Despite their years away, all of them still spoke with the typical Barbadian accent, called "Bajan."

I had just turned twenty-one and graduated from nursing school only three weeks earlier. My sister, five years younger than I, was also thrilled at the prospect of taking this, our first trip abroad. At the time, I recall feeling I was somewhat of a sophisticated, independent woman. After all, I was a legal adult, employed in a noteworthy profession, and travelling abroad.

My parents took my sister and me to the airport and lingered awhile to wish us well as we departed for Bim. They waited until our flight was called before leaving. Ma pressed a few dollar bills in my hand and told me to buy a few souvenirs of Barbados. We looked for the other travelers in our group, as planned. I spotted Aunt E. among a knot of people and was horrified by what I saw. For starters, in my opinion, they were dressed inappropriately for traveling. Ms. Lashley, the piano teacher, wore laced-up, brown and white flat shoes, a church dress, and a wide-brimmed, multi-colored, straw hat one would normally wear to the beach.

Maybe she wants to impress the folks who will be meeting her at the airport in Barbados, I thought to myself.

More important, beside the group was a mountain of suitcases, boxes, and bags of all shapes and sizes. I couldn't believe they intended to carry all that stuff on the plane. Marilyn and I stuck to the airline's rules and we each had only two suitcases and a carryon bag.

"Bring your things over here and weigh them with ours!" Ms. Bynoe, the secretary, commanded.

I could tell right away she wanted to spread the weight of those items among all of us —and, especially for us to share the overweight charges as well!

I answered, politely, "My sister and I would rather weigh our luggage separately."

Without warning, my usually quiet and unassuming father, angrily yelled at me for all to hear, "Will you keep your mouth shut and do as you are told?"

Shocked and humiliated, I extracted myself from the group and headed for the restroom. Arriving there, I broke down in floods of tears, not caring if I traveled that day or not. My father had burst the bubble and ruined my long-anticipated dream of my arrival in beautiful Barbados.

An hour later, Ma, who had been hunting for me around the airport, found me and retrieved me from the restroom. "Thank God I've located you," she exclaimed.

"How could Daddy have treated me that way?" I asked her. "What got into him?"

"Never mind," she soothed, as she escorted me back to the departure lounge. "You'll still have a good time. Your bags are already on board and they are making the final call for passengers. Aunt E. and Marilyn are waiting for you."

The trip proceeded without incident, with a brief stopover in Antigua, an island north of Barbados. Then, it was on onward to our destination, Bimshire.

"Are you ready?" asked Aunt E., as the plane landed. "You two are going to have the time of your lives."

As we exited the plane, I was assailed, all at once, by three forces: the oppressive mid-July heat, the Bajan dialect, and the flash of cameras.

A huge crowd of people, including several photographers from the local newspaper, were at the airport, despite the fact it was nearly midnight, when we arrived. Aunt E.'s grandson, Ricardo, had notified the newspaper she was coming home after several years away, and they wanted to get the story. They plied us with questions and followed us throughout the process of airport checkout. Hugs and kisses were exchanged, and tears were shed, as relatives of our group welcomed us to their island home.

"We're here in Bimshire, at last," I said to Marilyn. "This is going to be exciting."

A virtual caravan of cars, the small sizes of which I'd never seen before, carried us to the place where we would stay. On arrival there, Aunt E.'s son, Grantley, and daughter-in-law, Monica, our hosts, gave us a warm welcome.. Thus began my three-week adventure in Bimshire – a whirlwind of visits to people and places, beaches, shops and stores, fruit and vegetable markets, churches, town and country, monuments, tourist attractions, schools, homes, lunches, dinners– an all-inclusive submersion in the Bajan hospitality for which the island is famous.

I won't attempt to describe all our experiences, but I will certainly highlight those that, for me, were most memorable.

Bright and early next morning, I was awakened by roosters crowing outside our window. That was certainly new to me. I found out this happens daily and many locals depend on these domesticated birds as their alarm clocks.

No sooner had my feet hit the floor, I heard a woman outside at the front of the house calling out in a deep, almost sing-song, Bajan accent, "It is Louise here! It is Louise! Fresh bread for ya coffee now. Come please, it still hot. Come get ya bread!"

When I peered outside in the semi-darkness, the woman, indeed, was carrying a huge basket of just-baked, bread on her head. Granny, who ruled the roost where we were staying, went out to her and purchased several hot, round rolls for our breakfast. "Louise, the bread-seller, brought these," she explained.

They were delicious, and I looked forward to having them every morning thereafter, when Louise came.

Bread Sellers and Fruit Hawkers, 1960s Barbados

Photo Courtesy Old Barbados Archives.

Bajan Salt Bread, A Favorite[17]

I smiled the day after we arrived, when shown the newspaper write up. There was the story of our group's arrival at the airport, complete with photographs of us all. I must admit, it did make me feel like somewhat of a celebrity.

In addition to our visits to places around the Island, we enjoyed the friendly, ongoing banter between Granny and her precocious five-year-old great-granddaughter, whom we'll call M. I will, intermittently, share a few of their interactions throughout this narrative. One example:

Granny: "M., hush ya mout. You does give me de nerves!"

M: "All you don' laugh. She been tellin' me all week, my Granny from New York comin' and she ain't frighten for me. She will give me lashes right on!"

I'll never forget our first visit to Bridgetown, the Capital. We walked from the house, located on the outskirts, to Broad Street, the

---

17 My Bajan Cooking. Barbados. 2020.

main thoroughfare. The sidewalks were packed with people, hurrying here and there. Vehicles were everywhere. Women were laden down with bags and baskets of all descriptions on their heads. Barefooted men rode bicycles. Slow-moving donkey carts and overcrowded buses contributed to the traffic jam. I stood and watched with wonder.

I laughed out loud on several occasions as I overheard random conversations.

Two women were talking, and one described a certain man she knew, "He so fresh and black. So black till de blackness shinin' thru he clothes."

Two men were discussing evolution. One said, "Ya don' know we is from de animal kingdom?"

The other replied, "How so? If we does come outa monkey, why dey still here?"

I noticed several signs on buildings that were priceless:

"Mind your head."

"Anyone caught using these grounds for a urinal will receive a summons."

"Cheap-Cheap Grocery."

Public beaches surround the Island, and Aunt E. took us for early-morning sea baths. We went often and they were wonderful. The water was warm and refreshing. I was able to see far down into the ocean because of its clear, crystal-blue color. As the slow, incoming waves lapped the sun-splashed shore, I could see miles ahead into the horizon. As dark-complexioned as we were already, our beach escapades tanned our skins even more.

"Sea baths are good for everyone," declared Aunt E. "They sure help me feel better from my arthritis."

Grantley, graciously, took his vacation at the time of our visit to chauffer us around the Island. One day, before we left home, I asked what the letters on the license plates of vehicles meant.

M. answered immediately, "St. Michael take a M; You give a P for St. Peter; St. John take a J; and you give a X for Christ Church."

She was referring to the Parishes into which Barbados is divided, although she hadn't mentioned all eleven of them. To me, her response was still remarkable for a five-year-old. The remaining Parishes are St. Lucy, far north, St. Thomas and St. George, which are mid-Island and landlocked, St. Andrew, northeast, St. James on the west coast, St. Philip, southeast, and St. Joseph on the east coast.

A visit to my father's birthplace, in the Parish of St. Peter, in the north of the island was a must. We took a slow drive through Speightstown, the Capital, and made a brief stop in the Whim, where my grandparents farmed long ago. We paid a visit to their gravesite there. Next, it was on to Cherry Tree Hill, a nature preserve, and we stopped at two schools: All Saints Boys School, which my dad attended, and Aunt E.'s school, Black Bess Girls. I could tell by her smile, the latter brought back memories for her.

My Aunt was thrilled to be in St. Peter once again with her relatives who remained. We made the rounds at several and had lunch at Cousin Vera's. When Aunt. E. introduced us, our elderly cousin asked: "These Lutha's trildren? All two?" "He dead, eh?"

We explained to her, as she prepared the meal, our dad, who had left Bimshire many years before, was very much alive.

Our lunch menu was new to Marilyn and me. We had ham with Saltine crackers, and a salad called "Bulljaw," made with codfish and cucumbers.

Cousin Vera and her husband, Uncle Cecil, encouraged us to eat and drink more.

"Eat, eat, 'cause who don' eat goin' drop, and who eat, goin' stan' up."

"Dat juice is called Soursop. Put it to your head and drink it. Our mango tree ain't have neither one at this time."

"I cut up some cake dere. Use it!"

"It's good to know ya family."

A brief stop at Cousin Kit's house, was thrilling to me. She was then in her eighties, and eventually lived to be one hundred-and three years old. Her memory was clear, and we shared delightful family stories with her. I marveled how she remembered the details of my dad's birth. She had lived with his mom, my grandmother, to help take care of her newborn baby boy.

Cousin Kit

Upon returning home, we found M. and Granny in the midst of a disagreement. Whatever caused the problem, we heard them trading insults.

M.:   "Granny, you ain't pretty. You ugly like a mongoose."
Granny: "Ya wrong! Shut up ya mout, before I have ta pound ya. And stop tellin' lies outa one sida ya mout. Ya understan' what I meanin'?"
M.   "You does tell lies, too. You does show de backa ya hand for de front."
Granny: "I gon' put ya in a tree, and leave ya peeping thru de leaves."

Grantley was determined we visit every corner of the Island, and wanted to ensure we experienced each Parish. As we traveled, I was intrigued by how everyday items were described there, both verbal and written. They were certainly different than the words I knew back in America:

Bodice = Blouse   Snackette = Cafeteria   Black Lead = Pencil
Rubber = Eraser   Press = Closet   Queue up = Line up   Saloon = Salon
Groceteria = Grocery Store   Jeepness or Struggle Buggy = An old bus

Monica introduced us to typical Bajan fare. At the top of the menu was CouCou and Flying Fish, the national dish. She prepared a sumptuous meal for us one evening, which included, also, lamb stew, riced English potatoes, split peas and rice, and sweet potatoes.

She explained how Coucou is made, "Cornmeal is mixed with okra and seasonings, or one can make it from a local vegetable, called breadfruit, that grows on a tree. We make a gravy, and we fry, steam, or bake the fish, which we buy fresh-caught, from the fish market on the wharf."

We washed the meal down with Coconut Water and Ju-C, a local soda drink.

I was stuffed after the delicious meal. Retiring to the sitting room, we were invited to listen to a political meeting being broadcast over Rediffusion, a type of local radio station. This brief snippet was enough for me:

Person 1: "I bow to the chair."
Person 2: "What you talkin' 'bout bowin' to de chair? You must think in here is a circus."

Chairperson: "I will stand for no more of this pretentious myopia nor political buffoonery."

Granny told us she thought at least one of the speakers was a Bajan white man. Then she explained, "I don' dis play wid white people, ya know. As dey say, 'beans,' I ready to butter dem."

A highlight of my visit was a foray into Cheapside Market in Bridgetown. It was a buzz of activity as we entered the huge indoor location, where we found a variety of fruit and vegetables being sold. Women, with kerchiefs on their heads, and dresses overlaid by colorful aprons, ruled. They were known as "hawkers" by the locals, and sold their goods, brought daily from the rural areas, from enclosed wooden stands. It was a noisy place, as bantering among hawkers and calling out loudly to customers was the norm.

Cheapside Market, Bridgetown, Barbados[18]

Aunt E. certainly knew her way around the market and remembered the names of several hawkers. I was amused as Aunt. E. lapsed into a much stronger Bajan dialect with her old friends there.

"Hey Miss Agard, how you?"

"Miss E. You is back in de Island?" I ain't see ya fa donkey's years! What ya want today?"

"These two girls are my nieces from America. I here today for some plantains, okra, breadfruit, yams, and a few other things."

"I got plantains, but ya gon' have to go ova to Miss Thorne ova dere for yams."

It was clear, even in the market, there were loyalties to favorite hawkers. You dare not buy an item from one hawker, for example, ackees, small sour fruit, if you routinely buy them from another. If you do, the wrath of God will come down on your head. We witnessed the following exchange between two hawkers:

"Who you tink you are?"

"I's a child of God, das who."

"Well you sure ain't akkin' like it. You sold ackees to dat woman ova dere, when ya knew full-well she dis be my customer."

---

18 Lambers 2019. *Cheapside Market.*

"Essie Daniel, I oughta pull dat kerchief offa ya head and expose ya bald head for the world to see!"

Laughing, Aunt E. moved us on to the other side of the market. We left laden down with items for our eating pleasure.

On my last Sunday in Bim, Aunt E. took us to her former church, which was walking distance from the house. As we were leaving, Granny warned us of two things:

"When you walkin' 'pon de road, ya 'gon see some drunk people. Dey dis drink so much rum 'pon a Sat-dy nite, that Sundi mornin' you dis see dem snorin' in de street like dey was in a feather bed!"

"When you get to dat church, be careful dose folks don't get in de power and knock off ya head. I's a Roman Catholic. But the las' time I went in dere, a woman was standin' up prayin' like she growlin'. Another one let out some fluggabuga noise like she ain't had no sense."

I had to admit, Granny was somewhat correct. The goings on during the service were unbelievable and seemed like a scene from a movie. Several people recognized Aunt E. and interacted with her. One woman who was sitting in front of us, turned around and asked Aunt E.to scratch her back. When the Offering was being raised, a gentleman behind us tapped Aunt E. on the shoulder and said, "You from America. So, you have 'nuff money to put in for you and me."

A deacon announced to the congregation, "The Scripture will be read from the sixty-seventh, to the seventy-wonth verse."

When asked to lead in prayer, a woman prayed, "God, bless those who couldn't be at church today. Give them the absent portion."

When a woman was asked to sing a solo, she announced, "Well, this is a little haphazard, but I'll try. Pray fa ma."

Holy Communion was served that Sunday. After the service was dismissed, the Pastor announced, "This lef' ova bread and juice should not be wasted. I'm comin' 'round so all you can take some more til it all gone."

When I packed my bags on the final day of my Bim holiday, as expected, M. and Granny had an argument:

Granny:	"M., you dropped a black lead on the floor. Pick it up."
M:	"It ain't 'gon dead."
Granny:	"You ain' got a bit a understandin'."
M:	"An' you's a boss-idiot."

Since she had spent so many years away from Barbados until this visit, Aunt E. was not about to leave there after only three weeks. So, she planned her trip to allow her a six-week vacation. Marilyn was on summer vacation from school, so, Aunt E. suggested she stay longer, also, and they could return to the USA together. I, on the other hand, was scheduled to start my new job at the end of the three weeks.

I bade my sister and aunt goodbye, and boarded my aircraft home. Two of the women from our inbound group also returned on my flight.

I chuckled to myself many times as I winged my way back home. The trip had certainly been an eye-opener for me. I had lots of fun and the time was well spent. I vowed to myself, *I'll visit Bimshire again.*

Barbados, Where the Cool Breezes Blow, 2013

St. George Follies

Ivan Holder and his brother, Archie, were born and raised in the Parish of St. George on the Island of Barbados. They were the only two children of their parents, Doreen and Bindley, who farmed their land in a village called Market Hill.

These boys were mischievous fellows and their Schoolmaster, Mr. Johnson, at the local Boys School, complained bitterly about them to their parents, "They do not complete their lessons. They play too much, and they harass other pupils. You need to pull them up and get them in line."

As much as they tried, the Holders just could not get their sons under control.

"As soon as dey gets old enuff, I'm shipping both a dem off to England," Bindley told Doreen one evening, when their sons were asleep. "The cold weather over dere, and me brother, Everson, will surely straighten dem out."

"Why do they have to go dere?" Doreen asked in her thick Bajan accent. "I rather dem stay here where we can help dem."

Sunday after Sunday, at the local Nazarene church in nearby Workman's Village, Sis. Cadogan, the Holders' pastor, implored sinners to come forward and give their hearts to the Lord. "Come right up. Come to Jesus just now!"

Doreen, with glaring eyes, would glance over at her sons and nod them toward the altar. The boys pretended not to see her until they got a familiar knock in the ribs, which said, "I'll take you up there if you won't go on your own."

The routine was the same each time. With great reluctance, first Ivan, the older, then Archie, with heads down, would go up and stand before Pastor Cadogan.

"Why have you come forward?"

"To get saved," they said in unison.

After praying for them, the pastor dispatched them to their seats, amid loud shouts of "Amen!" from the parishioners.

Alas, by Monday, the boys were back to their old tricks. One morning, for an unknown reason, Archie threw a rock and broke a neighbor's window. Miss Eldean Pitt, a widow, was furious and reminded Bindley about his responsibility. "I want me window fix dis very week."

"Sorry 'bout dat, Miss Pitt, I'll get it fix real soon."

"It was a mistake, Father," pleaded Archie, as Bindley gave him a sound whipping. "I won't do it again!"

It was to no avail that Ivan hid himself. Although not involved in the rock- throwing incident, he received a few lashes as well. His father wanted to give him a warning.

Ivan already had an eye for the girls, though just in his mid-teens. His special fancy was Leotta St. Hill, who lived in neighboring Retreat Woods. Lottie, as she was called by everyone, was attractive, and had smooth, ebony-colored skin. Her beautiful smile revealed even, pearly-white teeth.

Although the walk was long, and they shortened the journey by cutting through the sugar cane fields, Ivan dragged Archie along with him to Retreat Woods every Saturday, on the pretext of playing cricket with the boys over there.

Lottie's parents were wary of the Holder boys and did not particularly like their parents either.

"Stay away from dem," Mrs. St Hill warned her daughter. "Lottie, dey nuttin' but trouble."

Mr. St. Hill chimed in, "Las' thing we want is you getting' wid child by one of dem boys. I'm warning you now, if it happen, out you goes from here," as he pointed toward the door. "I means it."

It was 1958, and, having a child out of wedlock, at that time, was a terrible thing. Also, Mr. St. Hill knew he and his wife would face severe discipline by their church if such a thing occurred. They would be "sat down" at the back of the church for at least three months for "failing to control their daughter." It had happened to others before.

Lottie, secretly, liked Ivan and was excited when Saturdays came. She loved the attention he gave her, and nothing could keep her away from him. She considered her parents old-fashioned and out of touch.

Archie also warned his brother, "Ivan, I don't think Lottie is the girl for you. You better think twice about calling her your girlfriend."

"What's that to you?" was his reply.

Some months later, the Holders heard a sharp knock on their door. The St. Hills had come to pay them a visit. Lottie, with head held down, trailed behind them.

"Come in," Bindley invited. "Have a seat, please."

Mr. St. Hill came right to the point "My girl, Lottie, here is with child. She say you boy, Ivan, is de child father."

"Come here, Boy," Bindley called to Ivan, who was eavesdropping in a bedroom.

"Des folks telling me dere daughter here is with child and you is responsible. Let me hear what you have to say 'bout it."

Ivan stood silent and held his head down. Without a word spoken, the truth had come out.

Mrs. St. Hill wiped tears from her eyes. "Lottie is a child, herself. What she goin' do wid a baby?"

Mr. St. Hill stood up, with resolve, and looked straight at Bindley. "You boy goin' have to marry my girl. We will not have her walking shame-faced 'round de village without a husband."

Bindley began to protest, "He's only a boy."

But Doreen, his wife, interrupted. "All right. What will be, will be. Since Ivan din' say he is not the child's father, he'll have to marry she."

Ivan looked at his mother with horror. "Marry, Mother? I want to go to England next year."

"Yes, marry. You big enuff to do what you did, you big enuff to marry she. England is completely out, for now."

"Dat settles it den," said Bindley.

"There's one more thing," Mr. St. Hill said. "I told Lottie long ago if she ever got with child before she married, she can't stay at my house no more. I am not goin' back on my word. I meant it den and I means it now."

"But she's still a schoolgirl," cried Mrs. St. Hill. "She needs to stan' home at us. She don't know a thing 'bout cookin', washin', or carin' a baby."

"She can stay here with us," Doreen declared. "She will now be our family. I'll help her wid de baby and learn her how to cook."

Mrs. St. Hill dried her eyes, visibly relieved. "God bless you all, thank you so much. We will talk later 'bout de weddin'."

The St. Hills and their daughter bid the Holders, "Good-day," and moved slowly up the road.

"I ought to beat you within a inch of you life," Bindley told Ivan, afterward. "You brought nuttin' but disgrace to we family."

"I'll get a job and care for her and the baby. I guess I'm a man now."

A few weeks later, the St. Hills visited the Holders again— this time to bring Lottie to live with them, along with a few of her belongings. The week before, they had all gathered for the marriage, held in Retreat Woods. Without much fanfare, Lottie and Ivan had said their vows before Pastor Lashley at the small Pentecostal church there.

Doreen was not happy over the whole situation, but made peace with it, nevertheless. The day Lottie came to move in with them, she welcomed her. The young woman and her mom embraced a long time. Mr. St. Hill and Bindley stood in silence.

"She gon' be all right here," consoled Doreen. "After all, the baby will be our grandchil' too. We'll see dat she keep in touch wid you all and I'll let you know when the baby comes."

Ivan found work after school in Bridgetown, the capital, in a small machine shop. He had a big responsibility now.

Lottie settled nicely within the Holder household, and appreciated the kindness her new mother-in-law, Doreen, showed her.

Months passed. At last, the big day arrived. Lottie was ready to give birth. In those days, midwives attended women at home. The local one was named Verna Brathwaite.

The house was a buzz of activity.

"Archie, you go get Miss Verna," Doreen ordered. "Ivan, cut through the canes and tell Mrs. St. Hill Lottie ready."

Eldean Pitt saw what was happening and poked her head in the door. "You need anything Miss Holder?"

"No thank you. We just fine."

Miss Verna arrived just in time to help Lottie gave birth to a lively baby girl.

"She sure can holler loud," declared Ivan, who had returned, in a flash, with Mrs. St. Hill. He glanced, with pride, at his baby daughter.

Lottie's mother, as usual, cried as she held her first grandchild.

They named the baby, "Jasmine Elaine," and she soon became the darling of the Holder household. Lottie's strong bond with her infant daughter was immediate.

Doreen Holder noticed her husband, Bindley, was not around at the time of the big event. She assumed he went out somewhere because he always said, "Birthing is women's business."

What she did not know, at the time, was that Bindley had taken a fancy for Mildred Bostic, who lived about a mile down the road. Mildred, who was childless, had separated from her husband a few years before, and he had gone to America to live, on a permanent basis. More amazing, Mildred and Doreen were cousins! Under pretext of going for a walk, Bindley would make as many quick visits as he could to Mildred's house, and Doreen suspected nothing. The two soon became wildly infatuated with each other.

One day, Doreen took the bus to Bridgetown to do some shopping. She ran into her long-time friend, Stella Greene, on Broad Street, where most people did their shopping.

After exchanging pleasantries, Stella came straight to the point. "What you gon' do 'bout dat woman, Mildred Bostic?

"Mildred? What about she?"

"You ain't hear, Doreen?"

"No. Wha' happen?"

Stella glanced left and right to make sure no one nearby could overhear what she said. "Mildred been entertaining Bindley, you husband. I hear she does have him at she house regular!"

Doreen froze and stared at Stella with disbelief.

"I'm sorry, Doreen, I really thought you knew, but had decided to do nuttin' 'bout it."

"I did not know, Stella. But thanks for telling me."

"What you goin' do Doreen?"

"You lef dat to me. Lef dat to me."

When Stella walked away, Doreen let the tears flow. The shock and pain of this news was overwhelming. She didn't finish her shopping but took the bus right back to Market Hill. On the way home, she thought of nothing else.

That evening after Supper, Bindley said to Doreen, "I goin' for a walk to get some fresh air."

"Okay. See you later."

Doreen, quite sure where he was going, decided to follow him. She stayed a reasonable distance behind, to make sure he did not see her. Her feet were tired, but she was determined to see for herself what her husband was up to.

Sure enough, as she approached Mildred's neighborhood, in the distance, Doreen saw Bindley glance around, then enter Mildred's house.

Doreen waited a few minutes, then rapped, sharply, on the door.

"Doreen, what are you doing here?" Mildred asked.

"I come for Bindley, my husband. Move outta my way and lemme in!"

Frightened, Mildred moved away from the doorway. There, in the front room, was Bindley, with shirt off, stretched out on the sofa.

Doreen's fury knew no bounds. "Wunna is two wuffluss rascallions!" she yelled. "Bindley Holder, what you doin' here at, Mildred?" "What you want wid my husband, Mildred?" "And to tink you is family to me!"

"Is not what you tink, Doreen," Bindley muttered, weakly. "I just came to help her wid some chores."

"Liar! Wid you shirt off? Helpin' wid chores at night?"

Mildred, trembling, uttered not a word.

"Okay, I've seen enough. De word spread 'bout you two all down in Bridgetown. I came to see for meself. I done wid you, Bindley Holder.

You can have dis wicked Mildred. I leffen here before sometin' bad happen."

Doreen returned home, enraged. Sleep was a stranger to her that night. Bindley came back in the wee hours of the morning but rose early and went out to tend the animals. No words passed between them.

Next morning, Doreen summoned Ivan, Archie, and Lottie, and told them what happened. The family was speechless. It was a lot for them to take in.

Doreen then, said, "I leavin' here and you father as soon as I can find a place to live. My marriage to him is over. He can have Mildred Bostic."

Ivan spoke up, "I don't understand, Mother. Can't you and Father work it out?"

"No, boy. I done. I feel nuttin' but hate for him. He can stay here without me. He brought it on himself."

Ivan continued, "Well if you're goin', Mother, I'm goin'. Lottie, Jasmine, and I, will go with you."

Archie was too stunned to say anything.

Over the next few weeks, Bindley and Doreen exchanged few words. He tried once or twice to persuade her to stay. Begging and pleading, he said, "I sorry, Doreen. Please forgive me. I leffin' Mildred out."

But Doreen had made up her mind and made her position crystal clear to her husband. "Dere's no going back, Bindley. I can't forgive you. We marriage is over. I am moving away from you and away from this Village called Market Hill. The Parish of St. George won't see me living here no more. I don't care what you and Mildred do. I plan to live my life without you from now on."

Soon after, Doreen announced to her family, "I found a place in town for us to move to. It's a nice house with plenty room for all of us. It's not too far from where Ivan works."

"That's good," said Lottie, "It will be nice to live near town, Mother Doreen, you'll be able to get to the market easily and to shop in nearby Bridgetown. Ivan can walk to work, and when Jasmine gets bigger, I'll look for a job to help out."

"I'm staying here with Father, for now," Archie said. "As soon as I finish school, I'm heading for England. They need Bajan boys to come over and work on the Public Transport there."

Moving day came. It was a somber time for the Holder family and few words were spoken by anyone. Doreen, Ivan, and Lottie had packed all their belongings for the move to their new abode near Bridgetown. Archie had a lump in his throat and couldn't speak. Bindley was out in the fields and did not come to say goodbye.

When the moving people arrived, Doreen took a wistful last look around the house that had been her home for so many years. She carried baby Jasmine in one arm and a kerosene oil lamp in the other, as she walked through the front door and boarded the moving van. Ivan gave Archie a brief hug. As he watched his family travel down the road toward their new home, Archie let the tears flow. He felt all alone.

Stella, Doreen's friend, who first brought Bindley's affair with Mildred to her attention, was glad when Doreen told her she had ended her marriage to Bindley. She believed Doreen deserved better. Although she was not asked to do so, she kept tabs on Bindley and Mildred for a while, and informed Doreen what was going on with them.

Doreen was glad to have Stella as a friend. She helped her settle into her new home and life near town. As a true friend, she accompanied Doreen to the airport a few years later when her son, Archie, left the Island to seek his fortune in Britain.

Doreen went on with her life and lived happily with her children. She helped raise Baby Jasmine, who was the light of her life. Ivan and Lottie made long-term plans to relocate to America and planned to take Doreen with them.

Bandits of the Caribbean

Looking back to 1972, some of my friends considered me bold and brassy, while others thought I was misguided. They were concerned because I accepted a job with an international agency to live and work in the Caribbean. Several contacted me when they heard about my plans.

"Do you think you're doing the right thing, going down there to live on your own?"

"To me, you're taking a big risk. The men in the Caribbean are known for their flirtatious ways, you know."

My aunt, who always had a ready word, weighed in, with a twinkle in her eye, "Who knows? You'll probably find a man there, get married, and never come back."

Despite their concerns, I continued to prepare for my departure.

I understood my friends meant well. At the time, few single women quit their jobs, uprooted themselves, left family and friends, and flew to a foreign country to live and work among strangers. Yet I did. It wasn't that I was looking for excitement and adventure. These came to me, unexpectedly. I welcomed the challenge and trusted God to go with me, protect me, and make me successful.

There was no way I could have envisioned what lay ahead of me, despite a robust orientation, first, in Washington, DC, then in Caracas, Venezuela, prior to reaching Barbados, my appointed duty station.

Washington, DC

My three-day stay in the nation's Capital entailed absorbing a host of bureaucratic information about the Organization that had hired me: rules and regulations, goals and objectives, and a laundry list of internal procedures.

I was also told the following:

"You will hear negative comments about your home country, the USA. Ignore them. It won't matter."

"Do not get involved in local politics when you reach the islands. It will not go well for you if you do."

"Be yourself, be authentic, don't patronize, be patient, be genuine in your desire to help, and you will succeed." The latter was an excellent piece of advice that remained with me and proved true.

Caracas

Janet, my new supervisor, had invited me to stay at her apartment, instead of at a hotel, assuming I didn't speak Spanish, Venezuela's national language. Because of what I encountered on arrival, thank God, I could speak a little.

After clearing immigration and customs at Maiquetia International Airport, Venezuela, with several suitcases and bags beside me, I searched in vain for Janet in the Passenger Arrivals Hall. I had sent her a cablegram a few days earlier, in which I accepted her lodging invitation and informed her of my arrival information. As my fellow arriving passengers scurried to their waiting modes of transportation, I soon found myself alone in an empty arrivals hall! I telephoned my host several times, without reply. It was, indeed, a scary time for me, alone in a foreign country. I was glad I had her local address though and decided to make my way on my own to her apartment.

Taxicab drivers barraged me as I exited the doors of the airport, each vying for my business. In halting Spanish, I showed them a paper with my written destination, and an older driver escorted me to his cab. I recall the hair-raising ride into the city of Caracas. It was clear no one obeyed the speed limit as vehicles of all descriptions careened in and out of traffic at ninety miles per hour!

"Dear God," I prayed, "Please get me to Caracas safely. I know it's not your Will for me to die on these roads!"

Upon reaching Janet's apartment building, I couldn't believe what happened next. A uniformed soldier with a drawn rifle approached the cab and demanded to know why I was there. I showed him Janet's name on my now-crumpled notepaper. Thereupon, he ordered the taxi driver to remain in his cab, WITH my belongings, while he escorted me upstairs. I trembled at the knowledge there was a rifle in my back and prayed I would find Janet at home.

I knocked and the door opened. Janet, a tall, middle-aged woman, stood there, looking quite surprised. I felt a tremendous surge of relief. In fluent Spanish, and in a slightly annoyed tone, she ordered my escort to bring my belongings upstairs. She explained to me he was the Concierge of the building, whom she knew well.

"I never received your cablegram," Janet explained later. "I had no idea you were coming today. In fact, something told me to return early from the beach where I was."

Her words reinforced that God was certainly with me. I knew, without a doubt, He would protect me and guide me safely to my destination.

Next day, I met the fearsome Zone Chief who headed the Caracas office of our Organization. It was obvious he ruled with an iron hand and demanded top quality work from his subordinates. His Office was responsible for projects in selected Latin American countries and the Eastern Caribbean. Although he was somewhat aloof, he welcomed me and said he had faith I would adjust well and provide excellent service to the people of the Islands.

I loved Caracas. The tree-lined streets, the quaint sidewalk cafés, and the delicious foods were wonderful. Janet took me to restaurants where we ate typical Venezuelan fare. In addition to Arepas, a corn cake of sorts, which immediately became my favorite, I loved the evening meals which I sampled over the four days of orientation. Pabellón Criollo, the national dish, was delectable. It consisted of Bistec (beef steak), Caraotas Negras (black beans), Arroz (Rice), Platano frito (fried Plantain), Yucca (a type of yam), and Ensalada Mixta (Mixed green salad). Venezuelan cooking stole my heart.

The food, the warm welcome, and the nuggets of practical advice from Janet, all combined to make me feel as if I was in- transit to great adventures ahead.

Barbados

My whirlwind orientation visits to Washington and Caracas left me exhausted. I looked forward to finally arriving at Barbados, my duty station and final destination. When I arrived, I was met at the airport by the Office Manager and another staff member. They welcomed me to the island and to the Organization. My stomach was a sea of butterflies as I contemplated the future.

My hotel was a welcomed sight that hot July afternoon, where I rested and recouped until next morning. Before drifting off to sleep, I reviewed the official business and government research I did on Barbados. I had visited there before on vacation, but moving there to live and work on a long-term basis, was completely different. I would not be living tourist-style by any means.

I recalled the island to be flat, densely populated, and surrounded by sandy beaches and crystal-clear water. It touches the Caribbean Sea on one side and the Atlantic Ocean on the other. Tourists love to visit the island because of its friendly, welcoming people and exciting night life.

Of interest, I learned from Janet, my supervisor in Caracas, "Many people from other countries, known as ex-patriates, live in Barbados and consider life there a Paradise. They have become permanent residents and have no intention of ever leaving!"

I slept fitfully, in anticipation of my visit next day to my new Office.

Over the following days and weeks, I was introduced to an eclectic cast of characters that worked in the Office, the likes of whom I hadn't met before. Each had the title of "Consultant," as I did, and was assigned to a particular work project. Most required frequent travel to neighboring islands, at the invitation of those governments.

Profession-wise, among them included an ex- college professor, an engineer, a health educator, two nurses, a dietitian, a statistician, and three physicians. They hailed from around the world. Several were from the USA and Canada, one from India, a few from Central and South America, and a diverse group originating from various Caribbean islands. As I got to know them over the months following my arrival, I dubbed them, privately, "Bandits of the Caribbean." It will soon be clear why.

Time, in this chapter, would not permit me to bring each of the characters to center stage. I will introduce a few, however, who deeply impacted me in some way. I can describe them, as a group, without exaggeration. While some were kind and had good intentions, most, in my opinion, were ruthless in their motives, flawed of character, misplaced in assignment to that corner of the world, and should not have been working for the Organization.

I was the youngest person, at the time, assigned to the Office. I arrived with enthusiasm and excitement about my new role. Had my work not required travel to the islands, I would have found little joy being stationed and working every day in that Office. It was soon clear to me the Office staff, consisting of a manager, secretaries, clerks, and a driver, struggled, as did I, to work, amicably, with the Consultants. Most of the latter were haughty, privileged, hypocritical, conceited, and frequently impatient and irate, for no apparent reason. To illustrate, allow me to introduce a few of them.

B.S.

This person, a tall, middle-aged, African American male, had been placed in temporary charge of the Office when I first arrived. He was asked to hold that position, while a physician was being recruited to represent the Organization throughout the islands. His job was to orient me to my new role. It became obvious he was more socially oriented than work oriented. He was unable to articulate the goal and mission of the Organization in the region and was quite inept at his job. It was later discovered he, routinely, shoved important documents which arrived at the Office, under the blotter on his desk and never responded to them. I'm not quite sure why he was hired, but he presented to outsiders an air of being a diplomat. My secret description of him was "Form without Substance."

K.L..

This fifty-something woman, with graying blond hair, hailed from the U.S. Midwest. She was incompetent at her job and did not know how to relate to her fellow nurse counterparts in the Islands. She avoided work travel as much as possible. Caucasian, single, and living alone, she was mean-spirited and clearly racist. I wasn't sure why she chose the islands in which to live and work. She employed a Black maid at her apartment, who did her every bidding. She, haughtily, gave orders, to the Office staff, but none of them took her seriously. I characterized her as "No Form, No Substance."

D.H..

D.H. had been declared a persona non grata in several countries of the region and had a reputation of being a rabblerouser. He was a short, diminutive man, in his mid-forties, of mixed racial origin, with slick black hair, and an olive complexion. He had no loyalty whatever to the Organization. His bent was always toward the "nationals" and not toward those who employed him. He was a busybody, a whisperer, and a newsmonger. Despite the Organization's policy to the contrary, D.H. was a close friend of politicians and ingratiated himself with them. He was happy whenever there was conflict anywhere and demonstrated a "Let's you and him fight" philosophy in the Office. I never felt as if I could trust him. My description of him was "Caution! program subject to change!"

Z.M.

Z.M. came from a family of businesspeople whose products were shipped throughout the islands. This convinced her she was from among the "upper class," and she had an exalted opinion of herself. Her work, however, did not match her self -concept. She was dull-witted, and produced little in terms of training, content, or otherwise, for the people of the islands. Though not involved in any way with my project, the Office staff advised me she was unrelenting in her criticism of my programs when I was not around. To my face, however, she always smiled. Within myself, I called Z.M. "Wicked Witch of the West."

My work in the Islands got off to a rocky start. Several incidents occurred which caused me to muster all the strength God gave me to tunnel through.

B.S. and K.L. were the colleagues who met me at the airport when I first arrived in Barbados. I'm not quite sure why the two of them were there. I suppose B.S. thought it his diplomatic duty, as Office Manager, to be on hand. K.L., a nurse like me, most likely came out of curiosity to ascertain what the new nurse looked like. She was asked to help orient me to the nursing profession in the region. From the moment I met K.L., she tried to gain the upper hand over me. Finally, I was forced to put her in her place. When I asked her questions about the work, she referred me to the files and told me it was better I did my own research. (Far be it from her to help me learn the ropes too soon!). Before I was able to purchase a vehicle of my own, K.L. refused to help me with transportation. She told me I would have to find my way, walking into the town, on the streets without sidewalks, on my own.

One day, B.S. invited the Consultants to lunch at a local restaurant. He said it was his way of welcoming me to the Office. "I'll treat," he promised.

At the restaurant, he told us, "Feel free to order what you like."

Alas, however, when the bill was presented at the end of the meal, B.S. told the waiter, "I'll only be paying for a cup of tea. That's all I had." He then passed the bill to the rest of the staff, I included, and asked us to take care of the rest of the bill. I could not believe this, nor could anyone else.

One Monday morning, K.L. and I flew to a neighboring Island on my first assignment. As I understood it, her role was to introduce me to the nursing staff and senior health officials. When we checked into the hotel, I prepared myself for a meeting later that afternoon. Imagine my surprise when I went down to the lobby to meet K.L. so we could ride together to the meeting. She was standing there in beach attire and sandals!

"Aren't we scheduled for a meeting?" I asked.

"Oh, no. I never make contact when I first arrive in the Islands. I relax on the beach first. I'll arrange for a meeting on Wednesday."

I returned to my room feeling awful. There was nothing I could do except wait until Wednesday. It was, indeed, my first insight into the contempt with which some ex-patriates held the people of the Islands.

In Barbados, D.H. made it his business to "introduce" me to Ministry of Health officials. When an official meeting was scheduled between them and me, it was clear they had "met" me before. Here is what they said to me:

"Oh yes, Dr. H. told us all about you."

"We understand you are very young and inexperienced, and will have nothing to offer us, at least for quite some time."

"The nurses in neighboring, less-developed islands will need your services more than we will here in Barbados. Therefore, It is probably best to spend most of your time in those locations."

I felt humiliated and undermined. When I confronted D.H. about those statements, he feigned being irate to hear them, and totally denied having made them.

About six months after I began my work in the Islands, a hair-raising situation occurred. The Zone Chief in Caracas contacted the staff in Barbados and issued this warning:

"I'll be taking the first thing moving from Caracas and arriving there day after tomorrow. Be prepared at 9:00am for a mandatory meeting. Heads are going to roll!"

When we met, the Zone Chief came straight to the point, "I'm not at all satisfied with the way this Office is functioning. I've already sent B.S. on vacation with his family. The date of his return is uncertain. Several upper level officials in the Islands have complained about the unsatisfactory assistance received from the Consultants in this Office. They said your visits to them have been intermittent and not connected to their program priorities. Correspondence has gone unanswered. There has been undue fraternizing with local people during visits to their countries. They have threatened to withdraw relationships with this Office."

Not a word was spoken in defense. The silence was deafening.

He continued, "The following steps will be taken, with immediate effect:

Number one, the entire staff in this Office is hereby placed on probation for three months.

Second, I have assigned a temporary Country Representative – a physician from our Washington D.C. headquarters –to supervise the staff in this Office and to monitor correspondence. He will be here by the end of this week.

Third, travel to the islands is suspended for one week. After that, travel requests will be screened for relevance by the Country Representative, before approval.

Fourthly, all files dated more than three years old will be removed and discarded. A new filing system will be implemented. Secretarial and clerical staff will oversee this activity.

Number five, Consultants will remain at home tomorrow and the next day, while a team of painters is here to paint this entire facility.

Lastly, I will return in three months to assess the status of these activities and any improvements derived therefrom.

Unless there are questions, the meeting is hereby adjourned."

I had not experienced such a sobering moment before. Staff was shaken to the core. Changes ordered by the Zone Chief were put into effect and a new sense of purpose prevailed in the Office.

At the end of the three months, probation was lifted, and routines were re-established.

Unfortunately, while attitudes of the Consultants improved, somewhat, their characters remained the same. They soon returned to their unacceptable behavior. Here is an example:

A year after I arrived in the Islands, I received my Performance Evaluation. My supervisor expressed how pleased she was with my work. She told me, in the short time I was there, I had developed in the Islands capacity to incorporate several new programs for mothers and babies. Demands for my assistance had increased. I was given an Outstanding performance rating.

Because of this, I was offered a promotion, which I accepted. My scope of work was expanded to cover wider health initiatives, including general nursing education, and Disaster Preparedness and Relief. My new position also included supervising the work of the other nursing Consultants in the area.

When Z.M., heard about my promotion, she became incensed and took steps to undermine it. This was, despite the fact she was not a nurse and had no relationship to my projects. I was informed her comments to the other nurses were as follows:

"She's only been here a year, and already she's being promoted. You nurses should complain."

"I understand her salary has gone up two levels. Now she's being paid far more than we who have been here longer."

"I'm going to contact my supervisors at the highest level in our main office in Washington, DC to see if we can get her promotion overturned."

Z. M.'s whining and her words caused no small stir among my nursing colleagues. Several agreed with her arguments and began to marginalize me. For quite some time, it was difficult to work in harmony with them, especially because I had to supervise them.

I continued to give the work my all. Thankfully, the Lord helped me keep my position for seven more years, until I resigned, voluntarily, from the Organization. I sensed, however, a continuing underlying thread of discontent because of Z.M.'s original stance.

Though difficult, I still thank the Lord for having met the Bandits of the Caribbean. He never promised us, His children, a smooth road in this life. Often, He places people and situations in our paths, to strengthen our faith and trust in Him. I certainly learned to pray harder and more sincerely during that season. At times, I questioned why I was there and why He allowed the struggles. I came to realize I had a responsibility to the "Bandits." God had granted me the opportunity to model Christianity through my responses to their attacks.

Bye Bye Birdie

'Twas the night before a Christmas many years ago, when I lived in Barbados, that I never shall forget. I had asked a friend of mine, who raised turkeys especially for Christmas, to reserve a nice one for me. On Christmas Eve I went to the farm, and a plump bird was waiting for me. It seemed just the right one to grace our table and serve our family and friends we invited for Christmas dinner.

"I'm going to wait until early tomorrow morning, on Christmas Day, to roast this turkey," I announced to my husband and kids that evening. "I want it have a "just-baked" freshness when our company arrives later in the day."

Aunt E., age 90, arrived at our home a few days earlier and was anxious to help with dinner preparations. She had presided over many Christmas dinners during her exceptionally long life.

"Don't wait until tomorrow to roast the turkey," she advised. "Put it in the oven tonight. I'll keep an eye on it and take it out when it is done."

"Are you sure?" I asked. "It's going to take a few hours to roast."

"Oh yes," she assured me, "I'll be glad to. I sleep little these days anyway."

Weary from the baking and decorating of the past several days, I thanked Aunt E. for her offer, seasoned the turkey, placed it in the oven to roast, as she suggested, then climbed into bed just before midnight. I was soon off to a very sound sleep.

About 6:00am next morning, I awakened to the acrid smell of smoke. I rushed out of bed and ran toward the kitchen, from which the smoke wafted. I bumped into Aunt E. on my way, and noticed she was fully dressed for the Christmas morning church service we had planned to attend.

"What's burning?" she asked with a troubled look on her face.

18

Arriving in the kitchen, I saw smoke coming from the oven. Right away, I knew what happened. My beautiful Christmas bird had been roasting the entire night!

"I'll get this," said my husband, who had followed me to the kitchen and turned the oven off. When he opened the oven door, we could see the charred remains of the turkey inside. Only bones were left!

"Aunt E.," I asked. "What happened? Did you fall asleep? You promised to keep an eye on the turkey!"

My aunt was annoyed I questioned her like this.

She replied with indignation, "I'm sure I heard you walking in the kitchen during the night. I thought you didn't trust me to watch the turkey, so I went to bed and let you handle it."

I struggled to control my anger toward my aunt. Not only had she spoiled our Christmas dinner, she refused to accept responsibility for what happened. However, because of her age, I forgave her.

"We'll have to serve chicken to our guests this year," I said to my husband. "Thank God, we have some of those birds in the freezer."

Just before our company arrived, we took the lovely roasted chickens out of the oven. They weren't the traditional turkey we looked forward to but were a great substitute.

Over the years, as we reminisce about Christmases past, we often laugh about the bird we lost at the hands of Aunt E.

At Home

Dolly Padmore was green with envy. An "At Home" party was being given for her cousin, Evadne Alleyne, and she was enraged.

With contempt, she declared to her mother, Daphne, "We seldom hear of "At Home" parties here in this island. Who is she to have one? Besides, I didn't have one. I never got to show off my wedding gifts to my friends."

Dolly, then, tore up the invitation to Evadne's party and threw it into the trash.

Daphne, who spoiled Dolly, her only child, only smiled. Dolly knew well why an At Home party would have been out of the question for her when she married two years earlier. Her wedding had not been announced to anyone, nor was her marriage made public. When she found herself with child, at age eighteen, she was taken by her parents before Pastor Springer, along with Calvin Padmore, the baby's father, who was accompanied by his mother. Calvin, twenty-three, was angry at being in this position and felt trapped into marrying Dolly. They knew they were not in love, so the marriage was not a happy occasion for either. They agreed to wed, thinking they had a duty to "give the unborn child a name." After repeating their marriage vows, the ceremony was over in no time at all.

In the 1940s and 1950s, At Home parties were not very popular in Barbados, but were well established in the USA. Bessie Alleyne, Evadne's mother, had taken a trip to New York, and was invited to an At Home party while there. She was so impressed, she decided to give such a party in Barbados for her daughter, Evadne, who was soon to be married.

"I know it will cost poor folks like us a lot to give the party," she confided to her husband. "But, after all, it is for Evadne. We must stretch ourselves and try and make it happen."

Bessie modeled the party just as she had seen it in New York. She invited friends to gather a few weeks after the wedding to view and admire all the gifts Evadne received.

The wedding was a grand occasion. Bessie and Gladstone Alleyne pulled out all the stops for Evadne, their beloved daughter. People came from far and near to their village church. Rudolph, the bridegroom, beamed with pride as his bride approached the altar. Her lovely, pale ivory gown, bedecked with tiny appliqués, drew approving nods from the audience.

Even the "lookers" came to view the affair. These were neighborhood folks who had not been invited, but who wanted to see the event anyhow. They crowded around the outside and peeped into the church through the open windows and doors. They were none too quiet in their comments.

"She does look too sweet!" remarked one.

"Indeed, and look at da fancy shoes 'pon she feet."

Dolly, with great reluctance, attended the wedding. She held back tears as she sat in the church, remembering her own situation. She couldn't bring herself to be happy for her younger cousin.

"Are you going to the Crane?" the invited guests asked each other, following the ceremony.

The Crane Hotel was THE place at the time for wedding receptions. Set high on a bluff in the Parish of St. Philip, overlooking pink sand and turquoise-blue water, the hotel was the ideal venue for the occasion. The cost of the reception was well beyond the Alleynes' means. However, Bessie, very resourceful, participated in the "sou-sou," a scheme for saving and borrowing money among close kin, when extra finances were needed.

Rudolph and Evadne spent their week-long honeymoon in St. Lucia, an island north of Barbados. Bessie wept with joy as they boarded the passenger boat that took them there. She was careful to store their wedding presents at her home until their return.

Daphne knew better and should never have listened to Dolly when her daughter shared her scheme with her. "I could use some of those wedding presents Evadne got. They sure were wrapped in pretty paper."

Daphne's heart pounded as she understood what Dolly meant.

"Mummy, I need you to help me get some of those gifts when Aunt Bessie goes to town this Friday. I'm sure she'll never miss them."

Together, mother and daughter conspired to steal a few of Evadne's presents. Dolly convinced herself and her mother she was worthy of some of them. After all, they were kinfolk.

When Friday came, Bessie rose early as usual for her trip to the market in the capital, Bridgetown. Mangoes, plantains, bananas, and breadfruit were among the items harvested from her yard for sale at the market. Her husband, Gladstone, had left home even earlier for his job at the factory.

Dolly and Daphne went straight to Bessie's house when they saw her head down the road for town. As expected, the door was unlocked, and they gained entrance easily. They found the gifts, still wrapped, in one of the small bedrooms.

"If we only take two or three, Aunt Bessie will never notice," Dolly exclaimed.

Daphne mumbled, "Okay."

In their haste to get what they wanted, neither of them heard footsteps approaching. Mrs. Mascoll, Bessie's aunt, had come to cook for her while she went to town.

At the sight of the gifts in Daisy's and Daphne's hands, Mrs. Mascoll went wild.

"What are you two thieves doing in here?"

The robbers trembled, having been caught red-handed.

"Wunna don't have one bit of shame! I ought to call the police and get wunna lock up right now!"

"Please, Auntie, give we a chance," pleaded Daphne, I'm sorry for my behavior."

"Give you a chance? You ought to be ashamed of wunna self. Stealing from you own cousin."

"Don't tell Aunt Bessie 'bout this," Dolly begged, weeping. "We never should have come here and I'm sorry."

"Put those gifts right back and get outta here now!"

The would-be thieves did as she told them and rushed down the road as fast as they could.

Mrs. Mascoll decided not to tell anyone about the near-robbery at Bessie's house.

The At Home party, held at Evadne's new flat, was a lovely affair. Bessie arrived for the happy occasion with teacakes, made by her very own hands. The guests "oohed" and ahhed" over the wedding presents. Daphne and Dolly, of course, did not attend. I reckon they had their own party "At Home."

Section D.
Winter Reflections

African Roots : A DNA Journey

For as long as I can remember, I have felt drawn to the Continent of Africa. Years ago, in my high school geography class, I learned the names of the countries and their capitals in that great part of the world. Despite the negative talk from teachers, such as, Africa being called a "Dark Continent," I was fascinated by what I read and by the few African people I met at the time.

"One day I'll go there." I said to myself. I knew in my heart it would happen.

My dream was fulfilled when my husband and I travelled to the Continent on a short-term missions trip. My heart thrilled as we landed on African soil. I couldn't believe I was finally there. Although our mission included ministry in one country, only, we gained much insight and knowledge about that corner of the world.

My penchant toward Africa was heightened, further, when I received, recently, the results of my DNA test. I learned my origins in Africa are 72% Nigerian; 10% Cameroon, Congo, and Southern Bantu Peoples; and 9% Benin and Togo. To learn where my ancestors originated, where they walked, the languages they spoke, the food they ate, and how they worshipped, brought me closer to them. I was able, also, to connect the dots from Africa to the Caribbean, where, relatively speaking, more recent generations of my forbears were taken on slave ships. I have been able to trace them, by name, to those who were born into slavery, then emancipated, as far back as five generations, in Jamaica and Barbados.This has brought me full circle.

The three essays in this section relate to people or situations that have their origins on the African Continent. You, my dear reader will find them interesting and enlightening.

> *"Princes shall come out of Egypt; Ethiopia shall soon stretch out her hands unto God."*
>
> Psalms 68:31. King James Version (KJV)

Three African Girls

A few years ago, I was privileged to celebrate the high school graduations of three of my dear friends—Shannon, Jada, and Danielle. Intelligent, focused, and ambitious, these daughters of African immigrants went on to excel in college and are working toward their career goals.

Shannon was Valedictorian of her high school class. Born in Zimbabwe, a country in the southern portion of Africa, she was named Nukiso at the time of her birth, meaning "the beautiful one," in her native Shona language. She was brought to the USA by her parents, Mariama and Augustine, at the age of two. When they arrived, the family faced a different lifestyle than the one to which they were accustomed, and worked hard to assimilate.

I met them after they relocated to Dallas, and sensed, right away, a curiosity and vibrancy in their five-year old, to whom they gave an American name, Shannon. I was certain, as she grew, Shannon would accomplish a lot. I was not at all surprised when I learned the four-foot ten-inch, mature young lady, had gained early admission to the renowned Vanderbilt University in Nashville, Tennessee.

She completed her pre-med studies with majors in the natural and life sciences, and, as of this writing, is currently in medical school. When she qualifies as a physician, she intends to focus on an area of medical research.

I was involved in the birth of Jada over twenty years ago. When I held her in my arms at the hospital, I had no idea what the tiny, first-born child of her parents would grow up to be. At her naming ceremony a few days after her birth, she was called Jaiyesimi, meaning "one who enjoys life".

I am amazed at what the tall, attractive young woman now has become. She is the pride and joy of her Nigerian parents, Emmanuel and Mercy, who immigrated here not long before her birth. Their daughter, now called Jada, went to a community college, then graduated from a four-year University with a Bachelor's degree in Nuclear Engineering. She is studying toward a Master's degree in her field.

My husband and I attended the lavish graduation party Trina and Solomon gave when Danielle, their third daughter, finished high school. We sampled the tasty dishes from their homeland, Sierra Leone, West Africa. In addition to a variety of meats, tastily prepared, there was groundnut stew, Jollof rice, cassava, fried plantains, and several other dishes.

When she is among her African friends, Dallas-born, Danielle, is also called Fatou, a name originating from her Krió people. She loves her name, which means "liked by all."

Danielle, a slender, fashion-conscious, free-spirited young lady, worked the room at the party. Lively music from the home country played in the background, as she greeted her guests, who attended from all around. Danielle graduated from Lubbock-based Texas Tech University with a degree in Marketing and Public Relations.

I'm so proud of my three young friends. They and their parents defy the prevailing stereotype about immigrants. The notion that immigrants come here only to take what the United States has to offer, without contributing to it, does not apply to them.

There's no doubt in my mind Jada (Jaiyesimi), Danielle (Fatou), and Shannon (Nukiso), will offer much to the progress of our complex and varied society. They will do so whether they use their African or American names.

Storm Clouds Over Mali

Timbuktu

Mary, a powerful wind gust, found herself in the throes of labor. She pushed with all her might, and delivered her baby, a small draft of wind. Regrettably, Mary passed away just after her child was born. However, before she died, she named her infant, David. This happened in early 1979, in a country called Mali, in West Africa, in a city called Timbuktu.

Mali, a landlocked nation, is located on the southern edge of the great Sahara Desert. Over time, sands swept down from the north, forming great sand dunes In Timbuktu, as well as throughout Mali and surrounding countries.

History tells us that In the twelfth and thirteenth centuries, in addition to its wealth from powerful gold reserves, Timbuktu was an oasis of culture in the middle of the desert. Several universities were there, with small gatherings of scholars. Into thousands of manuscripts, which still exist today, history, science, wisdom, and knowledge were poured by the scholars. The city of Timbuktu was also known, for centuries, as the center for the spread of Islam, Mali's dominant religion. After years of decline, caused by weather issues, including numerous severe droughts, sandstorms, and a host of political problems, Timbuktu, by the twentieth century, sadly, had evolved into a most impoverished place.

It was in twentieth-century Timbuktu, that David, the orphaned Wind Draft, was left to fend for himself. For a few months, he drifted here and there throughout the city, trying to make friends. The people walked the streets, ankle-deep in sand. It even threatened to invade their houses. David offered help to those around him by sending what he thought were cool breezes in the sweltering summer heat. But they complained about the "harsh winds", caused by David. He felt unwanted and unloved, and considered leaving Mali altogether.

One morning, a thought came to him. *"Why don't I head straight across the Atlantic Ocean and go to the tranquil islands of the Caribbean, which I've heard so much about? I think they might appreciate me more over there."*

David became possessed by the idea. He was not certain what he would do when he reached the islands but was sure he would come up with a plan on the way.

Bamako

Before leaving his country, David moved to Bamako, Mali's capital city of one million souls. His goal, while there, was to make concrete plans for his trip west to the Caribbean.

David arrived in Bamako in mid-August 1979 at the height of the rainy season, which lasts each year from June to October. As in Timbuktu, temperatures hovered around one hundred and twenty degrees, and the heat was oppressive. He soon realized he would have to step up his travel plans because the rains in Bamako were unrelenting. Although the landscape was barren, and the soil hard and scorched, floods were triggered throughout the city.

Daily thunderstorms occurred and the skies seemed deeply angry. David's investigation revealed that ripples of cold wind descend from the mountains of Chad, a country several hundred miles east of Mali, and collide with the warm air in his country. This confrontation leads to the violent weather and tempestuous storms in Bamako.

David had no way of knowing, however, that some storms do not die out, but, rather continue, after leaving Bamako, making their way west to the coast of Africa, and fall into the Atlantic Ocean many miles away.

Had he been human, young David, most likely, would have known meteorologists track African weather patterns and the conduct of storms every year.

Gentle David would have been aghast to learn:

- the not-so- unusual daily thunderstorms he encountered, could well be the culprits that spawn great hurricanes.
- rain from Mali and other West African countries, eventually, could be a curse to the Caribbean and the southern coast of the USA, wreaking destruction to property, dislocation of inhabitants, and loss of life.

David decided on August 15, 1979, *"I think I'll leave tomorrow and start my journey westward."*

He traveled from Mali, first as a Jet-Stream, meandering toward the nation of Senegal, on Africa's west coast, then out to the Atlantic Ocean proper. The warm ocean waters, at first, fed David with energy. He was enjoying the journey, so far. For two weeks, he slowly crossed the Atlantic Basin, gradually becoming more intense in the vast expanse of ocean.

On the twenty-second of August, David felt a strange foreboding. *"I feel as if I'm losing control of myself,"* he said, as his wind speed increased to thirty-nine miles per hour.

Weather gurus, by then, spotted him out in the Atlantic, and categorized him as a Tropical Wave. They sent warnings about him throughout the Caribbean Islands. The islanders knew, after years of experience, tropical waves play an important role and are seedlings in formation of hurricanes. At that point, no one in the islands knew at which island David would make land.

Dominica

Dominica is a mountainous Island, of volcanic origin, in the Eastern Caribbean. It has lush vegetation, which explains its nickname, "A Botanist's Paradise." With three hundred and sixty-five rivers, one for every day of the year, rain forests, and acres and acres of banana, coconut, and breadfruit trees, it has also been called, "Nature Isle of the Caribbean."

In 1979, the Commonwealth of Dominica had gained independence from Great Britain only the year before. Nestled between the French-speaking islands of Guadeloupe, to the north, and Martinique, to the south, Dominica's peace-loving people had no idea what would soon befall them.

On August 26th, meteorologists in the region renamed David a Tropical Storm, and warned, "A major storm, originating in West Africa, some five thousand miles away, has formed out in the Atlantic Ocean and is heading for the Caribbean. We predict it will hit Barbados. People on that island should begin to prepare. However, it is advised that all islands in the region remain vigilant, and begin to review their emergency procedures, should it become necessary to mobilize them."

Barbados is a flat island, of coral origin, some two hundred miles south of Dominica. They took the dire weather warning seriously, and began to prepare for the hurricane's arrival. On the island of Dominica, on the other hand, few precautions, if any, were taken. They continued to enjoy the balmy weather there and carried on their routine activities. They felt safe from the possibility of the storm's onslaught since there were no dark clouds evident, or any sign of rain. Further, the storm was predicted to reach Barbados, and not their island.

Meanwhile, David's winds rapidly intensified to seventy-four miles per hour, resulting in his upgrade to Hurricane status on August 28th. By reaching this level, he joined the infamous group dubbed "the most awesome, violent storms on earth."[19]

He began to spin faster and faster in a counter-clockwise direction, while a calm, clear, eye formed in his center. The eye was circular with a diameter nearly twenty miles across. The sea below became unsettled and formed huge waves over one hundred feet high. Bands of clouds converged around the eye, joining the moist air rising from the ocean's surface.

---

19   Braun. 2016. *How do Hurricanes Form?*

On August 29th, David intensified to one hundred and fifty miles per hour, rendering him completely out of control. Although he came close to Barbados, he veered away and moved in a northerly direction, for reasons unknown.

David careened ashore with a fury on the tranquil, sun-drenched island of Dominica that late-August morning. He was the first major hurricane of the 1979 Atlantic hurricane season and was assigned Category Five – <u>Major Hurricane</u> –status when he struck.

"I've finally reached the Caribbean," David said to himself, *"My dream has been fulfilled, but I never intended it to occur in this fashion. My only choice now is to walk through the island, meet people, and try to regain my calm."*

For six long hours, from nine o'clock in the morning, to three in the afternoon, David tramped through every corner and crevice of Dominica, destroying everything in his path.

The formerly placid, fun-loving David, upon reaching Dominica, morphed into a raging monster. He seemed possessed by something evil and was hell-bent on destroying everything in his path. He did not rest until this mission was accomplished. The sound of the wind he produced was deafening and frightening. When the eyewall, which surrounded his eye, passed over the island, there was a temporary calm in the wind. Within minutes, however, David began to rage again. He dropped ten inches of rain over the island, which caused numerous mudslides in several places. The coastlines were eroded, and roads were washed out. Seventy-five percent of the island's crops were destroyed. He raged until he had totally devastated the place.

Trees of all descriptions were uprooted, stripped from the mountains, and laid flat in the aftermath. Debris was strewn everywhere. There was no electricity or piped water. Roads and bridges were blocked. Contact with the outside world was completely disrupted. The shocked population sat motionless outside their flattened, mainly wooden, houses. Slowly, they soaked in the disaster that visited them.

Three quarters of the 75,000 people of the island were left homeless, and fifty-six people were killed.

A group of nursing leaders from throughout the Caribbean islands had gathered in Dominica the day before the storm arrived, to attend a Regional Nurses Conference. Although the hotel in which they stayed was damaged, they made themselves available as first responders immediately after the storm. These dedicated professionals rendered much-welcomed aid at the main hospital in Roseau, the capital. Thank God, they were there to attend to the nearly five thousand injured who showed up for emergency care.

A British military vessel, which happened to be in the region, sent their personnel ashore to also give assistance. They made repairs to the hospital, cleaned up debris from the streets in the town, and helped restore the infrastructure and essential services. The Dominicans were very appreciative of the help received from these two groups of outsiders.

When the hurricane was over, an eerie silence pervaded the island. No words could describe what people saw and felt. The hurricane had stripped them of everything –their food, their clothing, their shelter. Everything was gone. David left them feeling abandoned, alone, and cut off from the rest of the world.

Within days, international relief efforts began, and for many months afterward, the Island slowly moved toward normalcy. However, their lives were forever changed after David visited them. .

Whatever happened to David? you might ask.

Reports showed David continued his deadly assault for many days after leaving Dominica. Aside from the havoc he wreaked, he was silent and no longer shared his inner thoughts with anyone, as before.

Maintaining a Category Five intensity, he cut a path through the Leeward Islands, the northern Caribbean, including Hispaniola (Haiti and the Dominican Republic), Puerto Rico, Cuba, and the Bahamas, then on to the Southeastern coast of the USA. He caused massive loss of life –some two thousand deaths –in the Dominican Republic. As he battered and rammed his way through these countries, an estimated one and one-half billion dollars in agricultural and property damage was attributed to him.

David finally dissipated and died on September 8, 1979. His name was retired because of the untold devastation and high death toll he had caused. It was officially declared that the name "David" should never be used again for an Atlantic Hurricane.[20]

Post-Script

I was present in Dominica when Hurricane David visited the Island on August 29, 1979. I was there, along with my sister, and a group of nurses to attend a Nurses Conference. I experienced the onslaught and witnessed David's devastation first-hand. We barricaded ourselves in the main dining room of our hotel, and fervently prayed the storm would stop raging.

When David's eye passed over the Island, producing a temporary calm, we hurried to a nearby church, seeking better shelter, we thought. Thank God the door of the church was locked. We discovered after the storm, its roof had collapsed inward. Anyone inside the church, would have been killed, instantly. Thank God the church was empty of people at that time.

We retreated from the church and returned to our hotel, finding shelter in a storeroom on the grounds. We rode out the storm in those cramped quarters, until David stopped his tumult. We cherished the safety of that storeroom and it reminded us of Noah's Ark.

When David made landfall, he created a huge storm surge. His high winds, literally, drove the sea to the shore. That action caused water levels to rise and created crashing waves. We could hear the waves pounding as we sheltered in the storeroom.

When the hurricane was over and we exited our place of refuge, we attempted to walk through the neighborhood nearby. It was impossible to do so. The devastation we witnessed was indescribable. We stared in awe at what the forces of nature had done.

We were grateful that, unharmed, we nurses could serve as first responders at the national hospital. God gave us favor and stamina to

---

20 Wikipedia.1979. *David.*

utilize our previous medical knowledge and skills to serve the needs of the Dominican people.

Five days post-hurricane, the Lord opened the doors of a German cargo vessel which carried us, as well as critically ill patients from the hospital, to safety in Barbados.

Hurricane David's Destruction in Dominica, August 29, 1979.[21]

---

21   Photo courtesy of Brooks-LaTouche, Barbados.

Zambia for Jesus

Dedication

This Inspirational Essay is dedicated to the following Pastors and Ministers who welcomed us, showed us kindness, and ensured our comfort and safety during our Missions trip to Zambia:

Dr. Winston and Dr. Gloria Broomes, Grace Assembly of God, Atlantic City, New Jersey
Apostle and Mrs. Nelson Mumba, Lusaka, Zambia
Pastor and Mrs. Boyd Makukula, Chipata, Zambia
Bishop and Mrs. Sky Banda, Kitwe, Zambia, (both now in heaven with the Lord)
Pastor and Mrs. Ngoma, Fusheni Village, Zambia

The Mission

We arrived, at last, on the Continent of Africa, after a ten-hour flight from London. Although the journey was long and tiresome, my eyes never closed throughout the trip. My heart raced with wild anticipation as I contemplated what lay ahead. At long last, two lifelong wishes were being fulfilled: a visit to the mighty Continent, our Motherland, and a desire to do missions work abroad.

The year was 2005 when my husband, Neville, and I got the telephone call, inviting us to join long-time friends, Pastors Winston and Gloria Broomes, on a short-term missions trip to the nation of Zambia. The small country of 14 million souls is nestled in the southern portion of Africa, north of its neighbor, South Africa.

We accepted the invitation without hesitation and made plans to depart. Before going, I devoured every book and article I could find about Zambia. I read about its people, customs, languages, health care system, and a host of other tidbits to enhance understanding when we arrived there. The literature I read informed me Zambia is landlocked and is surrounded by eight neighboring countries, Democratic Republic of Congo, Malawi, Tanzania, Botswana, Namibia, Mozambique, Angola, and Zimbabwe.

As I read, I reflected on my old geography lessons in school. I recalled Northern Rhodesia (now Zambia), and Southern Rhodesia (now Zimbabwe), had been a single country before it gained independence from Britain in 1964. These two nations exist today as peaceful neighbors.

We obtained the required anti-yellow fever and malaria immunizations in preparation for our journey. We also raised funds among relatives and friends to help us bless the people to whom we would minister. The money would provide food and bring them items of clothing.

Finally, the big day arrived, and our journey began. We flew non-stop from Dallas to London, where we spent five days with friends. We continued our journey and landed in Lusaka, early in the morning. This teeming capital city of Zambia is inhabited by one million souls.

"I can't believe we are finally here in the Motherland," I exclaimed to my husband.

"Thank God for our safe journey," he replied, "Our dream has come true."

"Welcome to Zambia. Welcome to Africa," said a man who smiled broadly as he approached us.

The tall, slender gentleman was Apostle Nelson Mumba, one of the local pastors, and director of the Christian Radio Station, who came to meet us at the airport. He and his wife, Cecilia, hosted us and ensured we were safe and comfortable throughout our time in Zambia.

"Pastors Winston and Gloria arrived yesterday," he informed. "We are so excited to have them back with us in Zambia. It's been a long time since they have been here."

Our friends, the Broomes, were seasoned missionaries who lived in Zambia many years before. Their youngest son was born there. After Zambia, they were long-term missionaries to Kenya, in East

Africa, as well. They preached the gospel throughout those countries and established churches and bible schools.

As we traveled throughout Zambia, it was clear to us how much the Broomes were respected and treasured by the people. In fact, churches they established still flourished. Young people who accepted Christ under their ministry were now pastors and church leaders. What a privilege and honor it was to have been included in the mission with them!

Our three-week sojourn in Zambia took us to many corners of the predominantly rural nation. Despite rough, unpaved roads, absence of sanitary facilities, and dangerous checkpoints, our visits to those far-flung places were more than worth the difficult journeys. Though spent and weary when we arrived, the local pastors and their wives were always gracious as they greeted us.

The tiny village of Chipata was our first missions stop. We arrived there about eight hours after leaving Lusaka.

Pastor Boyd Makukula and his wife, Sarah, received us with open arms. "Welcome to Chipata. We're so glad to have you here with us."

Members of their congregation prepared food for us and had waited several hours for our arrival. In the worship service that followed the meal, they danced before the Lord, dressed in their colorful native apparel, and sang fervently:

Zambia for Jesus, hear the battle cry! Zambia for Jesus, we'll fight until we die.
We never will give in, while the people live in sin, Zambia for Jesus, we must win!
Chipata for Jesus, hear the battle cry! Chipata for Jesus, we'll fight until we die.
We never will give in, while the people live in sin, Chipata for Jesus, we must win!

They sang in English, first, then, in Chibemba, the language of the Bemba people —the largest tribe in Zambia. This catchy and meaningful tune remained with us throughout our time there. We sang it often in the van which carried us to various points of the mission.

Our greatest joy was ministering to the people there in Chipata who found Christ under the mighty and effective preaching of Pastor Dr. Winston Broomes. As we prayed for them on the altar, they cried out in confession of sins, and resolved to serve Him.

On our way back to Lusaka next morning, we stopped at Fisheni Village, on the outskirts of Chipata. Pastor Sarah Makukula accompanied us as far as this point. There we were able to experience authentic village life. We found a women's bible study in progress. Though seated on straw mats on the dirt floor of their church, without the benefit of chairs or benches, the ladies received the Word of God with gladness, with shouts of "Amen!"

Women's Mission, Fisheni Village, Zambia

As we moved further into the village, we watched as women worked outdoors. They pounded corn, known as maize, and pumped water from wells for their households.

Women of Fisheni Village, Zambia

We were introduced to Pastor Ngoma, of El Shaddai Temple there, and his wife. "Please come into our home. We are glad to have you here with us."

Their house had an intricately woven thatched roof. Its mud walls allowed the house to remain cool, despite the heat outdoors. Their children played outdoors, while we fellowshipped inside.

A few days later, our experience was quite different when we ministered in the small town of Kitwe. Bishop Sky Banda and his wife Sophie, who are both now in heaven, pastored a large suburban church in that area, known as the Copper Belt.

"This was once the location of a booming copper industry," Bishop Sky Banda explained. "Several of the mines here, once government-owned, now sit abandoned."

"Please tell us more about this," I asked.

"Years ago, the mines became privatized. Copper is now being extracted from some of the larger mines and is being exported abroad again. Zambian copper is said to be one of the purest in the world."

While in Kitwe, we gladly shared the gospel to young children and older youth. They listened with rapt attention as we spoke to them. It was clear their hearts were open to receive the Word of God. I marveled at how disciplined the young people were as they sat for a prolonged time, listening to our messages.

We learned from our hosts, and saw for ourselves, that people there still need the Lord.

A highlight of our Zambian visit was a trip to the hamlet of Livingstone, named after the famous British medical missionary and explorer, David Livingstone. He is said to have brought Christianity to Zambia in the nineteenth century. While there, we took a brief break from ministry for rest and relaxation.

After visiting the Livingstone Museum, we ate a wonderful lunch on the banks of the Zambezi River. The mighty Victoria Falls, dubbed one of the "Seven Natural Wonders of the World," cascades downward into the river and separates Zambia from Zimbabwe. Access to the Falls can be gained from either side.

The Glorious Victoria Falls, Livingstone, Zambia

The Zambezi, fourth largest river in Africa, originates in north-west Zambia and flows through six countries, en-route to the Indian Ocean. Running through many game reserves and national parks, it sustains animals, birds, and fish species along its banks.

As we viewed activities on the river, we saw tourists kayaking, canoeing, and white-water rafting. We watched to see if anyone was bungee jumping – a popular sport at that location. While there, we saw no one participating in this extreme sport. But a friend of ours, back in the USA, told us she had bungee jumped a few years earlier, at that very spot. It was her fortieth birthday, and, as a sports enthusiast, she gave herself this birthday present. With great excitement, she reflected on her experience as follows:

"At the center of the Victoria Falls Bridge, the Jumpmaster, first, attached ankle and body harnesses to me. I was then connected to a thick elastic bungee cord that was securely affixed to the bridge. Jump workers guided me to the edge of the platform for the count.

I could hear the roaring of the rapids of the Zambezi River, which flowed through the Bakota Gorge below. I was told the river was full of crocodiles, but I put that out of my mind. At the count of five, I extended my arms straight out in front of me, and leapt off the bridge. I plummeted, head-first, some 365 feet down toward the river. I saw rainbows coming from the Falls in the background. The cord bounced and swayed, allowing me to freefall a few times, for a few seconds. I experienced a spectacular adrenaline rush before it was over. Jump workers pulled me back up, then guided me to the underside of the bridge, unclipped my harness, and led me back to safety. Needless to say, it was the most awesome and unforgettable experience of my life."

It was clear bungee jumping is not for the fainthearted. However, we learned hundreds of people from all over the world go there to take the awesome plunge.

Next, we walked along a concrete footpath, then stood in awe and watched the power of the mighty Victoria Falls. The sights and sounds were thrilling. Local people call it "Mosi-oa-Tunya" – "the Smoke that Thunders." Extending 5500 feet wide and 354 feet high, it is con-sidered one of the world's largest waterfalls. We donned raincoats and head coverings to protect ourselves from the shimmering, rain-bow-colored spray that emitted from the Falls.

A few kilometers upstream, we took an exciting Safari – the adven-ture of a lifetime!

"My name is Buxton," a trained guide at the entrance to the for-est, introduced himself." I can see you are visitors, and you should not drive into the forest by yourselves. I can be your guide."

With a bit of caution, we accepted his services and he joined us in our vehicle. Buxton, who proved to be quite knowledgeable, led us deep into the mysterious wilderness.

We soon found ourselves up close and personal with the animals that inhabited the area. Before long, two mighty giraffes stood solidly in our path. Unlike the situation in a zoo, there was no barrier whatso-ever between us and them."Giraffes grow up to twelve feet tall. Baby giraffes are about six feet at birth," Buxton, calmly, informed.

We waited while the two giraffes observed us until they were ready to move on.

Safari, Zambia Africa

With much enthusiasm, over several hours, we filmed, at leisure, monkeys, elephants, hippos, rhinos, wildebeests, gazelles, zebras, and a host of other wonderful creatures, that lived there in peace and quiet together. We were told that no wild cats, such as lions, tigers, or leopards, inhabited that game reserve.

"Turn your vehicle around," Buxton, suddenly, cautioned our driver, in the late afternoon. "A herd of elephants has spotted us. The daddy elephant is flapping his ears, and this could mean trouble."

We certainly did not linger and followed Buxton's advice. We reversed our vehicle in a hurry and he led us to the far edge of the jungle. From there, we exited the park. All of us agreed it had been an unforgettable time spent.

We returned to Lusaka, the capital, as we neared the end of our mission to Zambia. You guessed it, my trip would not have been complete without a visit to the maternity ward of the University Teaching Hospital there. As a midwife, despite considerable red tape, I was granted an appointment.

My fellow midwives there were very gracious. "Midwives are the same all over the world, they declared. We are a great sisterhood."

I felt right at home as they toured me through the ward and demonstrated their techniques for bringing babies into the world. It was an eyeopener and a wonderful learning opportunity for me.

How thrilled I was when asked to preach in a large evangelistic crusade held on our final Sunday there. I was provided an interpreter, who translated my message into the Chibemba language. Although English is the official language of the nation, I was surprised to learn there are seventy-two ethnic groups in the country—each with its own language!

I will never forget the spontaneous village dance, in which the congregation engaged, before I began my sermon. It was lively and enthusiastic. We visitors joined in by moving to the lively music and catchy rhythms.

The people who attended the crusade received the Word of God and responded readily. Healings and deliverances were evident. I thank God for the privilege of having participated in that way.

My husband and I spent our final day shopping the busy streets and markets. We bought carvings, intricately crafted by local artisans, and souvenir items. These precious mementos are displayed in our home now—each one keeping the wonderful story of our trip to Zambia alive.

As we flew homeward, we indeed thanked God for the opportunity to have served Him on the Missions trip. Our hearts remain with the Zambian people. Apostle Nelson Mumba, and his wife, Cecilia, have become our lifelong friends.

Full Circle

Sometimes life brings us Full Circle. We start in one direction and follow a certain path. We are filled with ideas and visions of what we will encounter and what we will become. To our surprise, sometimes years later, we end up right back at the point at which we began. It's as if history has looped back on itself.

Why might this happen? It might be, as we moved on, life just got too busy for us to have noticed how far we had gone or what we had accomplished. Perhaps we got stuck in memories of a long-disregarded era, or in the fantasy world of childhood. We might have gotten caught up, nostalgically, remembering a life we lived with those who mentored or inspired us.

When we return to the place of origin, it's almost startling to see the parallels between what the beginning was and what is now.

> *"....and you shall return every man unto his possession, and you shall return every man unto his family."*
>
> Leviticus 25:10 Holy Bible. American Standard Version (ASV).

A Hospital in Harlem

Years ago, when I began my career as a public health nurse, I was assigned to a Junior High School by the Department of Health. My duties included screening students for health issues, assisting doctors during medical examinations, counseling parents on good family health practices, and serving as a resource for teachers and other school personnel. I worked there two days per week since I also had duties elsewhere, including mother-baby care in clinics, as well as making home visits.

The school was in East Harlem, New York City, on the edge of Marcus Garvey Park. I loved my work there and all the activities it entailed. The medical office was always a busy place. The students were ages twelve to fourteen, on the cusp of adolescence. Many were flapping their juvenile "wings" to see how much they could get away with.

The school was relatively well-organized by the then administrators. Teachers ran the gamut from those who had a genuine interest in their students, to those only holding down a job until something better came along. Although the ethnic mix of students comprised ninety percent African American, ten percent Hispanic, (largely Puerto Rican), and zero percent Caucasian, that of the administrators and faculty included ninety percent Caucasian, ten percent African American, and one percent Hispanic. Those disparate numbers made for frequent cultural clashes between students and faculty, and parents and administrators. There seemed to be no attempt to even the ethnic mixes to enable better understanding and communication.

At the time, Harlem was undergoing great transition. It was the late 1960s, and economic conditions were extremely difficult. Some parents left their children unsupervised, in the after-school hours, because they were at work. Thus, a fair number of young people were left to their own devices, and got into trouble with neighbors, peers, and the police.

It was the height of the Civil Rights and Black Power movements as well, with marches and demonstrations. Civil disobedience, led by leaders, such as Rev. Dr. Martin Luther King Jr., and Malcolm X, rightly, motivated the local citizens to demand equal rights.

The Vietnam War was also raging during that period, with many enlisting from the Harlem area. The war precipitated student unrest on college campuses, with calls for justice, also, on American soil.

Unscrupulous drug dealers saw vulnerable Harlem as an easy target, and slowly infiltrated the community with illegal drugs. At the time, heroin ruled as king. Dozens of young people died from overdoses of heroin and other drugs. Teenage pregnancy was high and so was the rate of school dropouts, even at the junior high school level.

Health in the Harlem community was at a low point. Diabetes, hypertension, and other chronic illnesses affected older members. Tuberculosis was rampant, as well as sexually transmitted diseases, among younger people. Nutritionally adequate food was scarce in the local supermarkets, because Black people were the predominant clientele. Merchants and shopkeepers reserved better quality food for White people, who lived downtown, or further uptown in Washington Heights.

It was against this backdrop of health and social decline, I worked back then. In the school, I struggled to teach students sound health practices, and pushed them to beat the odds, if they could, to become healthy, vibrant citizens. I encouraged teachers to make efforts toward instructing students on good physical and emotional health, as well. Parents came to me for advice even beyond the scope of medical issues. I was able to refer them to other social service programs. My medical office at the school, therefore, became a virtual Hospital in Harlem.

Fast-forward twenty years. A lot happened in my life as far as career development and training. I had also spent several years abroad providing health services in the Caribbean.

When I returned to the USA and lived, again, in Harlem, I discovered that the Junior High school, where my medical office was located, had been closed, permanently, by the local Board of Education. I learned that the still structurally-sound building had been placed on auction and was made available for purchase by the highest bidder. A church in the neighborhood, seeking larger facilities, bought, and converted it into a thriving spiritual oasis.

When my family and I looked for a place of worship, we felt led to join Bishop Ezra Williams, Pastor, in worshipping in the old school building, they had purchased, remodeled, and renamed, Bethel Gospel Assembly (BGA). Not only did it meet our spiritual criteria, but it was also located walking distance from where we lived. I knew, at once, I had come full circle to work and minister in a Hospital in Harlem.

By the time our family joined Bethel, the church had already established a plethora of programs, designed to meet the needs of the local community. Although, by then, the Vietnam War and the earlier civil unrest had come to an end, drugs, crime, homelessness, and decaying housing, were among the social problems that were decimating Harlem neighborhoods, creating urgent calls for help and assistance.

Harlem Hospital, located a few blocks north of the church, is one of New York City's public hospital centers. It has been operating since the late Eighteen-Hundreds, providing maternity care, as well as emergency, specialty, and general care to people in the surrounding neighborhood. It serves as a trauma, burn, heart, and asthma center. Daily, its emergency services are at capacity, and its operating rooms are at maximum functioning. The Harlem community takes pride in knowing Harlem Hospital is there as a monument of reliable care for the poor and underserved.

What is a hospital? It is a health institution that provides urgent care, by medical, nursing, and other staff, using specialized supplies and equipment. It attends to accident and fire victims, and those who require intensive or long-term care. It also meets the immediate needs of people with psychiatric emergencies.

Harlem Hospital provided the above-mentioned services to the poor and downtrodden of the area. But what happened to those discharged from the hospital? Thankfully, Bethel Gospel Assembly (BGA), among other agencies, churches, and social services, was there to meet the tremendous need for follow-up care. Indeed, they addressed the critical social and emotional needs of those directed their way.

In the late Nineteen-Eighties to early Nineteen-Nineties, the five-year period we were members of BGA, before relocating to Texas, not only were we thrilled to be part of the tremendous high-spirited worship, in which everyone participated, on Sunday mornings, but also the captivating preaching of Pastor Ezra, as he was affectionately known. In addition, we willingly participated in the astounding array of services offered the community by that sanctuary located on Madison Avenue and One Hundred and Twentieth Street.

BETHEL GOSPEL ASSEMBLY: A HOSPITAL IN HARLEM. 1980s.

Every Saturday morning, faithful church members, who were engaged in the Evangelism and Outreach Ministry, organized a feeding service for the homeless outside of Marcus Garvey Park. Lively gospel music was played to attract those in need. Preaching of the gospel was at the core. Food, including sandwiches, desserts, and hot drinks, comprised the breakfasts distributed to the hundreds who came. Those in need were directed to the Clothing ministry at the church. To those who found Christ, invitations were given to continue in the faith by attending services on Sundays.

An organized Christian Counseling service was made available to members of the community. The program provided individual, group, and family counseling, and served as a referral source for those in need of legal and other services. Several hundred individuals and families made use of the service.

I was extremely impressed by the in-house rehabilitation program for homeless men, located in ample facilities in the basement of the church. It was organized and run by a middle-aged couple, who lived on the premises with the men enrolled in the program. A requirement was attendance by the clients at all programs and spiritual services offered by the church. This included Sunday School, Worship Service, Bible Studies, and Counseling. The willingness of the men to incorporate themselves into these activities was amazing to me. Most of all, after the approximate six to-nine-month residence in the program, the majority remained and became integral parts of the church! Some even found partners among church members, married, and continued to live useful lives. It was a real success story.

A fully reformed ex-offender, and member of the church, had a heart for those incarcerated. He found an available house in the neighborhood, organized a fund-raising program, and provided rooms for temporary housing of those just released from prison. At the time, it was named Jericho House. His ministry and those who joined with him, were committed to ministering to ex-offenders and their families, through encouragement, education, and empowerment.

The church's Women Moved with Compassion ministry faithfully supported all these ministries. One service they provided, in association with the Clothing Ministry, was laundering and ironing the clothing donated. Periodically, they held an Iron-A-Thon, in which ironing ladies competed to see who could iron the most items of clothing. Prizes were given at the end.

Although our family moved to Texas with much anticipation, the change was bitter-sweet because of the disconnected feeling we experienced. Not only had we left close family and friends, we also said "farewell" to our Hospital in Harlem.

Oh, the Places You'll Go

My husband, and I adopted our son when he was six months old. Prior to that he lived in foster care. I am grateful to the foster family that took care of him. It appears they nurtured him well. When we finally met him, and the social worker placed him in my arms, I wept with pure joy. As I held him, he scanned my face for a moment, then smiled at me with his lovely brown eyes.

He seemed to be saying, "I've been waiting for you, Mom."

I said to myself, *I'm finally a mother and this is my baby to love forever.*

As our son grew, we noticed he exhibited delays in certain areas. He wasn't keeping pace with his peers with respect to achieving his developmental milestones. For example, he did not walk by the time expected. At his first birthday party, unlike his toddler pals who were stepping around, he was still crawling. He surprised us though on April Fools Day, when, at age fourteen months, with hands outstretched, he stood up took his first faltering steps alone down our hallway. With a twinkle in his eye, he appeared to say, "I was only fooling the two of you. I was waiting for this day to come, to surprise you."

By the age of three, our son was not saying words, or talking and speaking clearly. He only pointed at objects and made muffled sounds. We also were concerned about his motor coordination. Our pediatrician recommended speech therapy and music and movement classes.

"Will he ever walk steadily? Will he be able, someday, to cross a busy street by himself?" we asked ourselves.

Regarding academics, our son struggled with mathematics and reading comprehension. Both he and his teachers were frustrated. One of his teachers, who, no doubt, had no training in working with kids with learning differences, wanted to have him removed from her class and sent back to the grade he was in the year before. She seemed to want him out of her way. We insisted he remain in his proper grade and searched for resources to help him master the skills he needed.

We were disappointed to discover a dearth of information, at that time in the mid- 1980s, on strategies for helping children with academic delays. Such was needed to facilitate student learning, and, eventually, becoming successful in life. A counselor referred us to a small private school which had a motherly headmistress. He told us other kids he had referred to her previously were achieving success there.

Our hearts plummeted when we visited the location and discovered the "school" was the headmistress's converted garage! It was poorly lit, had a few worn desks and chairs, and little indication of a robust learning environment. Because of our son's easygoing attitude, he was willing to say good- bye to his friends at the school he was attending and transfer to this one. He understood how important it was for him to learn.

Due to the small teacher: student ratio, he had some degree of success. We knew his time at the school had come to an abrupt end after only one year of study there, however. We were horrified one afternoon at what we found when we picked him up after school. When I saw the raised weals on his arm, I demanded to know what transpired. The headmistress admitted, reluctantly, her adult, special needs son, had beat our child with a heavy tree branch because he hadn't referred to him as "Sir." Only pleas from the distressed parents kept us from reporting the school to the authorities. They promised to ensure no future contact between their son and any of the students enrolled.

Shortly thereafter, we found a school for our son which had programs and curricula designed for kids experiencing learning difficulties. The teachers had been specially trained in that area as well.

He worked hard to overcome every challenge, no matter how hard it was. He put forth great effort and his winning personality was also a sustaining factor. He had a positive outlook and an ability to quickly make friends. These served him well and endeared him to his teachers and his classmates. He formed lifelong friendships with several.

During the high school years, our son was able to access certain enrichment programs: one for African American youth, who had an interest in Broadcast Journalism; another for those with a flair for creative writing. Our son excelled at both, and even received the "Top Gun" Award for the former.

Another challenge came when he was diagnosed in mid-childhood with Attention Deficit Disorder. Not much was written about this issue back then in the early 1990s. We pressed and found research results which helped us better understand it. We learned people with this diagnosis can face lifelong challenges. Although, by adulthood, most learn to compensate in various ways, the underlying difficulties often persist, because it is a disorder of the brain. This could prove limiting for such persons when they enter the work situation.

This certainly proved true for our son, later, when working at certain jobs. At times, he encountered difficulty with supervisors, when they mistook his inability to stay focused, for carelessness or lack of interest.

My husband and I beamed with pride when our son graduated from high school and enrolled in our local community college. After completing two years of study, he attended a four-year college for two additional years. He then completed a technical program in Broadcast Journalism.

After a brief stint working at a radio station, our son found his niche in the Customer Service field. Right away, he clicked with clients and managers. It wasn't long before he received an award for Regional Best All-around Customer Service Employee. What a boost it was to his self-esteem! He returned home from the Awards Ceremony, held in California, with his engraved crystal trophy and his certificate in hand.

At age thirty-nine, our son called it quits with the single life and took to himself a bride. He found a companion who promised to be his helpmate. For years I prayed God would send someone who would help him stay on track, be supportive of him, and be kind to him, as he also is kind. Of Interest, the woman he married was also adopted as a baby. Although, growing up under entirely different circumstances, the two soulmates found each other, and, like homing pigeons, have come full circle home.

Not long ago, I attended the lovely marriage ceremony of my son and daughter-in-law, held in a beautifully converted movie theatre. As mother-of-the-bridegroom, I accepted the long-stemmed red rose he gave me. While we danced together, in my mind's eye, I was holding my baby boy once again and bursting with happiness. I could hardly believe my son had come of age, and turned out to be a stable, mature, and responsible man. My prayer has certainly been answered.

Allman Origins: Zoom Connections

A stranger, named Michael, sent me an email recently. I opened it because his last name, Allman, was familiar to me, and the email came through a reputable website. As I read further, he explained he was a genealogy buff and had been trying to connect those named Allman for a long time. He invited me to join him and several others, who have Allman roots, on a Zoom meeting scheduled within a few days.

Intrigued, I agreed to join the meeting. My birth name is Allman, and I have long been interested in family connections. I already had built a sizeable Allman family tree.

At the meeting, I was thrilled to see, again, or meet for the first time, several cousins with Allman roots, who live across the USA and in other countries. It was also good to meet Melanie, finally, a cousin in California, with whom I'd communicated in the past. I also saw my closer cousins, Edwina, Toni, Wilbert, Angela, and Ondre. These are spread throughout the corners of the USA and Canada, including Georgia, Texas, North Carolina, and Toronto. I had not talked with some of these folks for quite some time. I communicated with some after we had taken our DNA tests and emerged as cousin matches.

It's a fact that a large percentage of people with the name Allmans in the USA, like my dad, have roots in Barbados, in the Caribbean. When they immigrated here, of course, they brought the name Allman with them. What fascinated me at the first Zoom meeting I attended was the number of folks with Allman roots whose origins are in Guyana, South America. Years ago, my father told me relatives of his, named Allman, who, in prior generations, had moved to then, British Guiana, (now Guyana), stayed there permanently. Many had not been heard from again. Could our present group of Zoomers be part of that long-lost tribe of Allmans?

Perhaps, about fifty years ago, after my father had long immigrated to New York, he met two families who had the name Allman. Members of both families told my dad they had ancestors who had left Barbados for Guyana, before coming to the USA. Although these two families and my dad were never able to identify their exact connections, they became close and referred to each other as "family." They continued to visit each other for several years before they passed on.

My dad met another Allman group from Massachusetts, who originated in Barbados, although they had come from different Parishes in the island. They also became our "family." We attended family occasions, like weddings and funerals, spent vacations together, but never specifically identified how we were connected. There remain a few other people in that category. Uncle Percy, who has now transitioned, is one of these. He visited us from time to time during my childhood and we embraced him as family. We got to know his close family, Aunt Ilene, and Shirley in Barbados, also.

On the Zoom call, I was delighted to meet several new persons, who now live in different countries, who have roots in Guyana, and have connections with the Allman name. Alift, who has a strong British accent, which I love to hear, resides in England. Several others do as well. Michael, our fearsome Zoom Master, and others, reside in Delaware, California, New Jersey, Washington, DC, Barbados, and Guyana.

I was excited by the exchange of information regarding our Allman ancestors on my first Zoom call. So, I invited my siblings and other cousins to join us as we continue to meet. Among them are Marilyn, Luther, and Barbara. Marilyn, a retired university professor, is quite interested in having "centimorgan" connections explained among cousin matches. Centimorgan is a DNA term in which units measure genetic linkage.

Luther has been interested in the subject of slavery in Barbados for a while. He is trying to learn more about a White slave master there who had the last name, Allman. Luther is outraged that this man was paid money for each of his eleven slaves when he was forced to release them in 1838, four years after Emancipation in Barbados.

As a musician, Luther is also interested in ascertaining how many of our "cousin buddies" on Zoom might have music in their DNA.

He inherited his musical talent from our dad. We've already discovered several persons among our Zoom group who are in the nursing profession.

At a recent meeting, we shared our individual genetic experiences, and I was thrilled when Michael provided more information about a common ancestor, most of us have, named John Thony Allman. The majority already had him on our family trees. The records show he was born in Barbados around 1810, about twenty-four years prior to the abolition of slavery there, which happened in 1834. On my tree, he is identified as my fourth great- grandfather.

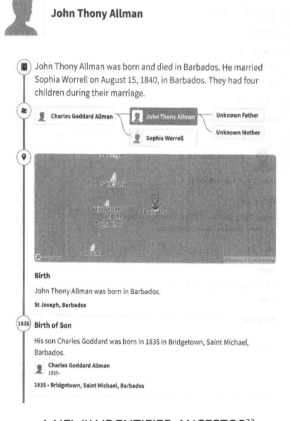

A NEWLY-IDENTIFIED ANCESTOR[22]

---

22 Ancestry Archives.

Once we highlighted this common ancestor, Michael was able to show us our respective progenitors, generation by generation, in Barbados. He identified three brothers in his own tree, who had left Barbados and were among those who migrated to Guyana. Finally, Barbados and Guyana were reunited!

Despite the documented John Thony Allman connection, there are several, among us who meet on Zoom, who yet are unable to identify exact ties with each other. There are also gaps in information among those who bear the Allman name in Panama, the USA, and other countries. We are confident, though, we will tunnel through these so-called "brick walls", as we continue to meet and evoke oral memories we've heard in the past from parents and grandparents.

We will continue to meet, "fortnightly," as our British kin would say. "See you in two weeks," say the Americans.

Pockets of Sunshine

During my thirty-eight years as a midwife, I was privileged to take care of thousands of expectant women, as they anticipated the joys of motherhood. Some were having babies for the first time, while others were already mothers of ten or more children. There were twins that arrived, unexpectedly, and some that arrived feet-first, rather than in the normal head-first position. Some mothers were ill with other health problems, while others experienced complications after giving birth.

My delivery logs indicate I helped moms deliver over four thousand babies into the world. Assisting them in taking their first faltering breaths, was always amazing to me. I thanked God every time for using my hands in this way in supporting brand-new life. I gave each one my blessing. Thank God, I never lost a mom under my care, and I never lost a baby. That was a miracle, in itself.

Besides the babies I delivered, there were many, in addition, I attended in other ways. These include my grandchildren, great-grandchildren, god-children, those I Christened and offered up to the Lord, and those whose parents I taught in Childbirth classes, following which, I served as Labor Coach, and helped them welcome their infants into the world.

I call my babies my Pockets of Sunshine. The memories of their births bring me much joy and satisfaction. They take me to a happy place. Several of these stand out. I Include in my "sunshine" group some special ones: a grandchild, my two great- grandchildren, one who called me "Church Grandma," and a newborn that required special care.

This section's essays allow you to hear my special babies tell their own stories. Listen, and you will find what they say inspiring.

As a mother comforts her child, so will I comfort you; and you will be comforted..."

Holy Bible Isaiah 66:13. New international Version.(NIV)

Marcus

Where were you, Doctor?

I, Marcus, arrived on an Autumn day, September 29, 1991, in New York City. My parents, Allison and Maurice, were filled with anticipation of my birth. I was their first child, and they wanted the best care they could find. My mom faithfully attended the doctor and ate all the right foods to keep me healthy as I grew inside of her. Grandma Dorothea, and Grandpa Ezra beamed with pride as they watched Mom getting larger in her middle section.

A nurse-midwife at the church was asked to conduct prenatal classes for the many families expecting babies at that time. The classes were great fun. I could hear the couples laughing as they exchanged common experiences. I laughed, too, although they did not know I was listening. In the classes, mom and dad joined the others, down on the floor, on pillows and blankets, as they practiced their breathing techniques, in anticipation of the birthing experience.

The couples huffed and puffed, trying to get it right. They asked lots of questions in the class and our midwife tried to answer them all. At the end of the six weeks of classes, mom and dad were ready for me to put in my appearance.

The morning of my birth, Dad took Mom to the hospital. The nurses notified her doctor she was there, in labor. It was a Sunday morning, and Grandpa, who was Pastor, and Grandma, went to church for the service. They asked Mom and Dad to call them just as soon as I arrived.

Meanwhile, our instructor midwife also went to church that morning. They, later, told me that Grandma went over to her during the service and let her know I was about to be born. Then, Grandma just stood there and gave her a look that said," I'd love for you to go to the hospital to be with Allison."

Our midwife did not hesitate and came right away to the hospital. Mom's doctor was nowhere in sight. In fact, he did not even make it there before I was born!

Moments after my midwife arrived, I pushed my way into the world. I guess I was waiting for her to get there! I let out a lusty cry for all to hear. Mom and Dad were ecstatic that I was healthy and lively. The news spread rapidly to the church and to our family.

I am so glad things worked out the way they did. My midwife called me her "special baby" and I called her "Church Grandma."

By the way, Where Were You, Doctor?

INFANT MARCUS LE GARE

ALLISON AND MARCUS

Twin Cousins

We Did It Again

Hello there, please allow us to introduce ourselves:

"I'm Alexis,"

"I'm Alexandria."

We call ourselves "Twin Cousins," and we approve this message.

"Twin Cousins." Sounds odd, doesn't it? You probably always thought twins were siblings. How, then, can we be twin cousins?

Let us tell you our story.

We were born on the same day, July 15, 1996, in Dallas, Texas. We looked strikingly alike for a long time after we were born, and people always thought we were twins. Our moms dressed us alike, we took photos together, and we got along just fine.

BABY TWIN COUSINS, ALEXANDRIA (Left) and ALEXIS (Right)

We think our grandma was more excited about us being born than our moms were. We were her first two grandchildren and she decided we should call her "Abuela."

Abuela was from Puerto Rico and could speak both Spanish and English. On the day we were born, however, she was so wound-up, she spoke only Spanish. She told us she'd prefer if the two of us would speak Spanish – especially to her, but our main language is English. We understand most of what she says in Spanish, though, and we're proud of our Puerto Rican heritage.

Alexis:

I arrived first—four hours before Alexandria did. Our moms gave birth in two different hospitals. But they were right down the street from each other.

Of course, Abuela was right there with my mom, her daughter.

Out in the waiting room, she chatted to my grandpa, in Spanish,

"No puedo esperar a ver a mi nieta. Quiero abrazarla, apretarla, darle de comer, y la aman todo a la vez."

("I can't wait to see my granddaughter. I want to hold her, squeeze her, feed her, and love her all at once.")

Together they prayed, asking for God's blessings as I was about to enter the world,

Querido Dios en el cielo, ayuda a nuestra hija, por favor
(Dear God in heaven, help our daughter, please.)

Meanwhile, at the other hospital, my uncle's wife was also about to give birth. He had called Abuela, his mom, earlier to let her know they were on their way to the hospital.

While waiting for me to arrive, Abuela grew curious about what was going on at the other hospital.

Me pregunto lo que está pasando allí. Tengo que llamar al hospital para averiguar."

(I wonder what's going on over there. I need to call the hospital to find out).

Before long, Abuela got her wish when I, her first grandchild, screamed my way into the world.

Alexandria:

Next, it was my turn to be born. Mom later told me she had a happy, healthy pregnancy and there were no complications. She asked my granny Grace, a midwife, to be there with her when I was born. Granny came right away and helped make mom feel comfortable. My dad was nervous because I was his first child and he had never seen a baby born before. Granny helped him stay calm also, while mom did all the work – doing the breathing exercises Granny taught her.

Mom had wanted to give birth to me without the help of drugs. She thought she could handle her contractions without them.

Years after, Granny told me, with a laugh, "Your mom wasn't as brave as she thought she would be. It wasn't long after her labor started, she begged me to get the doctor to give her some medications. When she got them, she settled right down."

Just as Mom was ready to push, the door to the labor room crashed open and who do you think came rushing in? Abuela, of course! She jabbered away in Spanish, but mom didn't know a word she said. My dad asked his mother to please calm down.

"You can push now, the doctor told Mom. Your baby is ready to come."

Mom gave a giant push, and out I came. I was a tiny baby. I didn't weigh a lot, but I was healthy.

Abuela was beside herself with joy, "*Dos nietas, nacidas el mismo día!*"

("*Two granddaughters, both born on the same day!*")

Alexis and Alexandria:

Over the years, the two of us drifted, somewhat, apart. We moved to different cities and saw little of each other, except on special occasions.

Fast forward eighteen years.

It was time for us twin cousins to graduate from high school.

Wouldn't you know it: although we attended different high schools, our schools scheduled our respective graduations on the same day! They would be held at different venues, however, and at different times of the day.

Once again, Abuela wanted to be at both graduations. She was so happy her two oldest grandchildren had reached this milestone.

"*Cómo vamos a hacer esto?*

("How are we going to do this?") She asked our grandpa.

"Supongo que tendrás que cortarte por la mitad!"

("I guess you'll have to cut yourself in half!"), he laughed.

Alexis:

My graduation ceremony was scheduled first. Abuela and Abuelo were right there and waived proudly as I marched in with my class. I winked at them as I went to the podium to receive my diploma. As I returned to my seat, I could see them hurrying out. I knew they were trying to get to Alexandria's graduation, thirty miles away, in time to see her receive her diploma.

Alexandria:

Well, graduation day is finally here. My friends and my family are here to see me march. I'm glad my cap and gown are red- my favorite color. I decided to wear five-inch high heels to make me look taller. I wonder if Abuela and Abueio will make it on time?

If they are here, I sure can't see them among the people in this huge crowd.

I couldn't believe what I heard when the Principal called my name, and I went forward to get my diploma.

"Esa es nuestra nieta! Gracias a Dios, gracias a Dios!"

("That's our granddaughter! Thank God, thank God!")

When I looked into the crowd, I saw both of my grandparents standing and waving, and shouting as loud as they could, the same thing over and over again. I was, somewhat, embarrassed, but I knew they meant well. I'm glad I made them so happy.

Alexandria and Alexis:

The day after our graduation ceremonies was a glorious day. We twin cousins celebrated in style. Our moms got together and planned a lovely luncheon, at a well-known restaurant. Those family members who could make it were there.

I'm sure you will have guessed by now, we twin cousins were the life of the party. We wore matching outfits, ate a lot, cut our cakes, and opened our many gifts.

Abuela, with tears in her eyes, insisted on making a speech:

"Recuerdo el día, hace dieciocho años, cuando nacieron mis dos nietas. Alexis vino primero, luego Alejandría. Aquí estamos, dieciocho años después, para celebrar sus graduaciones de la escuela secundaria. Una vez más, Alexis se graduó primero, luego Alexandria segundo - ambos en el mismo día. ¡Dios realmente tiene sentido del humor! Pero estoy muy orgulloso de ambos.

(I remember the day, eighteen years ago, when my two granddaughters were born. Alexis came first, then Alexandria. Here we are, eighteen years later, to celebrate their high school graduations. Again, Alexis graduated first, then Alexandria second, both on the same day. God really has a sense of humor! But I'm so proud of both of them.")

After the party, we twin cousins hugged each other, high-fived, cried, and said, "We did it again!"

After that, we went out to face the world.

TWIN COUSINS, ALEXIS AND ALEXANDRIA, All GROWN UP:
"We Did It!"

Yazmin

I Want to Say Thank you

My name is Yazmin. I arrived in this world on a windy March morning. Mom made it just in time to the hospital. After the midwife examined her, she told her there was no time to lose, because I was in a hurry to be born. Mom said her midwife was kind to her, held her hand, and helped her through her contractions.

Mom was shocked when she realized her midwife could speak Spanish. She had met few doctors, nurses, or midwives who could. For most, English was the only language they spoke, and it was hard, sometimes, for them to understand their patients' problems.

The midwife said to Mom, "Buenas días, Señora. ¿Cómo te llamas?"

("Good morning, Ma'am. What is your name?")

"Mi nombre es María. María Lopez."

(My name is María. María Lopez).

Although Mom was hurting badly, she was overjoyed, at last, someone could speak to her in her language. Mom told me she had not learned English back in Nicaragua, from which she had immigrated. When she got here to the United States, there was no time to study English. She had to find work to help support her family.

(¿Es tu primer bebé?")

("Is this your first baby?), the midwife asked.

"No. El segundo."

(No. The second).

"¿Sientes que el bebé viene?"

("Do you feel as if the baby is coming?")

"Sí, sí, Doctora, siento que el bebé viene ahora. Por favor, ayúdamé!"

(Yes, yes, Doctor, I feel the baby is coming now. Please help me!")

The midwife had no way of knowing that Mom had come to the hospital with a big problem. She wanted to talk to someone about it but didn't know to whom. Because she didn't speak English, she worried about the problem and was especially worried about me, her baby.

Just as they wheeled Mom into the delivery room, her midwife asked her, "¿Estaba todo bien con tu salud durante tu embarazo?"

(Was everything okay with your health during your pregnancy?")

Mom was relieved to finally let someone know what her problem was.

"Sí, Doctora, todo estaba bien conmigo, pero el bebé está enfermo."

(Yes, Doctor, all was well with me, but the baby Is sick.")

The midwife questioned Mom more closely,

"¿El bebé está enfermo? ¿Quien te dijo eso?"

("The baby is sick? Who told you that?")

Mom then had the chance to explain.

"Me hicieron uno ultltrasonido hace dos semanas y el médico dijo que el bebé tiene un problema con su corazón."

("I had a sonogram two weeks ago and the doctor said the baby has a problem with its heart.")

By that time, I began to press my way out of Mom.

Mom's midwife told her, "Manténla respiración y empuja, Mamá,"

("Hold your breath and push, Mama,")

"¡Dios mio, Ayúdamé!"

("¡My God, help me!"), Mom cried, as she experienced another powerful contraction.

With all her might, Mom pushed me into her midwife's waiting hands. She wiped my nose and mouth to clear my airway, and I let out a loud, lusty cry.

"Gracias a Dios! Gracias a Dios!"

(Thank God! Thank God!), Mom murmured.

Mom told me she watched as her midwife cut my umbilical cord, then she reached out her arms to hold me.

I snuggled up close to Mom and felt so happy to finally see her face. She talked to me often when I was inside of her. Now, this was the real thing. It felt so good as Mom held me close, not wanting to let me go.

The midwife told Mom, "La enfermera tiene que examinar a tu bebé, Maria.

(The nurse has to examine your baby, Maria)

When the nurse, who could not speak Spanish, completed her examination, she asked the midwife to tell Mom,

"Your baby is doing fine and seems normal. She is breathing nicely and moving her arms and legs. I'll take her to the newborn nursery very soon."

(Su bebé está bien y parece normal. Está respirando muy bien y moviendo sus brazos y piernas. La llevaré a la guardería de recién nacidos muy pronto.)

"What will you name your baby?" the midwife asked Mom.

(¿Cómo le darás nombre a tu bebé?)

"Yazmin Carolina Lopez."

("Yazmin Carolina Lopez"), Mom proudly told her.

Mom told me she took me home from the hospital a few days later.

Many years passed. When I, Yazmin, was a teenager, Mom told me a frightening story about my birth.

Estabas muy enfermo, y casi mueres después de nacer.

("You were very ill, and almost died after you were born).

"¿Qué quieres decir?

("What do you mean?") I asked her.

Estoy muy agradecida de que mi partera estaba allí para asegurarme de que obtuve una buena atención

("I am so grateful my midwife was there to make sure I got good care.)"

I looked at Mom, puzzled.

"Justo después de que naciste, mi partera estaba muy preocupada cuando le dije que tenías algo malo en tu corazón. Decidió saber más sobre lo que le dije. Dijo que estaba perplejada porque respirabas de inmediato y que eras muy activa".

("Right after you were born, my midwife was very worried because I told her you had something wrong with your heart. She decided to find out more about that. She said she was puzzled because you breathed right away, and you were very active.)"

"Así que fue al departamento de Registros Médicos para leer mi carta para saber más."

("So, she went to the Medical Records department to read my chart to find out more.")

Mom then told me the following:

The midwife read the report of the sonogram Mom had while she was pregnant with me. It said I had a hole in my heart. But before Mom had a chance to get a second sonogram, to confirm more what was happening to my heart, it was time for her to come to the hospital to give birth to me.

Mom continued, "Mi partera dijo que corrió a la guardería de recién nacidos tan rápido como pudo, con una copia del informe de ecografía en su mano. Vio a las enfermeras, cuidando tranquilamente de mí."

("My midwife said she raced to the newborn nursery as fast as she could, with a copy of the sonogram report in her hand. She saw the nurses, calmly taking care of me.")

'Este bebé tiene un problema grave", dijo mi partera al médico más cercano. "Su madre se hizo una ecografía hace dos semanas y aquí está su historial médico explicándolo".

("This baby has a serious problem," my midwife told the nearest physician. "Her mom had a sonogram two weeks ago and here is her medical record explaining it.")

Mom then related to me what the midwife told her next. It was quite worrisome.

"El personal de la guardería se dio cuenta de que tenían una situación de emergencia. Te dieron una radiografía de tórax e hicieron otros exámenes. Cuando la partera revisó más tarde, le dijeron que te habían llevado a cirugía de inmediato. Retiraron un crecimiento y repararon un agujero en los pulmones."

("The staff in the nursery realized they had an emergency. They gave you a chest Xray and did other examinations. When the midwife checked back later, she was told you had been taken to surgery right away. They removed a growth and repaired a hole in your lungs.")

Here is the rest of the story Mom shared with me:

The day after my surgery, her midwife returned to the nursery to find out how I was doing and to read my medical report. She was shocked by what she read.

After surgery, as they brought me back to the nursery from the operating room, I stopped breathing and died. The doctors and nurses worked on me for quite a while and brought me back to life. Within a few minutes, my breathing got better with the help of a breathing machine.

The midwife, then, told Mom something more.

While she was in the nursery reading the report of my surgery and what happened right afterwards, the head doctor approached her and asked, "Are you the midwife who delivered the baby?'

"I am," she replied.

"I'm so glad to meet you." he exclaimed and shook her hand. "You are a famous person here in the nursery. Because of you, this baby is alive. If you did not bring her mom's health record to our attention, most likely, she would have died a few hours after birth. We would not have known why. You're a great midwife!"

Mom told me, when the midwife told her the story of what almost happened to me, she listened carefully. The midwife expressed to Mom what a wonderful feeling it was to have heard the doctor give her credit for how she saved my life. However, she still praised God for prompting her to do something.

"When God urges us in a certain direction, we must obey,"

Mom told me, right away, she realized it must have been God's Will for me to be alive. Because she is not a religious person, I was surprised when Mom said,

"Dios me dejó caer en manos de esa partera."

("God let me fall into the hands of that midwife.")

Mom said that after my surgery, I healed fast and never had a problem with my lungs after that.

Now, many years later, Mom and I still talk about what happened at the time of my birth.

Nunca olvidaré a esa partera.

("I'll never forget that midwife,") Mom says.

"I wonder whatever happened to her?" I asked.

"No lo sé. Nunca la volví a ver.

("I don't know. I never saw her again.")

Whenever we talk about my story, I say to Mom, "Life is strange. Maybe one day you'll see her again. If I ever meet her, please introduce us. I would sure tell her 'thank you' for saving my life,"

Mom smiles at me and says, "No sé qué habría hecho si te hubiera perdido cuando naciste. No puedo imaginar lo que habría sido volver a casa sin ti."

("I don't know what I would have done if I had lost you when you were born. I can't imagine what it would have been like to come home without you.")

I thought about this for a long time. Now that I'm married and have my own children, I can imagine how awful that would have been for her.

I told Mom, "Creo que Dios me perdonó la vida por una razón. Mo"- Quiero darte las gracias por ser una gran mamá para mí. Creo que también diremos 'gracias' a nuestra partera, algún día".

("I believe God spared my life for a reason. "I want to say 'thank you' for being such a great Mom to me. I also believe we will both say 'thank you' to our midwife, someday.")

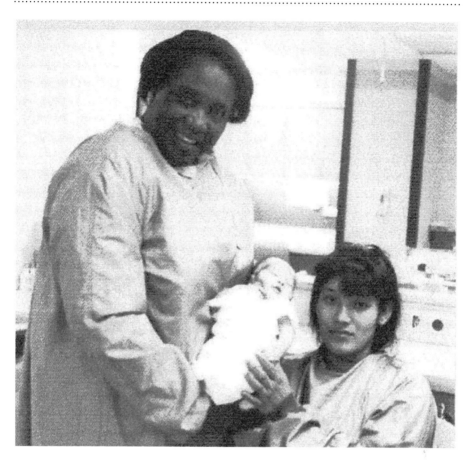

Midwife, Mom and Miracle Baby. Photo Courtesy of Parkland Hospital.

Char and Kay

The Legacy Continues

Charlotte Faith arrived in November 2015. I was thrilled on receiving the news,, especially since her birth marked the beginning of a new generation in our family. I can hardly believe I've become a great-grandmother. I never dreamed I would reach this stage in life, but it really has happened..

My husband and I, with excitement, drove seven hours to Little Rock, Arkansas where Charlotte put in her appearance. Her mother, our granddaughter, Grace, handed her to me, to hold, love, squeeze, and admire. She knew well the long--standing love affair I have with newborn babies. After all, I was present in the delivery room when she, herself, was born.

Charlotte's perfectly formed little body seemed such a miracle. Weighing six pounds, four ounces, her tiny arms and legs moved rhythmically as if dancing in thankfulness for the life God had given her. I wondered if those dancing movements *were* genetic, since Grace, her mom, is an accomplished professional dancer. Her recitals have been second to none.

Charlotte clasped my finger and held on tight, as if saying, "Nice to meet you, Grammy."

I am not saying this because Charlotte is my great-granddaughter, but she was one of the prettiest babies I had ever seen. She had a headful of jet-black hair, deep-set dark brown eyes, and a pair of full eyebrows that met in the middle. Conventional wisdom says this is a sign of individuality, that such persons are not overly concerned with the way they are perceived by others. Time will tell if this is true of Charlotte Faith. One thing she did that I could hardly believe, was, while only a two-day old infant, she raised her head up all by herself. This was quite unusual.

During our three-day visit with Charlotte, it was clear she would win the hearts of friends and family in the days ahead. She almost never cried, awakened only to get her feeding,, then drifted back to sleep. She seemed like such a contented soul.

It was refreshing for us, the older generation, to observe the young family —Charlotte's mom and dad with their new baby. It bespoke a continuation of the past and beginning of the future.

In less than a year after Charlotte was born, another great grand-child, Kayden Malachi, put in his appearance.

"Our legacy continues," I chirped.

My husband replied,, "Now we have a Miriam and a Moses, as in the Bible. By faith, I see a mighty woman and a mighty man of God."

I mused on what he said.. I believed the two would light the way for future generations in our family and well beyond.

Kayden's mom is my granddaughter, Alexandria. Their resemblance to each other has always been striking. In addition to their wonderful mix of African American and Puerto Rican features, they both have deep dimples, a ready smile, and a look of innocence on their faces. God blessed each of them with a rich, deep, tone of voice, unmistakable in a crowd of many voices.

Charlotte and Kayden have been good friends from the time they first met. They enjoy each other's company when they are together, although they live hundreds of miles apart. It is a joy to us, their great-grandparents, to observe these happy little ones together. Kay calls me "Gigi," while Char refers to me as "Bisabuela —Great grandmother in Spanish. Both call their great granddad, simply, "Papa."

We have high hopes for Charlotte Faith and Kayden Malachi as they start their young journeys in life. They each received our blessings when they emerged into the world. We believe and know God has His hand on them.

They are truly our rays of sunshine and we release them to their respective destinies.

Charlotte Faith

Kayden Malachi

A Brief Intermission

We pause to consider lessons learned from previous personal essays, and look forward to the themes presented in the formal essays to come.

Part II
Formal Essays

Section A. March Winds

In the Shadow of Lady Liberty

Lady Liberty stands on a pedestal in New York Harbor in New York City. She was a gift to the United States by France. She depicts a Roman goddess, called, Libertas, symbolizing freedom for all.

She holds a tablet in one hand and a torch, upraised, in the other. The tablet bears the date of America's Declaration of Independence, July, 4, 1776. The torch is a symbol of enlightening the world.

Among the immigrants who arrived in New York Harbor over many years during the late nineteenth and early twentieth centuries, several were fleeing religious or other persecution experienced in their countries of origin. Others sought a better life economically and socially. As they entered the gates of Ellis Island, they saw the towering statue, Lady Liberty. To all, she beckoned them toward the beginning of their uncertain journey in America.

The following three Essays describe arrivals by certain immigrants from the islands of the West Indies. All looked forward to their lives, and those of future generations, in their new land. As they disembarked from their ships, Lady Liberty pointed the way.

> *"Others went to sea in ships, conducting trade in vast waters. They saw the Lord's works, His wonderful works in the deep."*
>
> Psalms 107: 23 – 24. Holman Bible.

The Ship SS Avare

Over one hundred years ago, on March 9, 1918, the ship SS Avare set sail from Rio de Janeiro, Brazil, bound for New York City, on the first leg of its journey. Its initial load of passengers included affluent middle-aged US citizen visitors, as well as merchants, engaged in sundry businesses, making the return trip home from Brazil. Wealthy American and Brazilian family groups, on vacation with their children, were also among them. A few in-transit folks on their way to Canada, England, other parts of Europe, and even places in the Far East, were part of the group. These passengers were able to afford tickets that accommodated them in First Class on the upper decks of the ship.

A large group of students from Brazil's middle class also boarded in Rio. Most were swarthy, bright-eyed, single males who sought advanced education in the United States. Their goal was to become professionals after their training, and, thereafter, either remain in the USA, or return to Brazil and enter its upper class. The students' tickets assigned them to Second Class on the Avare, with accommodation in the middle decks of the ship.

The First and Second– class passengers were greeted with affection by Captain de Miranda himself, a native Brazilian, "Welcome aboard! Enjoy the voyage."

"Whatever you need, just let us know," chanted the fawning, uniformed stewards as they ushered those passengers to pristine, comfortable cabins or staterooms in their respective classes.

The Ship S. S. Avare was considered massive for its time. It was constructed in 1912 by German shipbuilders and weighed eight thousand gross tons. It accommodated sixteen hundred passengers. The ship became the property of Brazil five years later when seized by that government. It remained that country's possession for the next six years.

This grand vessel plied the waters of the South American – Caribbean corridor and stopped in various ports where immigrant people, bound for new lives in America, were received. This immigrant trade became the Avare's main source of income for several years.

The second and only stop the Avare made on that particular voyage, was in Barbados, the easternmost of the Caribbean island chain. One hundred souls from humble backgrounds had prepared for months for the ship's arrival. To them, the trip would be life-changing as they contemplated America, where a new life awaited.

The women passengers, for the most part, were young and unmarried. Among them were seamstresses, and domestics. A few housewives would be joining their husbands who had emigrated earlier to the USA. The men comprised tradesmen, including tailors, porters, carpenters and masons. A few teachers were also in the mix.

These passengers' decisions to make the journey had been bittersweet for all. The thought of leaving their families and seaside tropical clime, maybe forever, in exchange for a better economic existence in the great United States, had been gut-wrenching for them.

All had booked passage in Third Class—an area reserved for those who paid the cheapest fare. Little did they know they would experience Captain de Miranda's palpable disdain for them as lower-class passengers on his boat. The warm hospitality extended to those who boarded in Rio was not experienced by the ones who embarked in Bridgetown, Barbados.

Luther Allman, age twenty-one, from the Parish of St. Peter, was among the Barbados passengers, due to set sail from Bridgetown on the Avare on March 31, 1918. Although excited to go, he felt a gnawing ambivalence at the thought of leaving his parents, Charles and Clara, behind. He also felt a duty to his rural village folks to bid each one farewell, in person, not knowing whether he would return.

"Are you sure you shouldn't be on your way, Son?" his father asked the morning of his departure.

"I have plenty of time, Sir," was his polite reply.

Luther, tall and slender, with a full head of jet-black hair, embraced neighbors, church members, school mates, and others for quite some time before he returned home for the single piece of luggage he'd already packed. The most important item was his worn and weathered Bible.

"I plan to read my Bible every day," he assured his mother. "I know it will get me through the rough, difficult journey ahead."

Luther was shocked to learn he had missed the public horse-drawn carriage he had planned to take to the Port of Bridgetown.

"I guess I'll have to go on foot," he commiserated to his father. "It will take me about four hours to walk the twelve miles to town. I think I'll still make it, though. The ship doesn't leave until this evening."

Charles offered a prayer for his safety, while Clara brushed tears away on her apron, as their third-born son departed for America. "Will we ever see him again? How will he manage?" they pondered.

Meanwhile, down at the port, most of the passengers were already boarding the ship. Luther still trudged along to get there. These modest souls were directed, with impatience, to a space known as "the steerage" where they would be accommodated during the voyage. Most had heard rumors about the steerage in letters received from relatives who already made the voyage. However, nothing prepared them for the conditions they experienced when they were actually on board the ship.

Luther reached the great vessel within an hour of its scheduled departure. Apprehensive, foot-sore, and weary, perspiration pouring down his back, he presented his passport and ticket to the officers on shore. He was made to answer a list of questions related to his physical and mental health and confirmed he had at least twenty-five dollars with which to travel. A doctor made a cursory check of him from head to toe to detect any obvious diseases. Next, he and his bag were sprayed with a disinfectant and he was given a vaccination. At last, they waved him toward the gangplank at the ship's entrance.

"Good evening," he said to a ship steward.

The steward did not respond but eyed him with suspicion. With a swift gesture, he directed him to a receiving officer.

"Let me have your travel documents," the officer demanded.

Luther again presented his credentials. After examining them for a considerable time, he prompted the waiting steward, "Take him down to the steerage."

As he followed the steward, he felt the ship pull away from the shore. He paused to watch the distinctive Needham's Lighthouse, located southeast of Bridgetown, fade into the distance.

The steerage, located on the bottom deck of the ship and close to the engine, was accorded the least amount of service or privacy to those accommodated there. Luther later came to a stark realization: the wealthiest as well as the poorest travelers crossed the ocean on the same vessel only a few decks apart. But their respective experiences on board were as different as night and day.

Luther took a quick glance around the steerage deck to which he was taken. He noticed it was divided into three levels– each with large compartments for sleeping. The top level was for women without male escorts; the middle for men who traveled alone; the third was reserved for family groups.

When he entered his compartment in the middle area, he was taken aback by its sparseness and lack of ventilation. The heat was stifling. An iron frame, which he presumed to be his bed, a straw-filled mattress, a pillow, and a coarse gray-colored blanket were the only items there. No other passengers were assigned to his compartment, although it was apparent there was room for several more. He was disheartened when he later learned the compartments in the steerage deck would receive little or no cleaning or attention from the stewards throughout the entire seven-day voyage!

He was glad he listened to his mother and brought along towels, soap, and other toiletries. None had been provided by the liner. He noticed a few nails on the walls on which to hang his clothes.

Bathroom facilities in steerage were a nightmare. The smell was overwhelming. There were separate lavatories for men and women. But Luther's spirits fell when he saw, on the men's side, common rooms to be shared by several passengers. Each contained a few washbasins crowded into small spaces. There was a limited number of toilets with no provision for privacy between them, no bathtubs, no showers.

Luther was famished by the time he reached his berth. Just as he was about to search for the dining area, he heard a familiar voice in a strong Barbadian accent, "Is that you, Luther?"

He turned and was greeted by Thomas Walkes, a boyhood friend from his own parish, St. Peter. They smiled and embraced– each over-joyed to see a familiar face on the ship.

"Thomas, are you headed for America also?"

"Man, I'm sure glad to see you. It's great we are traveling there together."

From that moment, Luther and Thomas were inseparable as they made the thousand-mile passage to the Port of New York. They soon discovered each day of their journey was an experience in itself— filled with memories never to be forgotten.

Thomas, who had boarded several hours earlier, shared with him what he already found out during his brief exploration of the steerage.

"There's a small open deck available to we steerage passengers. At least we can get fresh air there."

"I guess we'll meet other Barbadians and visit with them as we travel. Right now though, I'm starved. I need to find the dining room."

Thomas let out a sarcastic laugh. "I got here in time for lunch today. Don't get your hopes up, Man. I got just enough to fill my stomach."

When a bell announced it was suppertime, Thomas guided Luther to a large room. Several long wooden boards set on tres-tles, with rough wooden benches placed in front of them, lined the side walls.

"Welcome to our dining room," Thomas declared.

The steerage passengers jostled for places in the food line. Stew-ards handed them eating utensils, a tin plate, and a cup. They served them the food from large tin pans. Boiled potatoes, meat, a vegeta-ble, and bread were on the menu, as well as coffee and tea. Milk was supplied for the children.

"It isn't delicious," Luther whispered to Thomas as they ate. "Rather bland, with not much seasoning, but I guess it will do."

After supper, they spent about an hour on the open deck, made a few acquaintances, then returned to their individual berths for the night.

Luther, exhausted, fell asleep right away. However, he was shaken awake in the early dawn by the chopping and churning of the ship. Fear gripped him as the boat rocked hard from side to side. He became conscious a storm had arisen during the night. As he peered out of the porthole through the gray mist and fog, he could see they were out in the wide- open ocean. No land was in sight. The angry sky lit up from time to time with ribbon-like sheets of lightning. Deafening claps of thunder and the continuous roaring of the wind shot waves as high as the porthole. The fleeting thought of the ship going down and being lost forever at sea was terrifying.

He began to pray out loud: "Dear Lord, please calm the storm and let it soon pass over. Don't let our ship capsize and we perish at sea!"

He felt so alone and wondered how Thomas fared. He longed for the company of someone with whom to ride out the storm. He decided to stay put, however.

Luther had been a keen geography student while in school. He reckoned, from the time they departed Barbados, they had reached the northern Caribbean, perhaps near Haiti or the Cayman Islands. He also knew this tempest was not a hurricane in its truest sense, since the hurricane season began in June each year in that region. It being April, he consoled himself, it was just a large tropical storm.

"Are you okay?" came Thomas' familiar voice some hours later. "I think the worst of the storm is over."

"Thank God," Luther replied, as shimmering rays of sunlight broke through the cloudy sky. "Although we couldn't see him, our captain kept our ship afloat with God's help."

"A lot of folks are seasick," Thomas informed. "We get most of the ship's rocking down here in the steerage, you know."

"I need to get out on deck for some fresh air. I can't stay in this berth another minute."

Luther heard a mix of accents from the folks who already gathered there: the rapid staccato of those from Barbados, the soft, almost melodious tones of St. Lucians, and those of other West Indians. Less affluent South Americans, also housed in the steerage, chatted among themselves in Spanish. He and Thomas joined the conversation about final destinations.

"I'll be staying in New York," Luther informed. "My brother, Charles, who lives there, will meet me when we land."

Thinking his friend was also going to live in New York, he was saddened when Thomas informed, "I'll be going on to Boston in Massachusetts. I'm scheduled to take a railroad train to my relatives there."

They were all conscious their ship was an artificial community of travelers. While they shared a common experience on board, their paths would diverge once they passed through Ellis Island. Their focus then would be on settling into a strange new land. Their brief shipboard acquaintances would fade forever into the past.

As Luther sauntered around the deck, he spied something folded up under a bench. He was excited to discover a two-page newspaper, of sorts, headlined THE GAZETTE, with yesterday's date on it. Luther, an avid reader, couldn't believe the treasure he found. There was no doubt the document had been produced on the ship. Typewritten information about Avare goings on was included. There were snippets of news from the outside world. He later learned the English-speaking Brazilian students in Second Class, each day compiled this newspaper to help chase their boredom.

World news, received by wireless telegram, was passed on to the students by the crew. Passengers in First Class were asked to provide input to the paper. Sadly, little interest was paid to what transpired in the steerage.

To Luther, the newspaper was a goldmine. He savored every word. Each day thereafter, for the duration of the voyage, he looked for and found on his deck a copy of the day-old paper. Although as a steerage passenger, he couldn't enter the upper decks, THE GAZETTE opened a window and helped satisfy his curiosity about life in those quarters. His biggest discovery, from the anecdotes shared, was this: although they had vast differences by social and economic status, the folks in the First and Second classes had the same hopes and aspirations for themselves and their families as those housed in the steerage.

Most of all, the paper helped Luther keep pace with world progress, in which he had an insatiable interest. World War I had just ended and Woodrow Wilson, the US President, was urging Congress toward a safer world through democracy.

"Did you hear that loud noise earlier?" Thomas asked Luther late afternoon the third day of the voyage.

"I did and I wondered what it was."

"Rumor has it, one of the boilers exploded in the engine room and a small fire was ignited. Thank God, the crew was able to get it extinguished before it got out of hand."

Luther shuddered. "I've heard many stories of explosions on steamships lately. Did you hear about the recent tragedy in Nova Scotia? Three boilers exploded on a ship traveling through that area. The boilers had not been inspected and repaired as they should have been. The fire spread so fast, the vessel was destroyed. It sank before help could arrive and all aboard were lost."

"We sure do take our lives in our hands when we travel. We must pray Almighty God takes us unharmed to our destination."

On the way to his berth that night, Luther heard the distinct sound of a young infant crying. He thought it strange since he hadn't noticed any very young babies or even expectant mothers among the steerage passengers. By that time, most of the travelers there had become familiar to each other. For, they existed in such close quarters.

The riddle was solved next morning at breakfast. The dining room was abuzz with the news. A baby had been born the night before right there in the steerage! Although there was a hospital on the ship, the mother was not taken there to give birth. Rather, a nurse who worked on the ship, who was also a midwife, helped deliver the infant boy in the mother's compartment.

"Mother and baby are doing fine," was the word passed along. "Thank God, there were no complications."

"I knew I heard a baby crying last night," said Luther to Thomas. "Since it was born at sea, I'm curious what its nationality will be."

Next day, Luther's question was answered when the baby's birth on board the ship was reported in THE GAZETTE. The paper explained the newborn's mother could report the birth at her next port of call and request a birth certificate.

Luther shared with Thomas, "Our baby's birth will be reported in New York and he will be given a birth certificate. That will make him a US citizen right away!"

On the fifth day of the journey, Thomas made a startling discovery. He rushed to find Luther and lowered his voice as he spoke. "There are prisoners aboard this ship!"

"How do you know that?"

"One of the stewards, with whom I made friends, divulged it when we were talking this morning. He made me swear not to tell anyone else, but, of course, I had to tell you."

"That's rather frightening to hear. I wonder what crimes they committed."

"I was able to get the whole story from my steward friend. There are five of them –all American citizens—who, separately, got into trouble with the law in Brazil. Each was arrested, tried, found guilty, and sentenced to years in prison. The US government, however, arranged to have them returned to the States and they will be taken to prison on arrival there. My friend, Pedro, told me at least one is a murderer and the others committed assault, theft, and other types of crimes."

Luther couldn't believe his ears. "Where are they holding them on the ship?"

"Right here in the steerage! Each one is assigned to an armed guard. Three are with their guards in one compartment and two are in another. They cannot leave their compartments for any reason whatsoever and will be the last to leave the ship when it reaches New York."

"I wonder how safe the rest of us here in steerage are with them aboard. I sure hope the guards can control them and there will be no incidents with them on this ship."

Luther was quite pensive upon awakening on the morning of April 6, 1918. It was the last full day of the journey to New York and his thoughts focused on their arrival. Yesterday's newspaper had informed they had reached the east coast of the USA and were somewhere near the Carolinas. He made his way to the steerage deck as soon as possible, where he imagined the talk would be all about Ellis Island.

As he entered the deck, however, he was stunned to find it in total disarray. Benches were overturned and fists were flying. Two, men who had goaded and taunted each other throughout the trip, had lost control and were punching and kicking each other. Members of the crew rushed in to pull them apart. The men, from Panamá and Colombia, had black eyes and were bruised and bleeding as they hauled them off to the ship's hospital.

"Those two disliked each other right away from the first night of the journey," Luther declared to the crowd that gathered.

Several folks nodded in agreement and murmured their embarrassment about the incident.

Soon afterward, none other than Captain de Miranda, himself, appeared on the deck. His face was stern and he did not mince words as he addressed the crowd. "You people should count it a privilege to have been even given passage on this ship. I know the voyage will end tomorrow, but I will not tolerate such an incident again. If so, there will be dire consequences. One of my officers will be here on deck at 4:00pm today to give you instructions about our arrival at Ellis Island."

There was complete silence as he stormed away without as much as a word of farewell or well wishes.

"It's sad the captain thinks so little of us steerage passengers," Luther mentioned to Thomas. "I guess the wealthier you are, the more you are respected."

Luther shared with Thomas what he read in the ship's newspaper about USA arrival procedures. "Did you know First and Second-Class passengers are not required to enter the USA at Ellis Island, but we steerage travelers must do so?

"No, I didn't know that. I thought everyone had to pass through there."

"Tomorrow, when the ship docks, inspectors will come aboard to examine the non-United States citizens on the upper decks for contagious diseases. If any are found, the persons will be quarantined on Ellis Island, pending further investigation. US citizens will not be examined at all."

As they waited on the steerage deck for the officer that afternoon, alarming stories and rumors were exchanged about rejections and deportations that occurred on Ellis Island.

At 4:00 o'clock sharp, an officer appeared, as expected. Each passenger was given a name tag with their manifest number written on it.

He announced, in a hurried fashion, "You will wear your name tag as you disembark. You will be taken in groups on smaller boats, along with your luggage, to Ellis Island. There you will be inspected by a doctor. If you do not pass your medical and eye examinations, you will be sent back to your home country. Children who do not pass the examination will also be deported. If you pass, you must answer a few questions to the satisfaction of the inspector. You will then be given a landing card to admit you to America. After that, you will be free to go."

No opportunity was allowed for questions. It was clear the officer's job was to deliver a well-rehearsed speech, then disappear.

"I'm sure glad this journey is almost over," said Thomas when the officer left. "I'm looking forward to seeing Lady Liberty though in the morning."

A chill was in the air next day as the Ship S.S. Avare glided her way into New York harbor. Luther was astounded at the sheer sight of the Statue. He stared at her with wonder. Others on deck clapped, cried, or shouted with joy.

"I hope we'll meet again sometime," he said to Thomas, as they shook hands and exchanged contact information.

"Perhaps one day when I visit New York, we can get together."

Luther clutched his landing card and took with him a few issues of THE GAZETTE. He searched the faces of the waiting crowd for his brother, Charles. Finally, in the distance, he saw him. They embraced a long time.

"Welcome to America, Charles greeted. How was the journey?"

Luther gave him a broad smile and said, "Thank God I made it without any problems. I'm looking forward to what lies ahead for me in New York.

Allman, Luther B.
Passenger ID 610018060009
Frame573
Line Number8

SHIP NAME Avare
ARRIVAL DATE April 7th, 1918

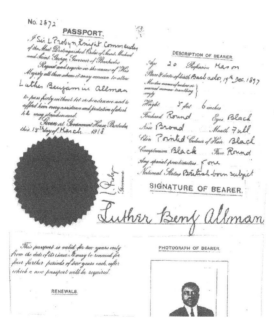

Arrival of Luther B. Allman in New York. 1918.[23]

23 Ellis Island/Statue of Liberty Foundation.1918

Three Wise Men: A-B-C

In the year 1918, World War I raged, and US President Woodrow Wilson struggled to bring it to an end. The war effort was tough on people, economically, and most worked hard to make ends meet.

Despite the hard times in America, waves of immigrants arrived in New York City from countries the world over, fleeing oppression and seeking improvement in their economic situations in "The Land of the Free and the Home of the Brave." Young people from the Islands of the West Indies were among those who came, arriving on ships of all sizes and descriptions. Lady Liberty, standing in regal grandeur in New York harbor, beckoned the vessels her way and offered them an entry point through Ellis Island.

Three young men in their early twenties sought more from life than their island homes could offer. So, around that time in the early twentieth century, they set sail for America, passports in hand. Luther Allman, tall and handsome, left Barbados and arrived in New York on the ship SS Avare; Edgar Bowen, of medium height and stocky, also a native of Barbados, was a passenger on the Ship SS Vandyck; Roger Collymore, serious and disciplined, bade farewell to his birthplace, St. Lucia, and reached these shores aboard the ship SS Advance.

Not knowing what lay ahead in the strange new land, each trusted God to bring him safely and open doors of opportunity when they arrived.

Allman, Bowen and Collymore, single, strong, and determined, survived the choppy and uncomfortable voyages aboard their respective crowded vessels and were filled with anticipation of the new life they would soon experience. They watched with sheer wonder as their steamers landed in the shadow of the great Statue and were cleared to disembark on the shore of their new homeland. As they landed, none of the three knew they would be joining and living among hundreds of their dark-skinned brothers and sisters from America's rural south, who also sought new opportunities in New York. They would later discover, by arriving at that moment in time, they were linked to a historical movement called The Great Migration.

Allman's brother, Charles, could not contain his excitement as he welcomed him to America. He took him home to his apartment in an area called Harlem. Stretching south to north from 110th to 155th Streets and west to east from the Hudson River to the East River in upper Manhattan, Harlem was known at the time as the world's most famous neighborhood. Indeed, it was the heart of the post- World War I African American cultural explosion called the Harlem Renaissance. It spawned musicians, artists, writers, and political activists. It included luminaries such as Marcus Garvey, Josephine Baker, Duke Ellington, Billie Holiday, Louis Armstrong, Marian Anderson, and WEB DuBois. These were among those whose gifts and talents were brought to light in Harlem. Excitement and energy were in the air as the world-famous Apollo Theatre on 125th Street offered many of them a start in the entertainment world.

The first Sunday morning after Luther's arrival, the Allman brothers walked a few blocks to a nearby church called The Christian Mission. The service was held in the upstairs parlor of a lovely Brownstone house. Most of the parishioners had also immigrated from the Caribbean and their familiar lilting accents brought back fond memories for Luther and a faint longing for home. Ladies in white dresses beat tambourines to the spirited singing. Prayers were loudly intoned, and the Pastor preached with authority and boldness. By the end of the service, Luther knew he had found a church home and was there to stay.

Edgar Bowen found work soon after his arrival in New York and settled in an area of Harlem known as Sugar Hill. More professional and prominent African Americans lived and practiced in that community and several Baptist and Episcopalian churches were located there. Young Edgar accepted Christ as His personal Savior and felt the call of God to ministry not long thereafter.

Roger Collymore surrendered his heart to the Lord in a street meeting conducted by women from a local Pentecostal church. He joined the church and worked there over the next several years. He served first, as Sunday School Teacher, then Deacon, street Evangelist, and Elder.

Alllman, Bowen, and Collymore were three young men who had profound intellects and were well ahead of their time. They proved themselves capable of visionary thinking and impressive community impact, over time. Not long after their arrivals in New York, they met one another and found they had much in common. Soon they were referred to as A-B-C: Allman, Bowen and Collymore.

Each of these young men evolved into a self-taught urban professional. Each had a love for people and an unquenchable thirst to minister the Word of God. Standing out from the crowds, each spoke impeccable English, and soon became quietly known as a force to be reckoned with. The three admired and supported one another in the respective Christian arena to which God had called each of them. All of them found wives, and, championed by these dedicated and educated Christian women, their ministries were launched and expanded.

Allman was musically gifted, playing cornet, piano and organ. His passion was classical music. At the urging of his wife, Mabel, a singer, he furthered his talent through teaching, and opened an evening music school in a storefront in Harlem. People showed up from throughout the community to learn what they had never heard or dreamed of before. Luther taught them Solfeggio, a music education method used to teach sight-singing and pitch. Indeed, his school became so popular, he soon formed a choir, followed by an orchestra, complete with brass, wind, and stringed instruments. Throughout the 1930s and '40s, this remarkable group sponsored many classical musical events around town. During this time, Luther continued to wear his other hat, Sunday School Superintendent, and capably taught and preached at his beloved Christian Mission church.

Meanwhile, in 1936, Bowen founded a new Pentecostal church in Harlem. Receiving his call by God to Christian Education, he soon inaugurated a Bible Institute which had emphasis on Evangelism. Edgar proved to be a capable educator. His unique ability to lay the foundational truths of the Bible spread like wildfire. People from throughout the five boroughs of New York, stampeded to this school to learn and grow under his tutelage. Students and parishioners joined Edgar in sounding their rallying hymn:

The Bible stands though the hills may tumble,
It will firmly stand when the earth shall crumble,
I will plant my feet on its firm foundation for the Bible stands![24]

After living and ministering in Harlem several years, Collymore settled in Queens, New York. A born leader, and concerned about declining spiritual values, he began community cottage prayer meetings and founded his own church in 1932. From then on, with the hand of God on his life, he was unstoppable.

Nine years later, Collymore's church purchased land and built a new house of worship. To reach a wider audience, he and his wife started, first, a Bible Institute, followed by a Radio Broadcast. Over the years, thousands completed courses and graduated from the Bible Institute. By means of the Radio Broadcast, hundreds accepted Christ or were strengthened in their faith.

Allman received advanced ministerial training and was elevated to Pastor of Ebenezer Gospel Tabernacle of the Christian Mission of USA in 1950. By then, the growing congregation had purchased a recently vacated, ornate Jewish synagogue providing ample space in which to worship. Luther, fluent with words, had a far-reaching vocabulary. Utilizing this God-given skill, he became a gifted expository preacher, elaborating, amplifying, and explaining the authenticity of the scriptures to his congregation. Sadly, after twenty years of marriage, his wife, Mabel, passed away suddenly. However, a few years later, God gave him a new wife, Daisy, who served, with excellence, alongside him. Although childless with his first wife, God blessed Luther with three children with his second wife. Over the next thirty years he was faithful to his family and to his call, while loving and serving the people of God.

---

24   Lillenas. 1917.The Bible Stands. (Public Domain).

In time, each of these men of God was duly elevated as they presided over churches and ministries, both local and international. Their titles became, General Superintendent Allman, Doctor Bowen, and Bishop Collymore.

As of this writing, the three churches, pastored and undergirded by the "Three Wise Men," are yet operational. Parishioners inherited enviable legacies from them. Although the three have now transitioned to Heaven, each lived well into his eighties or nineties, still proclaiming the gospel of Jesus Christ.

To these three, who launched out early in life from their homelands, and were obedient and unwavering in their defense of the gospel, we say:

"Well done, good and faithful servants.
You have fought a good fight. You have kept the faith!"[25]

---

25   Matt. 25:23; II Tim. 4: 7. New King James Version (NKJV)

Moving Your Tent

"**A**bram moved his tent. He went and settled by the Oaks of Mamre in Hebron. There he built an altar to God."[26]

"By an act of faith, Abraham said yes to God's call to travel to an unknown place that would become his home. When he left he had no idea where he was going. By an act of faith he lived in the country promised him, lived as a stranger camping in tents.[27]

One hundred years ago, in the early twentieth century, two families, the Allman family and the Wilson family arrived in America. Both groups landed in New York City, having something in common —that of being immigrants of West Indian origin. They, literally, had "moved their tents." At the time, the families were strangers to each other. On arrival, neither family had any idea what lay ahead of them.

The Allmans were from Barbados, the Wilsons from Jamaica, via Panama. The families came by boat at separate times. Both sailed into Ellis Island in Manhattan and settled north in a town called Harlem. At the time, Harlem was experiencing a cultural revolution, called the Harlem Renaissance.

Both families became submerged in the life and times of Harlem, while maintaining their Caribbean roots, and the strong Christian witness they brought with them.

Between the 1920s and 1940s, the Wilsons raised their children, sent them to school, founded a church, and participated in all aspects of life in their Harlem community. Their daughter, Daisy, became a Registered Nurse and, proudly, worked at Harlem Hospital. The parents looked forward to having grandchildren as their children found mates and established homes of their own.

---

26 Gen. 13:18. 2018. The Message Bible *MSG*.
27 Heb. 11: 8-9.2018. The Message Bible. *MSG*.

During the same time-period, the Allmans expanded and became a large family with many branches. Perhaps It might have been better to call them a Clan. All family members, resided in Harlem, initially, but only Luther remained there permanently. His siblings and their children moved to the neighboring boroughs of Queens, and The Bronx.

They maintained strong family ties, however, and visited each other often. All were members of Ebenezer Gospel Tabernacle in Harlem, and, in the early 1950s, Luther was elevated to Pastor.

Allman family celebrations were large and enjoyable. Weddings, picnics, birthdays, were wonderful occasions. Luther and his wife, Mabel, were childless, but they happily enjoyed twenty years of marriage together. Sadly, Mabel died suddenly after a brief illness, leaving Luther a middle-aged widower.

The Wilsons and the Allmans became happily intertwined when Luther Allman took Daisy Wilson as his wife in 1940.

Allman Family, 1940.

Living happily together over the next fifty years, they were blessed with three children. What follows are highlights of the story of this branch of the Allman family. Facing life against the highs and lows, ups and downs, of Harlem and the wider community, remarkably, they survived.

In this essay, their story evolves from the 1940s to the 1990s. Times were hard, and the family struggled on many fronts. The reader is invited to look in on this family. insights and information will be gained on two fronts: the social climate existing in their neighborhood and community, and, the strides the family made and their accomplishments, during each decade, despite the obstacles. It is, indeed, a narrative of resilience, undergirded by their faith in God and His promises. In the end, though battle-scarred and weary, they emerged victorious.

1940s

The Neighborhood:
Institutional racism in schools. Black students with Caucasian teachers. Unfair hiring practices toward Blacks. Adam Clayton Powell Jr. elected to Congress.
Public housing. Police abuse. Poor quality of schools.
The Great Migration: mass movements of Black people from the South.
High infant mortality rates. Christianity- a bedrock of the community.
Post-World War II economy.

The Family:
Birth of a son. Birth of a daughter. Birth of a daughter.
Family purchases Brownstone House. Become landlords.
Children's elementary school years.
Mary Jane candy. Dill and sour pickles after school. Cracker jacks.
Ice cream parlors and ice cream sundaes.
Father works two jobs as Postal Worker and Elevator Operator.
Mother works as Registered Nurse at Harlem Hospital.

Mother opens day nursery for neighborhood families.
Parents rent rooms upstairs for singles, couples, and families.

1950s

The Neighborhood:
Mass migration of Blacks from South continues.
Harlem overcrowded with growth of tenements and housing projects.
Black churches move uptown to Harlem. Growth of storefront churches.
Cult Leaders: Father Divine and Daddy Grace.
High death rates from Tuberculosis and other chronic diseases.
Drugs invade the neighborhood: Heroin injection is king!
Post Korean War times.
York peppermint patties; Jello salad; Spam.

The Family:
Son graduates from high school at age 15.
Daughter graduates from high school at age 16.
Daughter attends the Calhoun School, an elite girls school, on New York's Westside.
Daughter accepted at Houghton College in upstate New York.
Son attends College of the City of New York at age 16.

1960s

The Neighborhood:
Jewish mob and Italian Mafia emerge.
Harlem a major entertainment center: musical theatre, vaudeville, moving pictures. Apollo Theatre.
Home to over 400 churches.
Mass migration of Blacks from South continues.
Assassination of Dr. Martin Luther King, Jr., with race riot following in Harlem.
Black Panthers organize in Harlem.

Arrival of Black Muslims, Islam religion, and opening of mosques. Fruit of Islam. Muhammed Speaks.

Assassination of Malcolm X in Harlem at Audubon Ballroom.

Large influx of Puerto Ricans migrating to East Harlem from Puerto Rico.

Harlem Boys Choir.

Drug addiction rates higher than any in the city.

One-parent households the norm. High teenage pregnancy rates.

Chubby Checker and the Twist. Hula Hoops and Chemise Dresses. Rock 'n Roll.

Ernestine Cleveland Reems preaches. Tommy Skinner Boy Preacher.

Joe Bostic's Gospel Train and Mass choirs. Andrae Crouch. Gospel Music.

NAACP. SNCC. Freedom Rides.

Vietnam War. Kent State Killings. College unrest and student boycotts Hippies and Woodstock.

Horn and Hardart Automat cafeterias. White Castle hamburgers. Woolworths. Chock full O' Nuts. Muslim's Sweet potato pies.

The Family:
Father pastors church in Harlem.

Mother works as Nurse for New York City Department of Health.

Daughter graduates from Cornell University- New York Hospital School of Nursing, an Ivy League School.

Daughter graduates from Swarthmore College in Pennsylvania and earns Phi Beta Kappa Status.

Daughter graduates from Columbia University's Masters Program in Nurse-Midwifery, an Ivy League school, and achieves Sigma Theta Tau status: International Nursing Honor Society.

Daughter attends Harvard University in Cambridge, Massachusetts, an Ivy League school. Earns Master's degree in Mathematics.

Son marries Registered Nurse and blesses parents with three grand-daughters.

1970s

The Neighborhood:
Beginning exodus of middle-class Blacks to suburbs.
High infant mortality rates. Drug addiction with start of Crack epidemic.
Poor housing. Poor education.
Shuttered stores and shops. Abandoned buildings. High crime rate.
Vacant lots.
Poor sanitation.
Illegal gambling: "Numbers game."
Dance Theatre of Harlem.
High unemployment rates and poverty.
Evangelistic street meetings, tent meetings and feeding programs by churches.
Women's Lib and Feminism.
Good and Plenty candy. Carrot Cake; Fondue. Oh Henry! Candy bars; Hershey's Kisses.

The Family:
Daughter teaches at University of Rochester in Rochester, New York.
Daughter works for Pan American Health Organization/World Health Organization in Caribbean.
Daughter marries Engineer and blesses parents with three grandchildren.
Daughter marries Graphic Artist and blesses parents with a grandson.
Post-Vietnam War times.

1980s

The Neighborhood:
Jello Pudding Pops; Cool Ranch Doritos; Reese's Pieces; Sloppy Joes.
Auctioning off of many Harlem properties.
HIV and AIDS epidemic decimates community.
Section 8 housing.
Homelessness and high rates of mental illness.

Widespread use of Crack-cocaine.
Mother Hale and Hale House for addicted and abandoned babies.

The Family:
Parents continue to live in Harlem.
Parents celebrate forty years of marriage.
Father retires from Pastorate at Church. Becomes Pastor Emeritus.
Mother retires from Nursing.

1990s

The Neighborhood:
Crack wars and high crime rates.
Beginning gentrification of Harlem neighborhoods.
Lunchables. Chicken Caesar Salad. Jujyfruits. Fruitstripe Gum.
Operation Desert Storm and War in Iraq.
911: Bombing of World Trade Center in New York
Beginning of Internet and Information Super Highway.

The Family:
Family celebrates with parents fifty years of marriage.
Father transitions to Heaven, age 93.
Mother transitions to Heaven, age 81.
Family sells Brownstone Home in Harlem, a family treasure for over fifty years.

Post-Script

This family's story is an "I shall not be defeated" one. It was written, not to boast of its accomplishments, rather, to proclaim and demonstrate the goodness of God as they walked the journey of life. Like Abraham, they did not know where the path would lead them as they moved their tent, but they trusted God to walk with them. A final word to readers is, "We walked by faith, not by sight."[28]

---

28 II Cor. 5:7. New King James (NKJ) Version.

Section B. April Showers

Church Goings-On

What is the Church? In today's world we find a variety of definitions of what the word means. Some perceive "church" as simply a building, structure, or edifice, with a floor, sidewalls, and a roof. It may be ornate with stained glass windows, it may contain statues, or it may be adorned with lovely artistic works. It may be a simple brick or wooden building with basic furniture, including pews, a podium, and an altar.

Others believe the word church symbolizes more than just a building, but a gathering place, which can be located anywhere, as long as the persons gathered are there to worship. With this definition, they believe a church can be located at a home, a rented movie theatre, on the street, or even at a beach. To them, the focus is on the intent of the gathering, not on the building.

Mary Fairchild, in her article, "What is the Church?" affirms that how we understand and perceive the church is an important factor in determining how we live out our faith."[29]

I agree with her, because many people today attend church as a social exercise, or moral obligation. Sadly, their perception of church often is not at all related to faith in Jesus Christ, who established the Church. Perhaps this is why the sacredness of a church service, the sacraments within the church, and emphasis on the preached Word as our guide for living have come under attack in recent times.

---

29 Fairchild. 2020. *What Is the Church?*

There is an urgent need, for people who identify themselves as Christians, and claim to have a personal relationship with Jesus Christ, to model Christianity for all the world to see. Scandals and hypocrisy among pastors and church leaders have no place in the Body of Christ. Ungodly lifestyles among church members are contrary to biblical teaching. Congregants in churches have the right to expect the reflection of Christianity in their church.

There are six Essays in the section following. The first is a discussion of what makes a good Pastor as God has ordained. The next five discuss situations, unfortunately, all too common, that occur in many churches today. They are presented as Case Studies or Discussions designed to provoke thought and problem-solving.

> "For this I was appointed a preacher and an apostle (I am telling the truth, I am not lying), a teacher of the Gentiles in faith and truth."
>
> Holy Bible .I Timothy 2:7. (ESV)

The Making of a Pastor

The focus of this essay is an examination of the qualities God expects of the one who gives leadership to His people in the context of the church. I believe this assessment is necessary because of the many variations we are experiencing in the church of Christ today, in terms of pastoral calling, substance, and effectiveness.

Before I proceed, I would like to digress a bit to validate and celebrate the many courageous female pastors who impacted my life and still enrich our lives today. When I was growing up, most pastors were males. This is still true today. However, many more females, over the years, have answered the call of God, stepped out of their comfort zones, received advanced education and preparation, and have entered pulpits to give leadership in both mainstream denominational churches as well as in non-denominational ones.

Back in the day, especially in Holiness churches, lady preachers were called Evangelists or Missionaries. Many churches would only allow them to speak at women's events, such as Mother's Day, or at a special women's celebration. It is remarkable, also, some, otherwise, forward-thinking denominations, still prevent women from even standing in their pulpits if invited to bring the main message in a service. In these situations, the woman can speak, but only if the Pastor is present. Also, she must deliver the Word at a podium, at the level of the congregation –not elevated to the pulpit.

Churches supporting the latter thinking often cite the verse by the Apostle Paul, in First Timothy, which says:

"I suffer not a woman to teach nor to usurp authority over a man, but to be in silence."[30]

---

30   I Tim. 2:12.2012. *King James Version (KJV).*

They believe this to be biblical evidence supporting God's opposition to women holding positions of leadership in their churches.

Great efforts have been made to change such thinking and overcome this stance as enlightened thinking emerges. The recent Doctoral Dissertation of Rita G. Burnett[31] indicates and confirms several mainline Protestant denominations, over the past forty years, have embraced women as pastors and are supportive of their work among their churches and parishioners.

Churches which fully support lady pastors stand firm on the verse in Paul's letter to the Galatians:

"There is neither male nor female, for you are all one in Christ Jesus."[32]

I have been privileged in my lifetime to experience the teaching and preaching of many women who proclaimed the Word of God with knowledge and great clarity. Over one ten-year period, my life was radically changed and my Christian walk strengthened during annual meetings and conferences at which such women participated. Great pastors, who, temporarily, left their home pulpits for this mission include: Pastor Ernestine Reems, Dr. Claudette Copeland, Bishop Millicent Thompson Hunter, Bishop Barbara Amos, Dr. Pastor Cynthia James, Evangelist Iona Locke, and Pastor Jackie McCullough, among others.

Returning to the intent of this Essay, which, of course, is not what the gender of a pastor should or should not be, but, as indicated earlier, to highlight the qualities one should expect of our pastors, whether male or female. Are pastors born or are they made? Are they called of God or self-appointed?

As I thought about this, I became conscious of one person, who, to me, epitomized the characteristics of a good pastor. That person was my father, the Rev. Luther B. Allman, who is now at home with the Lord. Allow me to explain who Daddy was and why his ministry had great impact.

---

31 Burnett.2017. *Dissertations Paper 119.*
32 Gal. 3:28.2020. *New American Standard Bible (NAS).*

My father was forty-five years old when I was born. Therefore, I knew him as a dad who was much older than my friends' dads. Growing up, I viewed him as strict and distant. So, I really didn't have a strong relationship with him until I was almost grown.

I was always proud of Daddy, however. He was extremely intelligent and knew a lot about a lot of things. He read the <u>New York Times</u> newspaper daily and could complete its crossword puzzle in no time. Everyone knew it was the hardest puzzle around. He had a large, expansive vocabulary and possessed great oratory skills. He was a stickler for correct pronunciation of words and insisted my siblings and I use sentences grammatically correct.

Daddy was savvy politically and had an astute knowledge of what transpired in the world. On the personal side, he worked extremely hard, holding three jobs, at one point, to support our family.

Multitalented Daddy had an aptitude for music, teaching, and preaching. He conducted our church's choir and took special pleasure in leading an expanded choir and choral group annually. Each year a prominent work was performed, such as Handel's *Messiah* or Felix Mendelsohn's Oratorio *Elijah*.

Most of all, my father loved the Lord Jesus with all his heart. I've met few committed Christians like him. He was indeed a student of the Word of God and could expound on it spontaneously. A great Bible teacher, he was anxious to pass his knowledge on to others. He was not a demonstrative, fiery preacher, but people sat up, listened, and heeded when he began to preach and teach. I accepted Christ as my personal Savior under Daddy's preaching, the summer I turned twelve. He wanted everyone to accept and know Christ.

My father dearly loved his children and was proud to conduct all our marriage ceremonies with our respective spouses when we became adults. He dedicated each of his seven grandchildren to the Lord.

At the age of eighty, after pastoring over thirty years, my dad retired from the pulpit, realizing it was time to pass the baton to the younger generation. He remained highly respected by his parishioners and was given the title of Pastor Emeritus. He lived over ten more years in that role, mentoring and passing on his knowledge and experience to others.

On December 7, 1990, Daddy slipped quietly away to heaven in the presence of us all. In my mind's eye I could see the angels carrying him into the bosom of Jesus. He had a large and glorious funeral with friends attending from far and near. The accolades given were unprecedented. The choir sang of meeting him just inside the Eastern Gate in the New Jerusalem. His tombstone testifies of him resting from his labors.

When I think of Daddy and reflect on his life, most of all, I learned from him to incorporate God in every aspect of my life. Right before me, I saw the qualities God expects of those who accept the sacred calling of pastoring His people.

In sum, what qualities did I observe? How did Daddy's life demonstrate the making of a pastor? Here are ten of his attributes:

1. He listened to God, his Creator
2. He was intentionally quiet and limited distractions
3. He "heard," the music of his congregation, figuratively and literally
4. He demonstrated a Christ-like response to those who opposed him
5. He preached the Word of God in an uncompromised manner
6. He exhibited empathy –a genuine love for God's people, when sick, distressed, bereaved, depressed, as well as during good times
7. He incorporated his multifaceted personality and gifts into the life of his church and encouraged those under his leadership to do the same
8. He made his parishioners feel valued and loved
9. He welcomed visitors, strangers, missionaries, and evangelists, in obedience to God's Word
10. He loved his wife, children, and extended family members immensely, and always placed their needs ahead of his own

In my opinion, Daddy got it right where pastoring is concerned. I've proven him to be oh so right.

LUTHER B. ALLMAN, PASTOR, EBENEZER GOSPEL TABERNACLE MANHATTAN, NEW YORK, Photo Circa 1975.

When Ahab and Jezebel Lead Your Church

In the Bible, in the book of I Kings, the Israelites were ruled by a king named Ahab and his wife, Jezebel.[33] Together, they led Israel into idolatry and did more wickedness in the sight of God than all other rulers before them. Although the Israelites, from the days of Moses, had been warned not to marry idol worshippers,[34] rebellious Ahab, did so by marrying Jezebel, daughter of a Zidonian king. She worshipped a god named Baal.

In addition, this couple's personalities were mismatched, and their roles were reversed. Jezebel usurped Ahab's leadership role as king and took authority as she pleased. In several instances Ahab sat passively, allowing Jezebel to rule in his place.

Imagine being in a church today in which the church situation, personalities, and marital dynamics of the pastor and his wife were like those of Ahab and Jezebel. To others, they might appear on the outside to have a stable and healthy relationship, but the works of their hearts might prove otherwise. Let's take a closer look.

Pastor Ahab is a gifted preacher and Mrs. Jezebel an accomplished soloist. They pastor a mega- church and their congregation has grown rapidly. They are well-known throughout the community, and national Christian musicians often perform at their church services. Social activities for all age groups are the norm, and their children's ministry is second to none.

Meanwhile, behind closed doors, Pastor Ahab is very unhappy. An insatiable desire for money has led to greed and his mishandling of

---

33 I Kings 16:29 – 19: 29. 1982 King James Version (KJV).
34 Deut. 7: 3-4. 1982. King James Version (KJV).

the church's finances. Born and raised in poverty, Pastor Ahab vowed in his youth to get money wherever he could find it. Their church is on the verge of bankruptcy, but church members are unaware of this. Pastor Ahab is deathly afraid that news of their financial status will leak out.

Mrs. Jezebel ignores Pastor Ahab and has no sympathy for him. She is living the good life in her million-dollar home. She rules with an iron hand and makes all the decisions. She throws parties with friends outside of the church and is a frequent traveler. She has led church members to believe that she conducts women's conferences around the country because she is a sought-after speaker. She says her ministry operates independently of the church. The truth is, Mrs. Jezebel is heavily involved in illegal money transactions.

The only person who knows these pastors' secrets, is a trusted middle-aged woman who has worked with them for several years. They have given her the title of Executive Assistant, but she is grossly underpaid. She has no life of her own, and is blindly dedicated to their ministry. They are confident she won't erode their trust.

Please answer the following questions (This may be done individually or in groups):

1. What could be the consequences for the members of this church if the above scenario is the case?
2. How long do you think this church can continue to thrive?
3. If the truth is revealed, might irreparable damage be done to the name of Christ?
4. Can this church be rescued? Give reasons for your response.

Discussion:

Many Christians today face a peculiar dilemma, leading to the question: How do we find a solid, growth-oriented church that is suitable for our family?

Forty to fifty years ago, that question was seldom asked. People, for the most part, attended the family church where they were raised. Many were christened, reared, married, reared their children, and had their funerals conducted in the same house of worship. If the church was small enough, everyone knew one another and many of their families had lived in the same community for generations.

Today the situation is different. Families are much more mobile. Many move for employment or other reasons. Several end up living and working among strangers. Others are adventurous and move seeking changes in lifestyle and living conditions. Some retirees move to be closer to adult children and grandchildren.

People today are less tolerant of problems and situations which might arise in their churches and don't hesitate to move on. Such issues might include a pastor who has engaged in sin, such as infidelity, or financial misconduct. Differences in scriptural and theological interpretation among the church's leaders might emerge. This might become so intense, it leads to a church split. When these situations occur, members often leave the church feeling battered and bruised.

For those who know Christ, seeking and finding an ideal place of worship is a critical task. Many have a longing for the style of worship, preaching method, and familiar songs and hymns they left behind. For others, healing needs to take place because of mistrust developed from past experiences.

If you have left Pastor Ahab and Mrs. Jezebel's church, and are seeking a church home for yourself and family, here are questions you might ask when evaluating a church you are considering:

1. Is there a clear written statement of the church's doctrinal beliefs?
2. Is there an emphasis on praise and worship, prayer, and evangelism?

3. Does the pastor exalt himself/ herself, or does he or she appear to be a humble servant of God?
4. Is nepotism at the leadership level evident, where the pastor's family makes all the decisions?
5. Is there an emphasis on legalism, as opposed to focus on the cross of Christ and His work of grace?
6. Is there an over-emphasis on any of the following: finances, offerings, monetary donations, material prosperity, riches, and abundance?
7. Is there financial accountability and transparency? Are financial statements available to the membership?
8. Is an air of authoritarianism evident? Are unquestioned obedience and total loyalty to the pastor required?
9. Is there evidence of age, racial, and gender diversity, in which all people appear to be welcomed?
10. Does the pastor appear to be visionary with solid plans for the church's future?

Conclusion

Before a decision is made in favor of a new place in which to worship for an individual or family, much prayer is required. God's leadership in this situation is of utmost importance. He will show those seeking him in this situation His divine will and purpose. Once His guidance is clear, rest assured and be at peace.

Sexual Misconduct in Church: A Case Study

Mt. Pleasant Church was founded fifty years ago and has enjoyed a sound reputation in the community. Its present leader, Pastor Watson, is a man of integrity and a passionate preacher of the gospel. There are several prominent families in the church who have been members since its inception. The Pringle family is among these and Elder Pringle, the head of this family, is a friend of Pastor Watson. Chuck Pringle is the oldest son of Elder Pringle and is the church's organist.

Chuck Pringle is married to his wife, Denise, and they have three young children. Chuck is a dynamic worship leader and organist. His charismatic style has led several young people to join Mt. Pleasant. Pastor Watson likes Chuck and is pleased about his positive impact on the music department. However, he has failed to discipline him over the years when complaints about his sexual misconduct were brought to his attention.

For example, ten years earlier, before Chuck married Denise, Bessie Jackson, then age fourteen, told her parents Chuck had sexually assaulted her when she went downstairs to the restroom, while service was going on, and the pastor was preaching. She said Chuck grabbed her and forced himself on her in a darkened storage room. Bessie's parents complained to Pastor Watson about the incident, but he chose not to believe Bessie's story. He remembered she was known as a "fast girl" around the church. So, his only action was to speak to Chuck's father, Elder Pringle. He asked him to talk to Chuck and admonish him to "watch himself around the young girls at the church." Pastor Watson's philosophy is to "cover a fault and restore the sinner."

Bessie's parents waited for Pastor Watson to call Chuck to account for what he had done to her. They wanted him to face Bessie and be disciplined. However, none of this happened.

About eight months ago, Chuck's wife, Denise, came to Pastor Watson for counseling. She had heard complaints about Chuck's recent sexual misconduct with several young girls at the church. She also found pornographic magazines and videos in his closet at home. He frequently came home late from work. Denise asked Pastor Watson to discipline Chuck, suggesting he should be given a leave of absence from the music department, and be offered intensive counseling.

Pastor Watson told Denise he had already spoken to Chuck, who acknowledges he has a problem. Chuck told him, "I'm working on it." Pastor Watson feels Denise should "give him a chance."

Because of Pastor Watson's unwillingness to act, Denise stood outside of the church's annual meeting, and, as members went in, she distributed flyers to each of them. The flyers denounced Chuck's infidelities and the church's refusal to discipline him. She begged the members to raise the issue at the meeting to bring about action. The matter was not raised or even discussed at the meeting. Instead, after the meeting, by telephone, the members buzzed about the matter for a while, until it all died down. Chuck continues to lead the music department at the church.

Denise has divorced Chuck and has left Mt. Pleasant Church. Bessie Jackson, who, years earlier, reported Chuck's assault, has left also, along with her family, and they have moved to Florida. Other families, whose daughters were assaulted by Chuck have long gone.

One day, Bessie Jackson and her mother went to their new church in Florida. Bessie was shocked to see Chuck on the organ, accompanying the guest evangelist, who was visiting their church. Bessie swallowed hard and struggled to contain her anger. She pointed Chuck out to her mother, who became determined to confront Chuck after the service.

During the service, Mrs. Jackson, Bessie's mother, prayed for God's guidance about what to say. She thought about how Bessie, whom Chuck had raped at age fourteen, had had a stormy life of drug addiction and prostitution. By God's grace, she recovered and was moving on with her life. She was now stable, a widow, and the mother of four children.

Chuck recognized Mrs. Jackson right away as she approached him after the service and braced himself for a showdown.

Mrs. Jackson, instead, spoke calmly and said, "Chuck, I want you to know I forgive you for what you did to my daughter."

Shocked, Chuck broke down and wept. He lunged onto her shoulders, saying, "Thank you, thank you." He did not apologize or clearly acknowledge what he had done.

Action Plan for Mt. Pleasant Church

In groups of four or five people, discuss the following questions, then come up with an Action Plan for this church.

1. Reflect on the situation at Mt. Pleasant, then state three related scripture verses or biblical principles to form the basis of your discussion.
2. What responsibility does Pastor Watson have with respect to his handling of the accusations, past and present, against Chuck?
3. What would you have done as a Board member at the church's annual meeting when Chuck's wife appeared with the flyers?
4. How should Chuck be disciplined now?
5. Develop a Plan of Action for handling similar complaints in future to protect girls and women at Mt. Pleasant.
6. Mrs. Jackson has seen Chuck on Livestream, serving as Minister of Music at another church. He is in his late fifties or early sixties now.
   a. Is it worth her reaching out to the Pastor of the new church and exposing his past?
   b. Is Chuck's tearful drama with her enough proof that he has been rehabilitated?

Nepotism in Church:
A Case Study – How to Survive
in a Family-Run Church

Christian Witness Fellowship Church (CWFC) is located in a Mid-western city and was founded ten years ago by its present pastor, Rev. Thomas Rayfield. Although it is an independent church, it has a loose affiliation with a well-known mega church. Rev. Rayfield says this affiliation with the larger church provides a spiritual "covering" for his church.

The Rayfield family comprises Pastor Rayfield, Mary, his wife, their adult sons, Matthew, age 40, Paul, 35, Peter, 30, and their respective spouses. The entire family, including daughters-in-law, is employed full-time at the church and they are on the church's payroll. Each of them gives leadership to a ministry. Paul is responsible for the Music department and his wife, Lois, is Praise and Worship leader. Matthew is the Church Administrator and his wife, Dena, is over Finance. Peter leads the Christian Education department and preaches when his father is out of town. The Elders and Ministers report to Peter's wife, Sandra, who is titled Lead Elder.

Matthew Rayfield, the oldest son, emphasizes the importance of volunteering in the church. He presents it as necessary for the church's growth and development. When new people join the church, he urges them to sign up to become a "servant leader" in one of the church's ministries.

Mary Rayfield, the Pastor's wife, a short brunette, is always well-dressed in the latest fashions. She does not mix and mingle very often among the church's members. She retires right away to the "Green Room" after services. Her sons and daughters-in-law, however, are much more sociable. They are well known, approachable, and, for the most part, well-liked.

Mary's passion is interior decorating, and her home is located in an affluent, gated community. It is said to have exquisite furnishings and immaculate décor. Few church members have visited there or have been invited. Both she and Pastor Rayfield drive Bentley automobiles, and security personnel are in close proximity to them before, during, and after services.

Rev. Rayfield, a tall, blond-haired, imposing man in his early sixties, is a powerful preacher. He is known for his exegesis of the Bible. This has contributed to the rapid growth of the church which, at present, approaches two thousand members.

In addition to his preaching, however, this pastor does not hesitate to emphasize the importance of financial giving. In fact, in almost every service, he reminds the congregation that to withhold tithes and offerings is sinful. "The Lord loves a cheerful giver. Don't rob God," is his oft-spoken refrain.

When he launches a new construction project or program initiative, he doesn't hesitate to inform the membership, "It's your duty to contribute financially. Take a Pledge card and envelopes. God said, 'When you make a vow, you must fulfill it. ' "

In the ten years since its inception, there have been only occasional discussions about CWFC's financial status. No formal business meetings have ever been held with the membership. There is no clear indication of who comprises the church's administrative board, if one exists. It is obvious the Rayfield family holds all decision-making power. If members ask about the status of projects, the standard answer is, "Look around and you will see."

CWFC is led by the Rayfields, a Caucasian family. The church is culturally and racially diverse, to some extent, although predominantly African American. Although it is located in an upper middle- class neighborhood, its membership is blue collar working class. On the surface, the members seem satisfied with their church's leadership. They ask few questions, enjoy the worship, and seem proud to be affiliated with CWFC.

Over time, a steady stream of members and families has left CWFC. This has been truer among the more affluent or prominent ones. Few, if any, explanations have been given about why they departed. On one occasion, Pastor Rayfield, publically, referred to those who left as "disgruntled members." He urged those who were dissatisfied with the church to also leave. Little follow-up or outreach is made to these persons. It appears when new members replace them, and the gaps are filled, things continue as usual.

The pastor of the mega church, whom Rev. Rayfield says is his "covering," recently preached in a Sunday morning service at CWCF. At the end of the service, Pastor Rayfield asked the congregation not to leave right away and announced there would be an Ordination Ceremony. He asked them to stay until it was concluded. The congregation had not been notified prior to this and, therefore, was taken by surprise.

The visiting minister conducted the ceremony. Six candidates for Ordination, dressed in black and white business attire, were asked to sit on the platform in front of the congregation. The three sons of Pastor and Mrs. Rayfield and one of their daughters-in-law were among the candidates. Two other Elders were among the six. No explanation was provided about what criteria for ordination had been met, what offices in the church the newly ordained would hold, what their titles would be, or what additional functions, if any, they would have. The congregation, for the most part, appeared to accept what transpired, and congratulated the newly ordained after the service. Later, on the church's website, it was noted that the four ordained members of the Pastor's family had been given the title, "Associate Pastor." The two ordained Elders had been given the title "Staff Pastor."

Bob Williams and Betty Brown are two long-standing members of CWFC and both serve as Elders in the church. Bob approached Pastor Rayfield in his office about the lack of transparency and prior explanation about the Ordination that was held.

Pastor Rayfield became deeply offended at Bob and told him he was free to leave the church if he wanted to. Further, the fact that he questioned what was done, indicated that he had a "wrong motive." Elder Williams resigned from the church right away.

Betty was granted a meeting with Pastor Rayfield, by appointment. When she arrived at the meeting, she was surprised to see five people gathered there, including, Pastor and Mary Rayfield, two of their sons, and one of the new Staff pastors. Betty sought answers to questions she had about the ordination, in a respectful manner, and said she thought that nepotism was evident. She was shocked by their responses. Mary Rayfield, became agitated, rapped the table, rocked in her seat, took the lead, and told Betty that her husband, the Pastor, is alone qualified to make church decisions, and he is answerable only to God. Therefore, she is wrong to question anything he chooses to do.

Pastor Rayfield, in a hostile manner, informed Betty that God had shown him who his choices for ordination should be. He said, further, that on those premises, he, the pastor, rules supreme, as Moses did the Children of Israel.

Matthew Rayfield then told Betty she should have known by then that the Rayfield family had been "anointed and appointed, as a unit," to head the church. Further, that "nepotism is a 'bad word', and has nothing to do with church appointments."

Pastor Rayfield then accused Betty of being "disloyal" and said, because of that, he was suspending her appointment as Elder in the church for sixty days. Further, she would be relinquishing all other duties at the church. He said that during this period, he and his wife would be "observing her heart," while she sat in services, quietly, "meditating and praying."

The other persons at the meeting sat in stony silence. Betty left the meeting feeling battered and bruised.

Discussion

Please read carefully and discuss the above Case Study, then provide answers to the following questions:

1. Do you believe that nepotism is evident at CWFC? Why or why not?
2. What areas of concern, if any, do you have about this church?
3. Should Betty have asked for the meeting or should she have remained quietly accepting?
4. You are a member of CWFC. Would you have been as bothered by the ordination as Betty was?
5. If you were Elder Betty, what would your response be if you were in her position? Would you submit to the disciplinary actions?
6. Do you believe Pastor Rayfield and his wife were justified in what they said and did?
7. Does Betty have any responsibility to the other members of the church? Should she inform them of what happened to her when she spoke out?
8. Would you remain a member of CFWC or would you leave the church?

When Aunt Jemima and Uncle Ben Are Your Ministry Leaders

Sandra Long is an Elder at Eighth Street Church. Her father was a pastor while she was growing up, and she was always involved in various church ministries. She loves the Lord, and service to Him has always been a hallmark of her Christianity. Sister Terry Marshall is the Lead Elder at the church, and she, in turn, serves under Pastor Jerome Kingston, one of the Associate Pastors.

Sandra is having trouble with Sis. Marshall. It appears as if Sis. Marshall's only desire is to please Pastor Bradford, the Senior Pastor, and his wife. She notices Sis. Marshall ingratiates herself with the Bradfords by bringing food and gifts to them on a regular basis. Sandra hesitates to approach Sis. Marshall about difficult situations she encounters. For one, she has learned Sister Marshall isn't a problem-solver; second, she reports anything and everything she hears to the Bradfords.

Pastor Jerome seems to be intimidated by Sis. Marshall and Sandra realizes he is just a figure head. Prior experiences with him have taught her that he, simply, wants to maintain his position. More than once, Sandra has asked his opinion on issues.

His standard reply has always been, "I'd rather not discuss what I think at this time."

It is important to note that, at Eighth Street, the Senior Pastors, Rev. and Mrs. Bradford, are Caucasian and are leading a predominantly African American church. Although they deny being racist, their behavior belies this. For example, Sandra notices when White visitors come to the church, Sis. Marshall rushes over to them, gives them a warm welcome, leads them to seats right up front, and points them out to the Pastor. Pastor Bradford then makes a special point to welcome them, asks them to stand and introduce themselves, and encourages them to return. On the contrary, when African American visitors come, no such efforts are made for their comfort, no preferred seating is offered, and they are treated as ordinary.

Sandra once appealed to Pastor Jerome to help her deal with a difficult ministry situation, concerning Communion. At their church, Elders have responsibility for serving Communion. It is not served from a table located at the front of the sanctuary, as is the case in other churches. If congregants arrive before the start of the service, Elders distribute the Communion elements to them. During the service, when the Pastor indicates they have reached the moment of Communion, the Elders distribute it to those who have not yet been served. Sis. Marshall has told the Elders to place the Communion trays, filled with the sacraments, on the floor under their pews, until the Pastor announces it is time for Communion.

Sandra and the other Elders are appalled Sis. Marshall, Head Elder, would request this of them. They consider the Communion portion of the service a sacred rite and the elements should be handled with reverence. They have asked Pastor Jerome to speak to Sis. Marshall about the matter.

Pastor Jerome did not counsel Sis. Marshall, but told her, verbatim, every word Sandra said. He could have easily corrected the situation by suggesting to Sis. Marshall a better way of handling Communion. Upon hearing Sandra's complaint, Sis Marshall took offense and reported to the Bradfords that Sandra was hindering her from effectively carrying out her duties.

One Sunday morning, during their usual time of prayer before services began, Pastor Jerome chastised the Elders for "not owning their duties as Elders." He told them they "showed their true colors," when most did not attend the Pastor's mother's funeral, held at the church. Of note, the funeral had taken place on a weekday morning, when most of the Elders were at work. Further, the Pastor's mother was not a member of the church. Her funeral only had been accommodated there because of her son, Pastor Bradford.

At home, Sandra discussed with her husband, Peter, the problems she is experiencing at the church. Privately, they have labelled Sis. Marshall, "Aunt Jemima," and Pastor Jerome, "Uncle Ben."

To them, Sis. Marshall lacks self-esteem, and sees herself as servant to the Pastors, rather than as servant to God. They view Pastor Jerome as a security guard, whose job is to "protect" the White pastors from their Black parishioners. Sandra and Peter believe Pastor Jerome and Sis. marshall epitomize the feeling of lack of power, some African Americans experience when Caucasians are in leadership over them.

This couple would like to remain at their church. However, they are on the verge of leaving because they see no solutions to the problem. They believe it is too late for Pastor Jerome and Sis. Marshall to change.

Here is a question for discussion:

Do you believe Sis. Marshall and Pastor Jerome can change?

If so, what suggestions can you offer to impact the situation, positively, before Sandra and her husband give up and resign from the church?

Section C. May Flowers

Overcoming

The following three Essays cover different aspects of Resilience - the capacity to spring back from difficulties. It is the demonstration of toughness, and what enables a person or group of people to overcome and beat the odds. Life's situations can be sometimes ugly or overwhelming. Resilience fights back.

Reading the following essays will enable consideration of such virtues as perseverance, conflict resolution, problem-solving, responsibility, respect, anger management, self-esteem, empathy, among others.

> "Moreover, let us exult and triumph in our troubles and rejoice in our sufferings, knowing that pressure and affliction and hardship produce patient and unswerving endurance; and endurance (fortitude) develops maturity of character; and character produces joyful and confident hope of eternal salvation. Such hope never disappoints or deludes or shames us, for God's love has been poured out in our hearts through the Holy Spirit Who has been given to us."
>
> The Holy Bible. Romans 5: 3 - 5.
> Amplified Bible, Classic Edition (AMPC).

Brothers Grim: A Study in Conflict Resolution

"**B**rothers Grim" is an Essay which sheds light on a human weakness that has endured throughout generations: that of conflict among siblings and its consequences. There are many lessons to be learned. Prayerfully, the messages that emerge will provide hope for successful resolutions.

The Bible is replete with stories of family conflicts and difficult relationships among kinfolk. They provide insight into our own struggles. Several wives and husbands, for example, Job and his wife, had conflicts around many things which led to major issues.

Among the many family discords discussed in the Bible, however, animosity among brothers, specifically, is given considerable space. This compels us to pause and dig deeper into the root causes. Let's see what we can learn from the following "brothers grim."

Joseph was his father's favorite son. His dad, Jacob, made it clear to all how he felt about Joseph. In addition, Joseph was blessed by God with many talents and he boasted about his gifts to his eleven brothers. This deeply aggravated them and led to jealousy and hatred for Joseph. They desired to eliminate him from the family, so, with cruel recklessness, sold him to a band of merchants on their way to Egypt.[35]

Abel, the second son of Eve and Adam, was murdered by his older brother, Cain. Abel had done nothing to warrant this. Cain's wrath was intense because his fruit offering to God was not accepted, while Abel's animal offering was.

---

35   Gen. 37, 42, and 45.1982. King James Version (KJV).

God punished Cain for his awful deed and pronounced a curse on him.[36] In the Parable of the Prodigal Son, anger and jealousy were also displayed by the older brother. Luke Chapter 15 provides background.[37] The father demonstrated his joy at his younger son's return home from a life of degradation. He gave him gifts of a ring and a robe. in those times, these were symbols of royalty and authority.

This cut the older brother to the quick. "You never even gave me a baby goat!" he accused his father and refused to join the celebration.

His own standing within the family seemed of greater importance to him than his brother's homecoming.

Sibling rivalry and disdain were exhibited by David's older brothers in several instances:

- Seven brothers were rejected, before Samuel, the Prophet, accepted David, the youngest, and anointed him King of Israel.
- David, a talented harpist, was chosen by King Saul to play for him at the palace. No doubt, this was not at all pleasing to them.
- Three of the brothers, soldiers in the Israeli army, were furious at David because he came to check on them in the heat of the battle against the Philistine army:

    "Eliab his oldest brother heard when he spoke to the men and said to David, 'Why did you come down here and with whom did you leave those few sheep in the wilderness? I know your pride, and the naughtiness of your heart. You came down here so you could see the battle.'"[38]

- David triumphed and killed the Philistine giant, Goliath, and defeated their army. His brothers could only stand by and watch this happen.[39] This surely poured oil on their flame of jealousy.

---

36 Gen. 4.1982. King James . 1982.Version (KJV).
37 Luke 15.1982. King James Version. (KJV).
38 I Sam. 17:28. 1982.King James Version (KJV).
39 I Sam. 17. 1982. King James Version (KJV).

Nadab and Abihu were Moses' nephews.[40] They and their two brothers, Eleazar and Ithamar, as well as Aaron, their father, were anointed priests when the Israelites journeyed through the wilderness. The priesthood, a very sacred calling, was governed by strict laws commanded by God to Moses. Among these laws were specific instructions on the manner in which fire should be offered with respect to sacrifices.

Outwardly, all the priests appeared to have accepted their calling. However, inwardly, Abihu and Nadab did not. They colluded together and, in disobedience, offered fire their own way.

This stirred the anger of God, leading to their deaths by fire from God.

Rebekah and Isaac were blessed with twin sons, Esau, the first-born, and Jacob, second.[41] Scripture tells us Isaac loved Esau more, while their mom, Rebekah, preferred Jacob. This contributed to intense rivalry between the brothers. Jacob, the more cunning, twice deceived Esau and encouraged him to sell his birthright to him. Later, he also tricked their father into giving him the firstborn blessing, which, by law, belonged to Esau.

When Esau learned the irrevocable blessing had been bestowed on his brother, he fumed with rage and plotted to kill him. Jacob escaped his brother's wrath by running far away. Only years later, the brothers reconciled and had an amicable relationship.

Moses' older brother, Aaron, and his sister, Miriam, spoke against him because he had married an Ethiopian woman[42]. This prejudicial behavior was most displeasing to God. These siblings were also envious of Moses' calling and of his intimate relationship with God. They whispered together, forgetting, God, who knows all things, heard them. It isn't clear why only Miriam was punished with leprosy, but her chastisement shook Aaron to his core. He pleaded with Moses to ask God for mercy on her and she was healed.

---

40   Lev. 10: 1-7. 1982. King James Version (KJV).
41   Gen. 25:21-34; 27: 1-45. 1982. King James Version (KJV).
42   Num. 12. 1982. King James Version (KJV).

As we ponder the accounts of these 'brothers grim,' the green eye of envy appears to be a common thread. Why is this vice so prominent among brothers, in particular?

Jacob and Esau's story provides a clue. Favoritism on the part of their parents, led to serious family problems. Neither parent seemed to appreciate each son as individual and special, who brought something unique to their family unit. When parental favoritism is displayed, jealousy and envy are prone to rear their ugly heads. As these boys grew, it appears as if they, themselves, adopted their parents' attitudes and had difficulty accepting each other's differences. It was inevitable, conflicts would ensue.

Of interest, in several of the narratives, it was the older brother, more often than not, who had issues with his younger brother. This was true of the older brother(s) of David, Joseph, Moses, Abel, and the older brother in the Parable of the Prodigal Son.

A question to ponder is: What might have led to the dysfunction in those families?

Anger appears to be a root cause. Perhaps the older brother had set high expectations for himself. When the younger brother surpassed those expectations, he could not handle it. Cain's rage was so extreme, he killed his brother.

Additional Lessons:

Of what else can the 'Brothers Grim' remind us? God's Word, in Ephesians 4, provides a wealth of information[43]:

- First, we are told to "be angry and sin not." Anger may be justified but must be kept under control.
- "Endeavoring to keep the unity of the Spirit in the bond of peace." This must be worked at within families.
- "Speaking the truth in love." Jacob lied and deceived his father, claiming to be Esau. His lack of love for his brother was evident, as was Esau's disrespect for his family.

---

43 Eph. 4. 1982. King James Version (KJV).

- "Let no corrupt communication proceed out of your mouth," as was the case with Aaron and Miriam. We must be vigilant in this regard.
- "Grieve not the Holy Spirit of God," as did Nadab and Abihu. God requires total obedience from His children.
- "Be kind to one another, tenderhearted, forgiving one another even as God for Christ's sake forgave you." This verse speaks for itself.

Conclusion:

The Essay, "Brothers Grim," gives us insight into one of our own human struggles — that of animosity and jealousy among siblings. God, in His infinite wisdom, knew that we, who would live generations after these brothers, would need to consider and resolve this issue also.

What have you learned from the "Brothers Grim?"

Carl and Clive Callender

Carl and Clive Callender are two of the most remarkable people I know. From humble beginnings, they rose to high achievement and have made an indelible mark on the world. It was often said, "Nothing good can come out of Harlem," an African American enclave in New York City. But these two pioneers proved the naysayers wrong. It is clear to everyone who has known them, they were selected by God for greatness. Although beset by many disappointments along the way, several unexpected opportunities also came, which they gratefully accepted, and surpassed expectations.

Born in 1936, the identical twin boys arrived in time between the Great Depression and World War II. Their first major setback occurred on the very day they entered the world. As their mother struggled to give birth to them in a New York hospital that cold winter's day, she passed away and went home to be with her Lord. Baffled and overwhelmed by the death of his wife, their father, Joseph Callender, placed his healthy, robust sons in foster care for a while, until he could get his bearings.

Three years later, Joseph re-married and the toddlers came to live with him and his new wife. However, their stepmother had to be hospitalized, and Joseph, again, was unable to manage them alone. Thank God, their deceased mother's sister, their Aunt Ella Waterman, whom they called Auntie, stepped in, took them in, at the age of seven, and provided them with a happy home.

As the boys grew, their intelligence and quick wit became obvious to everyone. Their harmonious singing also made them well-known in the community. Aunt Ella, a strong Christian woman, and a member of Ebenezer Gospel Tabernacle in Harlem, insisted they accompany her to church on Sundays and participate in children and youth activities. That initial grounding in Christianity paid off in tremendous ways as the boys navigated through life. At an early age, they came to faith in Jesus Christ. Clive accepted Christ at the age of seven, and it was then his dream of becoming a medical missionary became his life's dream. This reality came about after he heard a sermon which spoke of ministering to the souls and bodies of mankind.

Ebenezer church was where I first met Carl and Clive and they became like older brothers to me. The parishioners were, for the most part, immigrants from the Caribbean. They embraced Carl and Clive as if they were their own children. They mentored the twins on the importance of getting a sound education. The boys soon realized education, indeed, was the steppingstone for success in life. They excelled in academics and seemed almost driven to achieve as much as possible. To them, the sky was the limit.

As life would have it, however, when the boys were in their midteens, two more major blows occurred —blows so severe, other young people, no doubt, would have been knocked off course. Auntie passed away after a brief illness, and Clive was diagnosed with pulmonary tuberculosis.

At age fifteen, Clive endured a horrific eighteen-month hospitalization requiring surgery and removal of one-third of his right lung. The last six months were spent in Otisville, New York, in a tuberculosis sanitarium, a long-term care facility, located there.

Later, he recalled, "people were dying all around me. To my left and to my right, people succumbed daily to this disease."

Despite this experience, God still had a plan for Clive. As many physicians crossed his path in the hospital and in the sanitarium, he felt inspired by God, and was reminded of his calling to become a medical missionary, one day, to help the poor and downtrodden in Africa.

Meanwhile, Carl, his twin brother, undaunted by these setbacks, with dogged determination, faced life as it came. He enlisted in the United States Air Force, serving in France and Germany, and was honorably discharged three and one-half years later. He attended New York's prestigious Hunter College, one of the top colleges in New York, and obtained his Bachelor' degree. Selecting Law as his lifelong profession, he entered Howard University Law School and earned his

Jurisprudence Doctoral Degree. During that time, he earned the title, Most Improved Student.

Carl and Clive never forgot their roots in Harlem and never failed to give thanks to Ebenezer Gospel Tabernacle. Year after year, they came back to let us know what they were doing and what they were accomplishing in life. They especially revered my father, Rev. Luther B. Allman, then pastor of our church. They credit him for being a surrogate dad, when, as young men, they were alone, because of the unfortunate events that came their way. What joy we always felt as we celebrated the career paths of this dynamic duo, who were envisioned, no doubt, 'least likely to succeed,' when they arrived on this earth.

Clive survived his tuberculosis experience and had no setbacks after his long recovery period. Following discharge, he graduated high school, then, gained admission to Hunter College, as previously noted, a college of excellence in New York. He earned his Bachelor's degree with majors in physiology and chemistry. After this, he was unstoppable. Meharry Medical College in Nashville, Tennessee was his next port of call.

He completed his training and received his Doctor of Medicine degree in 1963, finishing as the Number One student in his class. I am sure his mom and Auntie, together, looked down from heaven, smiling, as he received his credentials.

After serving one year as instructor in surgery, Dr. Callender had the opportunity to realize his life's dream, by becoming a missionary surgeon to Nigeria, West Africa. He along with his wife, Fern, a Nurse, went there to assist in medical recovery efforts in the aftermath of the Biafran Civil War. They returned after nine months of service there.

Clive completed a two-year Post- Doctoral Fellowship Program, through the National Institutes of Health, to study Organ Transplant Medicine at the University of Minnesota. Thus, he began his illustrious career as a leader in kidney and liver transplant surgery. Over the next several years, he impacted this field throughout the world.

Meanwhile, Carl pursued his legal career in New York City, opting, at first, to give back to his community by providing ten years of service as an Attorney in a Legal Services Program for the poor. He could well have practiced at a prestigious law firm, but chose to serve in this capacity. Hundreds of his former clients have testified of his kindness and of the successful outcomes they obtained, due to his untiring efforts on their behalf.

Dr. Clive Callender returned to Howard University Medical School in Washington DC in 1973 and founded the University's Transplant Center. After conducting hundreds of transplant surgeries, he came to realize this fact: the greatest obstacle in transplant medicine is the scarcity of donors.

As a result, his passion became two-fold: the education of African Americans about the critical importance of organ donation; and increasing the number of African American organ donors.

In the late 1980's, Dr. Callender was honored by the Dow Chemical Company, a major contributor to his program, for the amazing impact of his work. The resplendent affair at the Capitol Hilton Hotel in Washington, DC, was attended by thousands.

My dad, Rev. Allman, was invited to be one of the speakers. However, due to advanced age, he was unable to fulfill this invitation and I was asked to take his place. it was a great honor for me to highlight the character and achievements of my long-time friend, this accomplished, yet humble, physician.

In 1991, he founded the national Minority Organ Tissue Transplant Education Program (MOTTEP). He was successful in obtaining several million-dollar grants, which enabled him to develop a Minority Donor Strategic Plan for implementation in twenty-five cities throughout the country

Dr. Callender's work was so outstanding, it led to his promotion to the position of Professor of Surgery and Chairman of the Department of Surgery at Howard University's College of Medicine. He also became foremost spokesperson for organ donation in the USA. He authored over one hundred and fifty scientific publications on transplantation, and appeared on numerous national television shows, including the Oprah Winfrey Show, Nightline, and CNN News, among others.

Lest we think Dr. Callender, the younger twin, left his older brother in the dust, we must think again. After many years of practice, Carl Callender, Esquire, rose to the rank of Deputy Commissioner for the Housing Preservation Department of New York City. Following that, he directed the Bedford-Stuyvesant Community Legal Services Program in Brooklyn. His strong history of legal practice, along with deep affirmation by the community, earned him the position of Administrative Law Judge with the Sanitation Department of New York City. For the next ten years, thereafter, Judge Callender served as Housing Court Judge. I was thrilled to have been a quiet observer in his courtroom, one day, as he sat on the Bench, black-robed and serious-faced, settling cases that came before him.

"What ever happened to Carl and Clive Callender?" you might ask.

I am delighted to let you know, as of this writing, they are both alive and well, are in their mid-eighties, and are as vibrant and engaged as ever.

Dr. Clive stepped down as head of the Department of Surgery in 2008, but now serves as Professor of Surgery at Howard University's Medical School. He teaches transplantation, professionalism, ethics, and takes care of transplant patients. His daughter, Elana, one of his three children, followed in her father's footsteps to the field of Medicine, and has become a sought-after Obstetrician-Gynecologist in the Washington, DC area.

Judge Carl retired from the Bench a few years ago. He continues to serve as an Ordained Minister at his local church, where he directs a youth and sports program. He administers a scholarship initiative within that program.

The Callender brothers both continue their financial donations to projects sponsored by their beloved Ebenezer Gospel Tabernacle in Harlem and visit when they can.

God has a plan and purpose for each of us. When we find out what these are and pursue them, like the Callender twins, our accomplishments will be immeasurable.

DR. CLIVE AND JUDGE CARL CALLENDER, CIRCA 1990.

Onward and Upward Against the Odds

A woman named Daisy gave birth to a baby girl at Sloan Hospital for Women in New York City in the 1940s. Little did she know at the time her baby would one day circle back to Sloan, the same hospital in which she was born, and manage the deliveries of babies there.

I was that baby. The road from newborn to career fulfillment was by no means an easy one for me. The struggle for a sound education became my rallying cry over the years.

With the help of my loving, supportive family, I pushed through the racism I experienced in my early childhood and high school years. Such incidents included, suggestions by teachers that I quit school; the withholding of grades, awards and prizes I had duly earned; and a general lack of interest and support by those charged with leading me toward accomplishment of my educational and career goals.

I was always conscious God was on my side, however, since I knew Him personally. I knew He had called me to undertake the wonderful career path ahead of me. However, nothing prepared me for the trauma I would experience as I navigated higher education.

Early College Years at Houghton

Houghton, the Evangelical college I attended in Upstate New York, had high academic standards. Nothing less than these requirements would do for Daisy, my mother, who deemed me too young, as a sixteen-year-old, to live away from home on a college campus. As a young high school graduate, I was focused on the nursing profession as my career goal. My mom wanted nothing to distract me from moving forward. When she realized an older cousin was also studying at the school, she allowed me to enroll.

I had never lived in a predominantly Caucasian environment before. Most of the professors and classmates I met at the college had few, if any, experiences with "Colored People" or "Negroes", the then ethnic identifiers. While some extended themselves and were friendly on the outside, to most, I was an anomaly, and it was best to treat me as an "unseen" guest at the college. Some never spoke to me in the two years I was there, despite the "everybody knows everybody" environment there was at the small, one- thousand- student body campus. One or two of them, however, became long-term friends.

At the invitation of a friendlier classmate, I spent a weekend at her family farm. Upon arrival at the dinner table, after blessing of food was said, my colleague's five-year-old brother pointed a toy gun at me and exclaimed, "Bang, Bang, Negro!"

The silence in the room was deafening.

My saving grace while at Houghton College was Kathleen, my Black roommate, to whom I was assigned. I suppose school officials placed us together, without either of our inputs, assuming because we were both Black, we would automatically get along.

Together, Kathleen and I processed the many slights, insults, and difficulties that came our way, daily. We prepared a strategy of responses.

"Watch out for John D. He refused to work with me during Chemistry lab today. He walked away and left me to do the experiment by myself."

"That group of girls stopped talking as soon as I entered the classroom. I knew they were discussing me when they eyed each other knowingly."

"We can't plug in the hot comb to press our hair. It will cause a shortage in the dorm's electricity. If we take the chance and it happens, we can't let them know it came from our room. What shall we do?"

Meanwhile, the Black students on campus were in a separate category. Back then, Black was not considered to be beautiful and few Civil Rights heroes had yet emerged. A further unofficial subdivision was native Blacks versus foreign Blacks. The foreigners were primarily on scholarship from Africa or the Caribbean, and thought it their duty to behave as if they should show eternal gratefulness toward Whites—both students and faculty alike. To have identified with the native Blacks, therefore, would have been a sign of ingratitude and completely out of order.

One Kenyan brother went as far as to declare, "You all are bastards, and not pure Black. You let the White man run all over you. You don't fight back. We Africans are the pure ones with brains in our heads."

A female student from Nigeria looked down her nose at Kathleen and me and never saw potential for collegiality with us. A very light-skinned Black American female student, blatantly, was trying to pass on campus. She displayed marked discomfort whenever a potential for friendship showed itself.

"Watch out for the guy from Kenya," my roommate and I were warned, by a fellow Black student. "I invited him home to spend Thanksgiving with my family, and he tried to rape my sister. My dad did not press charges but sent him back to campus."

This cautioning came from the student who pretended to be friendly, but only dated White girls, especially the blondes. In fact, although there were many opportunities for dating on and off campus, including musicals, concerts, roller-skating, and other entertainment offerings, neither I nor my roommate was ever asked out on a date. It was an extremely hard pill to swallow.

The most egregious issue on campus, for me, was the avowed profession of Christianity, outwardly displayed via fervent chapel prayers, lusty hymn-singing, and a predominant focus on missions, but the concomitant demonstration of the opposite. *Where was their love for others? How did they reconcile their ungodly behavior with God's love?* I asked. Unexpectedly, I had collided with a different brand of Christianity than the one I had been taught, and to which I was accustomed at my church back home, which had an all-Black congregation.

I had mixed feelings when I completed my two years of Nursing prerequisite courses at Houghton. On one hand, the exposure of living away from home for the first time was good, and the "Christian" atmosphere was protective. However, on the other hand, despite the advantages of being in a rigorous academic program, the joy of the social life most students look forward to on campus, was never experienced. No attempt was made by the college to ensure a pleasant experience for minority students. I do not reflect back to my time there with much enthusiasm.

Against this backdrop of White racism and Black racial isolation, I, Daisy's daughter, fought to get a higher education. More was yet to come.

My Years at Cornell

Acceptance into Cornell's professional nursing program was a great achievement for me. The opportunity to study at the prestigious Cornell-New York Hospital Medical Center, located in the heart of New York City, was huge. At the time, few admissions of "other" racial groups were allowed, Affirmative Action was unheard of, and, again, no efforts were made toward advancing the concept of racial diversity at the school.

On the first day of class, once again, I was largely ignored. My ninety-three other smartly-attired classmates, drawn from highly academic institutions around the country, regarded me with suspicion. None came forward to introduce herself and I, in turn, regarded them all with cautious optimism.

Once again, a reluctant African classmate was among those admitted. She sat aloof, clad in full, colorful, native garb, wearing a gele head wrap high on her head - the type typically worn in West African countries. Her stance said to one and all, "Don't move a step closer. I am a queen, and I deserve to be here."

I still approached her, however, asked her name, where she was from, and if there was anything needed.

Her crisp reply was, "I'm from Liberia and I speak perfect English. My family ranks high in my government back home and I don't need any help."

I backed off at once and left the young Liberian woman to her own devices. I felt sad that a warm, collegial relationship was not established. We never exchanged words after that, and, within six months, the African student did not make it academically. She failed the program, dropped out of school, and was never heard from again.

Except for the presence of a Chinese student, and a friendly Black student in the class above me, I remained a "party of one," in my class and had to fend for myself.

Of interest, throughout my three full academic years at Cornell, I encountered five Black faculty members. They were a mixed bag. In my first year of the program, I studied under two of them, both of whom were from Jamaica. One was smart, pleasant, and a capable instructor, but, obviously, not accepting of her own Blackness. She in no way identified with me as a young Black student, whom she could mentor. It appeared not to matter to her whether I succeeded or failed in the program. My interactions with her were purely about academics.

The other, who was fair-skinned, and maintained a strong Jamaican accent, was adored, and fawned over by the White students. She ingratiated herself with them, and totally ignored me throughout the duration of the program.

During my second year, one Black faculty emerged who was friendly and supportive. She happened to have graduated from the same Nursing program from which my mother, Daisy, had graduated. She was proud I was in the program at Cornell and was helpful. She kept me afloat during stormy times.

In my final year, a warm and caring Black faculty member appeared. She looked out for me and went out of her way to give advice. She became a real friend and advocate, even during off-duty hours.

Upon getting to know me, about one-third of my classmates fully engaged with me, and, ultimately, became my lifelong friends. One-third remained indifferent, being fully absorbed in their own issues, and not regarding me as "one of us." The remaining one-third were outright hostile and made life exceedingly difficult for me. Their racism was palpable, and they did not care. It was the actions of this group that made me debate whether I should give up and throw the proverbial towel in on the program.

For example, one hostile classmate almost caused me to drop a patient on the floor in a clinical ward of the hospital. We were both assigned to the patient, who had multiple physical and treatment needs. The two of us were supposed to combine our strength and lift and turn the patient, who was completely bedbound. I rolled up my sleeves, shifted my weight to maximize the situation, and did not notice my classmate was simply standing there watching me doing all the work. When I attempted to lift the sheet under the patient and move it upward, the full weight of the patient fell on me. Not only did the patient almost tumble out of bed, but the discomfort in my back afterward was, for a long time, intense. My colleague gave me a veiled smile, no verbal apology, and moved on. It was as if she regarded me as a beast of burden who should carry all the weight.

At my next weekend visit home, I told my mom, "I don't think I'm going back, Ma. It's too hard to make it in that environment. It's clear they don't want me there."

Ma, who always took the bull by its horns, grabbed me by my shirt collar, looked straight into my face, and said, "You're going back, Girl! Don't even think about dropping out. That is not to be in your vocabulary. You're smart, you are successful in your subjects, and you WILL graduate."

The conversation was over at that point and was never returned to again. I went back to school with renewed determination to press on.

The classmates who were outwardly friendly, still didn't "get it," however. Although I was their classmate, with equal academic qualifications as they, they just could not reconcile me as equal. For example, they dated, (and several married), young men who were studying at Cornell's medical college across the street. When a new elevator operator was employed at the nurses residence, several classmates referred me to him as a good "catch" for a husband. In their minds, they were "do-gooders," and needed not bother discovering the young man already had a wife and kids!

My saving grace was the support of the ancillary staff at the hospital, including janitors, cafeteria, and laundry personnel, among others. The visual of "only one of us" at the school made them feel so happy. They pampered, applauded, and encouraged me. That made all the difference in the world to me and bolstered my self-confidence..

Of interest, several Black nurses, already graduated and employed at the hospital, were not at all friendly toward me. Looking deeper, it was clear this indifference came primarily from those from the South. Many of them had even graduated from historically Black schools of higher education and knew what racism was all about. Those from the North were much more hospitable and extended themselves more readily toward me when I worked on the hospital wards.

Most of my White nursing instructors had not yet learned or internalized the concept of equality for all, in their patient care and in their teaching. Insensitive comments were the norm. For example, one dermatology instructor, with marked sarcasm, advised the students, "You'll have to depend on your sense of touch to determine if the patient has a rash. Some of them are so dark-skinned, you can't even see the rash."

An even more worrisome problem was the belief some instructors held that Black people's laboratory results were to be interpreted differently from those of Whites. For example, one instructor told us students that low hemoglobin readings, signifying anemia, do not mean the same for Blacks as they do for Whites.

"Black people can tolerate having much lower readings, without being sick or needing treatment," she said.

Such comments were chilling, and, although I questioned my instructors when they made these racist statements, almost always, I was ignored or rebuffed.

On graduation day, the hospital's support staff turned out, en masse, to see me, the only young Black student in my class, accept my Registered Nursing Diploma and Bachelor's degree. My parents' joy was over the top and their tears flowed. They knew I wasn't the first Black student to receive these credentials, but those who earned them were few and far between.

Onward and Upward to Columbia

After I had a few years of nursing practice under my belt, I went to Columbia University to study for my Master's degree. I decided to major in the Nurse-Midwifery program they offered. Again, I was the only Black student enrolled in the program, although a few Black nurse-midwives, already graduated, worked in the hospitals where I obtained clinical practice.

I was delighted to discover that practice in my chosen profession would begin at Sloan Hospital, the same institution in which I was born.

"You certainly have come full circle," Ma declared upon hearing I would be practicing at Sloan.

I was thrilled to find the records of my birth among the hospital's medical record archives.

I will never forget the first baby I delivered at Sloan Hospital. The mother was a frightened Black girl who had no family support. I worked with her, calmed her down, and presented her baby to her when she gave birth. I knew, then, God had blessed my hands to provide care in this profession which dated back to ancient times.

Some classmates in the Master's program had come to New York from Southern states to study. By then, Dr. king and Malcolm X were at the forefront of marches and racial protests. These students, determined to maintain the racial status quo, were not having it. They openly challenged the societal changes and demonstrated their discontent as often as possible. For example, one student went home on vacation to Alabama and returned to class with a doll, who had the face and clothing of Aunt Jemima. Her full bright-red lips, and the handkerchief on her head, were the butt of jokes made by the students. They laughed out loud when they saw it. The owner passed it around the class for all to get a closer look, not caring about my feelings or reaction.

When the doll reached me, I stopped it in its tracks, saying, "This doll has gotten this far but will go no further. You will not insult me and the people of my race. How dare you bring this back to class?"

The room went silent. The student who brought the doll seethed with rage, visibly, but did not utter a word in response. I believe a change took place in my classmates that day, with a new respect for me, prevailing. I went on to complete the program with honors.

I practiced my chosen profession of Nurse-Midwifery for several years after completing Columbia's program. Many infants passed through my hands as they were born and took their first breaths of life. Mothers were grateful for my assistance. My mom, Daisy, lived to see me practice my profession for over twenty years, before she went home to be with the Lord.

It is important to know those years were not without an abundance of racial discrimination toward me, however. Even after gaining promotions to the level of Director of Nursing, some subordinates, even those I had trained in the art and science of Nurse-Midwifery, resented my authority over them. Some openly questioned decisions I made, refused to cooperate, and once even formed a group and met, secretly, with my Vice President to have me dismissed from my job. Thankfully, my superior and the Human Resources department found their charges frivolous and unfounded, and I maintained my position, successfully.

Although I had the necessary credentials and earned my appointment to a faculty position at a prestigious medical center university hospital, some, who worked under my supervision, chose to ignore my qualifications. They openly questioned my knowledge of high-risk and other conditions in patients for whom they were caring, and did not respect my experience. The word "challenging" does not adequately describe the unwarranted resistance I felt from them daily. It was clear they did not accept having an African American person in a position of authority over them.

God, in His mercy, however, helped me complete the career plan He had for me. I retired when I deemed it time to do so. I had held academic positions and taught at several outstanding colleges and universities. I delivered over four thousand babies into this world over thirty-eight years. Against the odds, it was a wonderful and highly rewarding time spent.

Post-Script

Eventually, still higher education beckoned. After raising my children, I resumed studies and completed a Doctoral Program in Theology at Jacksonville Theological Seminary. Since my studies were, primarily, via distance learning, I was not in a geographical space with some who might have been racially hostile toward me.

This advanced education strengthened me in areas required to fulfill my spiritual callings. I was ordained and became involved in practical areas of ministry, while I still, for a few years, carried out my chosen Nurse-Midwife profession. The Lord also blessed me with the gift of writing, and, I write for His glory. Indeed, God does all things well.

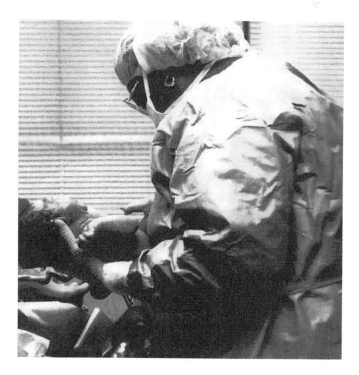

MIDWIFE, GRACE BURKE[44]

---

44   Photo Courtesy PARKLAND HOSPITAL.1994.

GRACE BURKE, WRITER

Grace Burke (center), Director, Parkland Nurse- Midwives, 2006[45]

45   Photo Courtesy Parkland Hospital. 2006.

Epilogue

"In the midst of winter I found there was in me an invincible summer. And that makes me happy."[46]

---

46   Maquet, Albert. 1958.

Works Cited

BBC World Service. 2001. *The Land of Twins*. British Broadcasting Company.*UK*.

Braun, Scott. 2016. *How do Hurricanes Form?* Precipitation Education. NASA. Greenbelt. pp. 1-6.

Burnett, Rita. 2017. *The Evolution of Women Pastors in Mainline Protestant Denominations. Dissertations.* Paper 119. Kentucky.

Fairchild, Mary. 2020.*What Is the Church?* Learn Religions, learnreligions.com.

Fawcett, John.1782. *Hymnary.org.* Public Domain.

Hussey, Jenny 1921. *Lest I Forget.* Public Domain.

Lillenas, Haldor. 1917.*The Bible Stands.* Public Domain.

Maquet, Albert. 1958. *Albert Camus: The Invincible Summer.* George Brazilier, Inc. Herma Buffault (Translator).

Negro Spiritual. *Jordan River.* Author Unknown. Public Domain.

Newell, William. 1895. William Reed. *At Calvary.* Public Domain

Newton, John. 1725-1807. *December's As Pleasant As May.* Public Domain.

Shakespeare, William. 1611. *The Tempest.* London. UK.

University of Texas. 2019. *Twin Project.* Population Research Center. Austin, TX.

Wikipedia.org.1979. *David. DP Express.* Dominica.

Wikipedia.org. https://en.wikipedia.org+Pig_Latin+899788329

Bible Citations

Holy Bible:
Amplified Bible Classic Edition (AMPC). Lockman Foundation. 1901.
English Standard Version (ESV). Good News Publishers. 2016.
Holman Christian Standard Bible (Holman). Holman Publishers. 2004.
King James Version (KJV). Thomas Nelson, Inc. 1982.
The Message Bible (MSG). Eugene H. Peterson/Tyndale House Publishers. 2018.
New American Standard Version (NASV). Lockman Foundation. 1995.
New International Version (NIV). International Bible Society. 1984.
New King James Version. (NKJV). Thomas Nelson.1982.
New Living Translation (NLT). Tyndale House Publishers, Inc. 2015.

Selected Image References

(Those not created or owned by the Author. Used by permission.)

Ancestry.com. *John Thony Allman*. Ancestry Archives. (Public Domain). 1804.

Brooks-LaTouche Photography. Bridgetown, Barbados. 1979.

Landers, Michelle. Cheapside Market. Blog post. Barbadosmedstudent.com. Feb. 18, 2019.

My Bajan Cooking. Barbados. 2020.

Parkland Hospital. Dallas, Texas. *Midwives*. Parkland Highlights.1994.

Parkland Hospital, Dallas, Texas. *Parkland Nurse-Midwives*. 2006.

Statue of Liberty – Ellis Island Foundation, Inc. SS Avare. (Public Domain).1918.

Taneica and Sherica. *History of the Hot Comb*. Blog post. Shatterproof Glass Dolls. *4 September 2010*.

The Breakdown of the Hot Comb. The Evolution of Hair. April 17, 2014.

Traje Typico Panameño. Pollera of Panamá. Rep. de Panamá. 1973.

Vintage Hot Combs and Curling Irons. Google. Under Creative Commons License.

Ware, Deidre. *Fried, Dyed and Laid to the Side: Memories of the Hot Comb!* UrbanGeekz. Newsletter. July 14. 2015.

About the Author

Grace Allman Burke earned Diplomas in Writing for Children and Teenagers at The Institute of Childrens Literature. Her published books include *Couples of the Bible,* a bible study for young adults, which analyzes the marriages of nine biblical couples; *Delights by Daisy,* a recipe book comprising fifty of her mother's delectable recipes; *Caribbean Adventure,* a novel for young people; *The Stranger's Son,* in the genre of biblical historical fiction, won two Christian Literary awards in 2016; and *Broken Pieces...Mending the Fragments Through Adoption,* a memoir.

Dr. Burke holds advanced degrees in Nursing and Nurse-Midwifery from Cornell University and Columbia University, respectively. She earned her Doctor of Theology degree from Jacksonville Theological Seminary. She is also an Ordained Minister. Before retirement, she practiced as a Nurse-Midwife for thirty-eight years and delivered over four thousand infants. She worked in the Caribbean as an international Health Consultant and has held faculty positions at colleges and universities in the Caribbean, New York, and Texas. She lives with her husband in Dallas, Texas.

Dr. Grace Allman Burke

Made in the USA
Monee, IL
03 September 2023

42044253R00199